THE FINISHED WORK OF CHRIST

The
FINISHED
WORK *of* CHRIST

THE TRUTH OF ROMANS 1—8

Francis A. Schaeffer

CROSSWAY BOOKS • WHEATON, ILLINOIS
A DIVISION OF GOOD NEWS PUBLISHERS

Library of Congress Cataloging-in-Publication Data
Schaeffer, Francis A. (Francis August)
    The finished work of Christ : the truth of Romans 1-8 / by
Francis Schaeffer.
      p.   cm.
    ISBN 1-58134-003-6 (hardcover : alk. paper)
    1. Bible. N.T.   Romans I-VIII—Commentaries. I. Title.
BS2665.3.S212   1998
227'.107—dc21   98-22416

11	10	09	08	07	06	05	04	03	02	01	00	99	98
15	14	13	12	11	10	9	8	7	6	5	4	3	2	1

TABLE OF CONTENTS

INTRODUCTION

By Udo W. Middelmann,
The Francis A. Schaeffer Foundation

T he studies of the first eight chapters of Paul's Letter to the Church in Rome you hold in your hands belong to the earliest systematic studies of Dr. Francis A. Schaeffer. These studies are of special significance because they express most of the essential ideas and truths that are foundational to all of Dr. Schaeffer's works and the content of his later books. As such these studies provide fresh insights into Schaeffer's work, but much more than this, they help us see the timeless significance of God's Word for every new generation.

In a more immediate sense, these studies grew out of Dr. Schaeffer's personal interaction with students and the discussion of the critical ideas of our time. In-depth, give-and-take discussions such as these were typical of Schaeffer's basic method in all that he did. Thus Schaeffer's insights were hammered out in these often lively exchanges, where honest questions—no matter how perplexing— were given honest, compassionate answers based on the unchanging truth of God's Word.

These studies were first given in a student flat in Lausanne, Switzerland in the 1960s. On the same day each week Schaeffer would go down the mountain to take a discussion among university students who met for lunch in the "Café Vieux Lausanne," just a few covered steps below the twelfth-century cathedral.

There, around 1526, the French reformers confronted the views of the Roman Catholic church with the Bible's teaching. In a famous debate, the citizens of Lausanne listened to both sides and then voted in favor of the reformers' teaching. Their views were based on Scripture, free from the distorted traditions of Rome. Just to the side of the Cathedral lies the old Academy, where those same reformers later would place the University. The University was still there when Schaeffer gave the biblical answers to questions from students nearby in the "Vieux Lausanne."

At night he would teach the Roman class in Sandra Ehrlich's flat before rushing to the station for the last train and bus home in the mountains. Harold, a Dutch economics student, and students from many nationalities joined them for the evening. On the tapes of the original recording one can hear Harro, as he was called, translate for a Swiss student and frequently ask questions himself. Mario from El Salvador, a South African girl, an Italian art student, a Czech, an American, and my wife Deborah were some of the others who spent two hours every week studying the book of Romans verse by verse. Dr. Schaeffer always made the studies interesting as he applied Paul's letter to the intellectual questions of Paul's day, as well as ours, often the very ones discussed earlier in the Café with agnostic and atheist students. For in the fundamentals of the problems of human existence and questions there is little difference from the Greeks to our own twentieth century. As originally given, these lectures were in the "give and take" style of lecture/discussion at which Dr. Schaeffer excelled. This text has been edited to remove repetitions and comments from the audience, while maintaining the style and content of the original tapes.

The Letter to the Romans answers all the basic questions of Man in any age about his origin, the problem of a moral God in an evil world, and the questions about significance and true humanity. In a systematic way Romans addresses the kinds of questions any thinking person has in a world like ours, where problems are often recognized, but the proposed solutions rarely go to the core of the disease.

Schaeffer pointed out that, until recently, Romans was studied in American law schools in order to teach students the art of presenting an argument. A reasoned case is made for a foundational proposition.

Counter statements are considered one by one, and refuted. Romans is not about a leap of faith but presents a comprehensive argument for the central proposition: "I am not ashamed of the gospel, for it is the power of God for the salvation of everyone who believes: first for the Jew, then for the Gentile. For in the gospel a righteousness from God is revealed, a righteousness that is by faith from first to last, just as it is written: The just shall live by faith" (Rom. 1:16, 17).

Paul, the author, under the direction and inspiration of God's Spirit, addresses our relationship with God, giving real answers to real questions. What we think we know about the universe, man, meaning, and morals, needs constant nourishment and correction. Without the correction and reproof found in God's Word, sinful man will inherit foolishness in all the central areas of life. This always begins at the place of what men believe about God.

Schaeffer understood Romans to be a completed sermon of Paul's, much like other sermons that he presented wherever he preached. After the introduction follows a proposition, then the exposition of that proposition. We see this in Acts 17, where Paul was unable to finish a similar sermon in Athens. He left and went south to Corinth, where he wrote Romans. In each city he visited he taught a whole circle of truth, covering the basics in a complete and integrated way.

Romans is just such a systematic teaching Paul sent to a church he had not seen in person. The church in Rome began in much the same manner as the church in Antioch. Both churches began through the witness of believers who had been present in Jerusalem during the events described in Acts 2, where 3,000 were converted on the day of Pentecost. Cornelius in Acts 10 had become a God-fearer through conversations with believers. In each case, the church was not the result of "professional" teachers but of believers reaching out to others.

Romans differs from all the other letters in the New Testament in one important way. No other New Testament writing gives such a systemization of the doctrine of the gospel. All others are addressed to churches or people who had heard sermons when apostles had visited personally. All the others address specific problems, special needs, or dubious practices. They address believers with specific teachings and admonitions against the backdrop of what they had already heard in the body of belief.

In Rome, however, no one had ever preached the complete gospel. Therefore, the Roman letter can be said to be a unified statement of what the Old and New Testaments present concerning our situation before God and in the world. The entire truth is summed up in the theme verses in chapter 1, verses 16 and 17. The rest of the letter is an unpacking of these two verses: Why they are true, what is the dilemma, what is the solution, and how to live now. Paul declares that there is no reason to be ashamed of Christianity, neither intellectually nor in the experience of life under God.

Through the years since Dr. Schaeffer delivered these lectures/discussions thousands of students have studied the "Romans" tapes, straining their ears to follow the study from a dismally poor recording. They were glued to it because Dr. Schaeffer applied Paul's teachings to the basic questions of Man at any age. Schaeffer himself frequently returned to Romans in discussing the intellectual bleakness of modern life.

This is a verse by verse study of the text. Woven into it are pointers to the central problems we face in our generation. Everyone who is concerned about a supposed absence of God, or about the truthfulness of God and His moral rightness, discovers a God in the Bible who grieves over the sins of the creature, but who is not responsible for their sin. We come face to face with the anger of God due to our sin as well as His compassion in providing justice, salvation, and a future restoration through Christ. Each member of the Trinity—far from being merely an item of theological interest—is intimately and powerfully involved in our redemption through history.

Along the way, it is interesting to see how much weight Schaeffer puts on the sinfulness of man, which provokes the wrath of God. Yet never is there a hint that this sinfulness destroys the humanity and rationality of man as created in the image of God. God is not the author of evil, and evil does not diminish the obligation of Man to seek after and choose God. Schaeffer does not fall into the theological trap of extreme Reformed advocates who say that depravity has removed humanity from Man, thereby absolving Man from the responsibility to repent or to seek after God. Like Paul, Schaeffer pleads with his neighbor to bow before the known God and to accept "the finished work of Christ" for his salvation, for his present battles against sin in the Christian life, as well as for the hope of a final resurrection and righteousness on the Day of the Lord.

Man is fallen, but he is not a zero, he is not worthless. Man has great value as created in the image of God. At the same time, however, all of our being has been tragically affected by the Fall, including our will and intellect.

Here is a God who does battle for us. There is no arbitrary solution or esoteric mystery. Paul does not shy away from tough questions. He answers them from the wholeness of God's work in history. By inviting people to believe God (not "in God")—His existence, His being, and His promises about God's solution to our guilt from sin in the finished work of Jesus Christ—Paul shows God to be the One who is morally just and the One who will justify those who believe.

1

INTRODUCTION AND THEME
(1:1-17)

☙

The book of Romans falls into two distinct sections: chapters 1—8 and chapters 9—16. There has been great discourse among Christians through the years as to whether there is a relationship between the two sections. One may find a relationship, but this is not the important point. Both sections are worth studying by themselves. In this study we will deal only with the first section, chapters 1—8.

In several books of the Bible there is a verse or verses that constitute a theme statement, and this is very plainly so in the book of Romans. The key to understanding this first section of Romans is found in 1:16-17:

For I am not ashamed of the gospel of Christ: for it is the power of God unto salvation to every one that believeth, to the Jew first, and also to the Greek. For therein is the righteousness of God revealed from faith to faith: as it is written, The just shall live by faith.

With that theme statement in mind, we will begin our study of Romans by looking at Paul's introductory remarks in 1:1-15.

Paul, a servant of Jesus Christ, called to be an apostle, separated unto the gospel of God ... (1:1)

Paul identifies himself as a servant, or slave, of Jesus Christ. He says this specifically and with great care. He is writing to the church at Rome, and Rome knew a great deal about slaves. Slavery was legal in the Roman Empire. The world understood what it meant to be a slave, and Paul begins by declaring himself a slave of Christ.

There was a great distinction, however, between the slavery of the Roman Empire and Paul's slavery to Christ. Slaves in the Roman Empire were slaves not because they wanted to be, but because they had to be. A heavy iron band would be welded around a slave's neck, something he could not possibly remove by himself. This marked him as a slave for as long he remained a slave.

Paul's slave relationship to Jesus Christ, however, is something quite different. He is a slave not because he has to be a slave, but because he wishes to be one. Paul had an iron band around his neck, not because it had to be there but because he held it there by the fingers of his own will. We too must adopt this attitude if we are to be fruitful in the things of God.

Just as the slave must "will" the will of his master, our usefulness to Jesus depends on the extent to which we will the will of God. We are not robots. Rather, in love we choose to return to the position of obedient dependence on God in which He created us. This may seem an unpleasant idea to some, but as God's creatures this "slaveness" is the only place of joy and the only place of usefulness.

Paul was human. It hurt him just as much as it would hurt us to be beaten and imprisoned for his faith. It hurt him just as much as it would hurt us to be thrown to the beasts. His shipwreck was just as wet, just as windy, just as uncomfortable as it would be for us. Beheading was surely not pleasant to anticipate. And Paul could have escaped all of this simply by forsaking his servanthood. So when Paul introduces himself in this way, it is not just a pious expression. Rather, it introduces a theme central to Romans: that after accepting Jesus as our Savior, we are to live for Him.

... separated unto the gospel of God ... (1:1b)

As Christ's servant, Paul is "separated unto the gospel." Separation always has two actions: separation from and separation to. Separation from is easy to understand. Many things can keep us away from God, and it is not possible to be separated *to* God unless we are separated from such things. It is a means to the end of being separated to God to preach to the Gentiles. Paul was separated from the normal comforts of life, such as marriage (1 Cor. 7:8). That doesn't mean every Christian will be called to forego marriage, but every Christian should be willing to do so. Nor will every Christian be asked to die for the gospel, but every Christian should be willing so to die. The willingness is the crux of the matter.

Paul calls himself a "servant of Jesus Christ" but then speaks of the "gospel of God." The gospel relates to all three persons of the Trinity. It is the good news of the Trinity to a lost and fallen world. Jesus is the Lord of our redemption; however, the gospel is the good news of the entire Godhead, the Trinity.

(Which he had promised afore by his prophets in the holy scriptures,). (1:2)

The phrase is in parentheses, yet there is really no interruption of thought in the first three verses, and verse 2 is important. It expresses the unity of the Old and New Testaments, a theme emphasized constantly throughout the Bible. Paul says God promised the gospel "afore" in the Holy Scriptures. How far back does that go? Romans 16:20 will give us a clue: "And the God of peace shall bruise Satan under your feet shortly." Surely this refers to Genesis 3:15, which states that the woman's "seed" is going to bruise the serpent's head. Jesus Christ is the seed of the woman (compare Gen. 3:15 with Gen. 22:18 and Gal. 3:16). He is the one who crushed the serpent's head. Yet, by identification with Jesus, we look forward to the Second Coming and shall also bruise Satan under our feet. The gospel goes back literally as far as we can go. As soon as mankind sinned in the Garden, before twenty-four hours had passed, God promised the Messiah. And it looks forward to the Second Coming on the basis of the finished work of Christ.

People often try to pit the Old and New Testaments against each other. But the emphasis throughout the New Testament is on its unity with the Old. This was true in Christ's preaching, in the book of Acts, in Paul's epistles, and in all the other epistles. There are not two messages, only one. The Old Testament people of God looked forward to the Messiah revealed fully in the New Testament. Paul knew that the church in Rome included Jews as well as Gentiles, so it was important to remind them that there is just one message.

Concerning his Son Jesus Christ our Lord, who was made of the seed of David according to the flesh; and declared to be the Son of God with power, according to the spirit of holiness, by the resurrection from the dead. (1:3-4)

Paul shows both the human and the divine side of the Incarnation. He certainly believed in Christ's deity, but the fact of His being truly divine does not change the fact Christ was also a true man and came down through the natural line of David. Again, Paul probably has his Jewish readers in mind. It is extremely important for them to be reminded that Christ is indeed the son of David, because the Old Testament prophesied specifically that the Messiah would come through Abraham and David.

. . . the seed of David according to the flesh . . . (1:3b)

Obviously, by "flesh" Paul means "human." He does not have in mind the sinful connotation of that word, as he will later in 7:5.

Paul says nothing of Christ descending through David's son Solomon. God's promise to David was absolutely unconditional: He would be the ancestor of the Messiah (2 Sam. 7:16). Solomon wanted an unconditional promise too, but God's promise to Solomon was conditional. In essence, God said, "*If* you do so and so, then you will carry on the line" (1 Kings 9:4ff.). But Solomon didn't do so and so, and neither did his royal descendants, so God denied him involvement in the fullness of the promise. If one takes the genealogy in Matthew as referring to Joseph and that in Luke as referring to Mary, one finds that Jesus came through David on both sides. He came on Joseph's side through Solomon, establishing a legal continuity with David. But as far as His actual conception by the Holy Spirit through Mary, He came through Nathan, a son of David other than Solomon. Both the unconditional promise to David and the conditional promise to Solomon were thus fulfilled in exquisite detail.

On the human side then, Christ came through David. But there is more than the human. He was also "declared to be the Son of God with power" (1:4a). "Declared" in this place is better translated "determined." Determined means it is certain. It is certain that Christ is also the Son of God. Why? Because of a particular "power" (1:4). Christ's deity, to be believed, must be demonstrable. The thing that demonstrated with certainty that Christ was God was His "resurrection from (or of) the dead" (1:4).

Before considering the resurrection itself, notice that the Resurrection was "according to the spirit of holiness" (1:4). The spirit of holiness can be seen as the work of the Holy Spirit, or as the Holy Spirit Himself. Much is said throughout the New Testament of the relationship of Jesus Christ to the Third Person of the Trinity. That relationship resulted in a holiness of life on Christ's part. Paul says elsewhere that Christ was "justified in the Spirit" (1 Tim. 3:16). The writer of Hebrews says that Christ "offered himself without fault to God . . . through the eternal Spirit" (Heb. 9:14) and spoke of Christ, "who in the days of his flesh, when he had offered up prayers and supplications with strong crying and tears unto him that was able to save him from death, and was heard for his piety, his godly fear. . ." (Heb. 5:7). When He was on earth as a true man, Christ operated through a commitment to the Holy Spirit. Because He did this, God heard Him.

Jesus was declared to be the Son of God "by the resurrection from the dead" (1:4). This can be translated either "from" or "of" the dead. What is the difference? Resurrection "from the dead" would seem to refer solely to Christ's own resurrection, while resurrection "of" the dead would seem to have in view our future resurrection as well. Either way it would be enough to prove Christ's deity—He is determined to be, declared to be the Son of God by the marvelous fact that He has been raised physically from the dead and that there shall be the Christian's future resurrection from the dead.

By whom we have received grace and apostleship, for obedience to

the faith among all nations, for his name: among whom are ye also the called of Jesus Christ. (1:5-6)

Paul and his colleagues received grace and apostleship for a definite purpose: "for obedience to the faith among all nations, for his name." Paul's mission is not only to Jews, but to "all nations." He is leading up to 1:7, where he states that he is now writing to Rome, the capital of his known world. He now faces away from himself and the "we" of 1:5 and turns toward those to whom he is writing: ". . . among whom are ye also the called of Jesus Christ." These are the Christians, Jews and Gentiles alike, making up the church at Rome. They all have a place "among the nations" that Paul has been called to reach.

To all that be in Rome . . . (1:7a)

We are now brought face to face with the church in Rome, probably meeting in a home, a church perhaps founded by laypeople rather than by an apostle. Paul had not been to Rome, and neither, despite the traditional Roman Catholic view, had Peter. If Peter had been in Rome, it is inconceivable that Paul would not have mentioned him in this letter. Yet the church was there, a united church of Jews and Gentiles in the world capital of Rome. And this should not surprise us, for the church at Antioch of Syria, perhaps the greatest of the early churches, the one that sent out the first missionaries, was also started by laypeople (Acts 11:19-20). It is reasonable to think that the same thing could have happened in Rome. If you go to Rome today you can see the traditional site of Priscilla and Aquila's home, where a church met. To me this is the ideal. It is the way the church would have continued to function if the Holy Spirit had been allowed to work—wherever Christians go, they proclaim the gospel and little churches spring up.

To all that be in Rome, beloved of God, called . . . saints. (1:7a)

You will notice that I have left out the words "to be" in the phrase "called to be saints." The KJV includes these words in italics, but they are not there in the Greek; they were added by translators to make the English flow more smoothly. When we read it as "called saints," however, we are brought face-to-face with the fact that here in Rome, in the world capital, there are those who are saints in God sight. As soon as we accept Christ as our Savior, we are saints in God's sight. This is based first upon Jesus' passive work, His passive obedience in taking the punishment for our sins. But it is based also upon His active obedience in perfectly keeping the law for us. Christ's mediatorial work for us began at His baptism, when His public ministry started. From that time on, what He did, He did not only for Himself but for us. When we accept Him as Savior, His active obedience means that we have a positive righteousness with God. We are clothed with the righteousness of Jesus Christ. Our guilt is gone on the basis of His finished work on the cross, His passive obedience. But we are also clothed with His perfect righteousness, based on His active obedience. This being so, we, like the Romans, can be called saints right now.

Paul likewise addresses the Ephesian and Philippian Christians as saints (Eph. 5:3; Phil. 1:1). The Ephesians passage is especially intriguing: "But fornication, and all uncleanness, or covetousness, let it not be once named among you, as becometh saints." This speaks of something quite different than the traditional Roman Catholic view that a saint is someone special. The New Testament teaches that you are a saint as soon as you accept Christ as your Savior. Christ has taken your guilt and you are clothed with His perfection. If a little boy puts on his father's overcoat and buttons it above his head, you see nothing but the overcoat. Likewise, when God looks at us, He sees nothing but the righteousness of Jesus Christ that covers us.

But since you are a saint, says Paul in Ephesians, you should live like a saint. Likewise he says elsewhere, "If we live in the Spirit, let us also walk in the Spirit" (Gal. 5:25). Be what you are in the sight of God. This is the very antithesis of salvation through works. Everything depends upon the finished work of Jesus Christ. Our calling is to live in keeping with what we already are in God's sight—and as we will be one day in history, at Christ's Second Coming. This is the great lesson of chapter 6, where Paul explains sanctification. There we will learn more about this great truth.

Grace to you and peace from God our Father, and the Lord Jesus

Christ. First, I thank my God through Jesus Christ for you all, that your faith is spoken of throughout the whole world. (1:7b-8)

News of the little church at Rome and the reputation of their faith had become known throughout the Christian world. It must have been a great encouragement as word came back that in Rome, the capital of the world, there was a faithful church of Jews and Gentiles.

For God is my witness, whom I serve with my spirit in the gospel of his Son, that without ceasing I make mention of you always in my prayers; making request, if by any means now at length I might have a prosperous journey by the will of God to come unto you. (1:9-10)

There are three steps in Paul's prayer for the Roman believers: He thanks God for them (1:8), then prays on their behalf (1:9), then makes a specific request regarding them: that he might get to see them soon (1:10).

For I long to see you, that I may impart unto you some spiritual gift, to the end ye may be established; that is, that I may be comforted together with you by the mutual faith both of you and me. (1:11-12)

Paul is not distant or aloof from the people he writes to. Rather, he longs to be with them. His desire that they be "established" parallels Luke's desire that his friend Theophilus might "know the certainty of those things, wherein thou hast been instructed" (Luke 1:4). Paul knows that such maturity will bring sweet and wonderful fellowship between himself and the Romans. He expects to receive a blessing from them as well as giving one to them. This is surely true among Christians always. When the relationship is what it should be, the blessings run in both directions.

Now I would not have you ignorant, brethren, that oftentimes I purposed to come unto you, (but was let hitherto,) . . . (1:13a)

The educated reader should have few problems with the King James translation, but "let" is one such problem. It meant "hindered." Today it means the exact opposite. Its meaning of "hindered" survives only in tennis: When the ball strikes the net we have a "let ball," meaning that the ball was hindered. Paul was "let," or hindered, in his desire to visit Rome.

. . . that I might have some fruit among you also, even as among other Gentiles. (1:13b)

Paul has expressed his desire to impart a spiritual gift to the Romans (1:11), but he expects from them a harvest of spiritual fruit. It is two ways of saying the same thing: The gift is the cause, while the fruit is the effect.

I am debtor both to the Greeks and to the Barbarians, both to the wise, and to the unwise. (1:14)

Paul considers himself a debtor to both educated and uneducated, the wise and the unwise. This is an entirely different mentality than that of most Christians. Most Christians think they are doing something special when they tell others about the gospel. But Paul understands that such witnessing is not something special, for he is a debtor (1:14) or a "servant" (1:1) of the gospel. We, like Paul, should feel ourselves indebted to preach the gospel to everyone. It is a debt we can never escape. There is no neutrality or convenience in Him, for we are debtors to preach the gospel. At the end of this introduction to Rome, Paul then concludes:

So, as much as is in me, I am ready to preach the gospel to you that are at Rome also. (1:15)

He is ready to preach the gospel wherever the Lord takes him, regardless of the cost. There's no doubt that Paul was eventually killed in Rome, so his desire to preach the gospel there did, indeed, cost him greatly. Yet there is really no other way to preach the gospel to a lost and dying world. As you give your life to the Lord, there will be a cost. "Paul, a servant . . ." (1:1). "I am debtor" (1:14). "So, as much as in me is . . ." (1:15). We are not playing games.

For I am not ashamed of the gospel of Christ: for it is the power of God unto salvation to every one that believeth, to the Jew first, and also to the Greek. For therein is the righteousness of God revealed

from faith to faith: as it is written, The just shall live by faith. (1:16-17)

With these verses we begin the first main section of Romans, chapters 1—8. These chapters are really an exegesis of 1:16-17. You never get beyond these two verses. 1:1-15 is the introduction; 1:16-17 is the theme; then 1:18—8:39 is the exegesis of that theme.

Paul is "not ashamed" of the gospel. Later, he will say that "hope maketh not ashamed" (5:5). He uses basically the same Greek word in both places, but with a slightly different emphasis. After we have accepted Christ as our Savior (in Chapter 5), we experience a hope that will not disappoint us or make us ashamed. But even at the beginning, there is no need to be intellectually ashamed of or disappointed in the gospel as a system. Paul is not speaking to backward or primitive people. He is surrounded by the Greek and Roman world with all its intellectual understanding, yet he is not ashamed of what he is preparing to speak about.

Jesus warned us not to be ashamed of the intellectual content of His teaching (Luke 9:26). As if answering Jesus, Paul says, "I am not ashamed of the gospel." Paul was not ashamed as he stood on Mars Hill (Acts 17). He was not ashamed when confronting the religious leaders of his day. He was not ashamed to preach while imprisoned in Rome. So also we, surrounded by our intellectual world, should not and need not be ashamed.

It is a very serious thing to be ashamed of Jesus and His teaching (Luke 9:26). In his last letter to Timothy, Paul reminds us that this includes not being ashamed of those who truly stand for Jesus and His word: "Be not thou therefore ashamed of the testimony of our Lord, nor of me his prisoner" (2 Tim. 1:8). We should proudly identify with all who identify themselves with Christ. Paul cites the example of Onesiphorus, who "oft refreshed me, and was not ashamed of my chains" (2 Tim. 1:16).

Paul tells Timothy of his own suffering for the gospel's sake, concluding, "Nevertheless I am not ashamed: for I know whom I have believed, and am persuaded that he is able to keep that which I have committed unto him against that day" (2 Tim. 1:12). "That day" is the Second Coming of Christ. We should be unashamed of Christ for as long as we live (2 Tim. 4:1) or until He returns, not just when things are going well, but even when the gospel is in ill repute. And we shall not be ashamed in experience either. That was certainly the case with Paul as he wrote to Timothy from prison.

We should then not be ashamed of the practice of Christianity, but also not of the teaching of it in its intellectual concepts. There is an imperative here, not just a passing thought. It is a lifelong experience not to be ashamed.

For . . . the gospel of Christ . . . is the power of God unto salvation. (1:16)

We often use the word *salvation* as though it were parallel to *justification*. Perhaps we ask, "Are you saved?" when a more accurate question would be, "Are you justified? Is your guilt gone?" There are biblical reasons for using "saved" in this way, yet when Paul is being explicit he uses *justification* for this concept. When we accept Christ as our Savior, we are justified. Justification addresses a legal problem. It means God declares that our guilt is gone on the basis of the finished work of Jesus Christ. But our salvation is much wider than justification.

Salvation includes three tenses: past, present, and future. Romans 1—8 covers all three tenses of salvation. Chapters 1-4 deal with the past act of salvation for the Christian, which is justification. Romans 5:1 through 8:17 deals with salvation's present aspect, which is sanctification. Then, in a brief but very striking way, 8:18-39 speaks of the future aspect of salvation, which is glorification.

Salvation includes all of this on the basis of the finished work of Christ.

. . . for it is the power of God unto salvation. (1:16b)

Literally from the Greek, the gospel is God's *dunamis*, His dynamite by which He brings about salvation, all of it: justification to remove guilt, sanctification in the present life, and at the Second Coming glorification.

. . . the power of God unto salvation to every one that believeth, to the Jew first, and also to the Greek. (1:16b)

Paul's next words make this concept of salvation very large but also very limited. It was very large: ". . . to every one . . . to the Jew first, and also to the Greek." The Jews had thought of salvation as applying only to themselves. Paul emphasizes that this is not so. Salvation, he says, applies to Gentiles as well as Jews. But it would be just as correct for us to say that salvation applies to Jews as well as Gentiles. It is a completely open circle. The whole world, people of all skin colors, people under all flags, the door is open to them all for salvation. The circle of salvation is as big as one can imagine. It includes the world's entire population, throughout all time. It is totally universal. It is the power of God unto salvation, to everyone. Earlier Paul spoke of the Greeks and Barbarians (1:14), meaning the educated and the uneducated. The circle of salvation is as large as us. It's the whole world. The educated, the uneducated, the Jew, the Gentile; wherever you find a lost person, the circle of salvation is as big as that.

Paul says the gospel is "to the Jew first," and of course his practice, as seen throughout Acts, was to preach in the synagogue first and then, when they rejected him, to turn to the Gentiles. Today, unfortunately, we Christians often just leave the Jewish community alone. Even if we don't follow Paul's practice of going to Jews first, we certainly should not leave them till last or ignore them altogether.

The circle of salvation is large, but it is also very small. There is a definite limitation: ". . . to every one that believeth." The circle is as big as the world, but includes only those who believe. Each individual has the choice of either accepting or rejecting the gospel.

The gospel is the power of God for that total salvation to all who believe that to them accrues the active and passive obedience of Christ. But it is limited to those who believe.

For therein is the righteousness of God revealed from faith to faith, as it is written, The just shall live by faith. (1:17)

This carries us along to see that salvation involves more than justification. We are justified by faith, but we are also to live in the present by that same faith—not just concerning finances but in all areas of life. Martin Luther proclaimed justification by faith alone, and of course that is taught throughout the Bible and is included in what Paul says here. But he goes further: After being justified by faith, we are to live by faith. It is the second aspect of salvation, our sanctification, that Paul will explain in 5:1 through 8:17.

"The just shall live by faith" is a quotation from Habakkuk 2:4 in the Old Testament and occurs two other times in the New Testament (Gal. 3:11; Heb. 10:38). As we observed in 1:2, there is a unity in the message of the Old and the New Testaments. There are not two religions in the Bible, not two ways of salvation, only one. Habakkuk says, "Behold, his soul which is lifted up is not upright in him: but the just shall live by his faith" (Hab. 2:4). He is contrasting the person whose soul is "lifted up" on the basis of his or her good works with the person who lives "by faith." Paul is drawing the same contrast. It isn't only the contrast of becoming a Christian through faith rather than through moral or religious works; it applies to the present aspect of salvation as well. The person who waits to be saved on the basis of his or her own righteousness will wait forever. Likewise, if we wait to grow spiritually on the basis of our own prideful efforts, there will be no spiritual growth.

"The just shall *live* by faith." Beginning in 4:17 and especially in chapter 5 and on, *life* and *death* will become key words. Paul will constantly contrast being dead and being alive. And though he doesn't really begin to develop that theme till then, it is at the very heart of what he is teaching in these introductory verses. Already we have seen the phrase, "the resurrection from the dead" (1:4). If, as we suggested, this is translated "the resurrection *of* the dead," then Paul is already thinking in terms of our complete salvation—the total life that is ours in Jesus Christ. We are to "live by faith" now. In chapters 5 and 6 Paul will develop this into a call to fullness of life on the basis of the blood of Christ, by faith, now. It isn't just being justified, it is something much more than that.

PART ONE

JUSTIFICATION

(1:18—4:25)

2

THE PERSON WITHOUT THE
BIBLE: GUILTY
(1:18—2:16)

꽃

For the wrath of God is revealed from heaven against all ungodliness and unrighteousness of men, who hold the truth in unrighteousness. (1:18)

When Paul says that the gospel is "the power of God unto salvation" (1:16), the unsaved person may well ask, "Why do I need salvation?" Luther pointed out that the gospel really includes both gospel and law: There is no use telling men that they must be saved (the *gospel*) until they feel a need for salvation (a need that the *law* reveals). Christianity in the Old and New Testament teaching is unique in emphasizing the need for salvation. Other religions stress that you need a guide or some other kind of help to teach you how to live or how to die. But these other religions do not emphasize the need for salvation from guilt. Our problem is not metaphysical, but moral.

In 1:18 Paul begins explaining why all people need a Savior. He explains the need for salvation first as it applies to Gentiles (1:18—2:16), then as it applies to Jews (2:17—3:8), then as it applies to all humanity, Jew and Gentile alike (3:9-20). I like to describe it this way: Paul speaks first to the person who does not have the Bible, then to the person who does have the Bible. That, after all, was the main difference between the Jews and Gentiles of Paul's day, and those two categories will certainly help us apply Paul's teachings to our world today. Why does everyone in the world need a Savior?

To the Gentile (the person without the Bible) who asks, "Why do I need salvation?" Paul says, with finality (v. 18), Because "the wrath of

God is revealed from heaven against all ungodliness of men who hold the truth in unrighteousness!" You are under the wrath of God—that's why you need salvation. Mankind needs a real salvation. We don't need a spiritual guide or the inspiring example of a martyr. We need a real Savior because we are under God's very real wrath. In mentioning God's wrath, Paul introduces the first key word of the Christian vocabulary: *guilt*. He discusses guilt in 1:18—3:20. Then, in 3:21—4:25, he will discuss the second key Christian word: *substitution*, that is, Christ's substitutionary death for our sins. People of other religions have no concept whatsoever of the Christian significance of these two words.

We need salvation because we are under the wrath of God. We need a real salvation because we are guilty. That wrath of God will come to fruition at the judgment at the Second Coming of Jesus (2:5). The Second Coming in the future is our focus point in the same way as we look back to the day of Jesus' death. This is parallel to the Lord's Supper with its emphasis on the death of Christ in the past and the looking forward to the day He will come again.

There is another question that the unsaved person without the Bible asks. It has been asked in every generation, though perhaps never shouted louder than in our own generation: If God made me, why am I now under His wrath? If God made me as I am, how can He consider me guilty? Is He not unjust in doing so? Where does evil come from? God is unjust if He made us this way and holds us guilty. This takes us right back to the words of the Bible's teaching of a historic Fall. If you remove the record of a historic Fall in Genesis we will lose all contact with the Christian message. Without that answer to the origin of evil, the book of Romans would have no meaning, the death of Christ would have no meaning. Why should God hold us under His wrath if He made us the way we are? If He had made us all four feet tall, would He judge us for not being six feet tall?

Paul answers that question:

Because that which may be known of God is manifest in them [those without a Bible]; for God hath shown it unto them. (1:19)

That which is known of God is obvious, even to the person without the Bible—for God has shown it to them. He has shown it, first of all, through their conscience, as Paul explains later: "Which show the work of the law written in their hearts, their conscience also bearing witness, and their thoughts the mean while accusing or else excusing one another" (2:15). Everyone has a conscience. Paul will speak later of the fall of Adam and Eve, but he begins by dealing with the individual non-Christian and non-Jewish reader, the lost man or woman. He is dealing with individual man as significant. He is dealing with the individual man or woman standing before him in the Roman world, or with the individual man or woman reading his words in the twentieth century. And he says to that person, "You ask why you are under God's wrath, but look at you! Don't you have a conscience? Don't you know very well that you are not the person you should be?" Paul doesn't allow the distraction of endless arguments. He keeps it on the level of the individual, a significant man.

He says to the Gentile nonbeliever, "Even though you have never seen a Bible, you have a conscience and you know that you have violated it. You're not a machine. You're not a robot. You're not an animal. You can't excuse yourself by animal psychology. You know you have a conscience and you know that you have violated it."

For the invisible things of him from the creation of the world are clearly seen, being understood by the things that are made, even his eternal power and Godhead; so that they are without excuse. (1:20)

Not only does the nonbeliever have a conscience, he should know there is a God simply by observing the amazing creation all around him. He is not living in a dark cave. He can see creation all around him and surely he must wonder where it all came from. And yet, men would rather believe a gigantic lie that they are really nothing than believe the reality that there is a God. The Bible emphasizes many times that creation is a testimony to God. Even those who do not have the Bible should be able to conclude from creation that there is a God. As the psalmist says, "The heavens declare the glory of God; and the firmament showeth his handiwork. Day unto day uttereth speech, and night unto night showeth knowledge" (Psalm 19:1-2). Notice it is *knowledge* that creation reveals. As Paul shows, creation reveals knowledge to the rational person—who can't escape his rationality even though he is a rebel. "There is no speech nor language, where their voice is not heard" (Psalm 19:3). There is one voice that is heard wherever humans live, with or without the Bible. It is the voice of creation. And creation is not speaking to the sticks and the stones, it is not speaking to the animals, it is not speaking to machines; creation is speaking to the rational creature who is a rebel against the Creator, even while he is still a rational creature.

In its original language Psalm 19:3 reads, "There is no speech nor language without their voice heard." It doesn't make smooth English, but the thought is that you can just feel it. It comes like a great weight against you. "There is no speech nor language without their voice heard."

Paul quotes from this Psalm in Romans 10:18 and expressed similar thoughts about creation's witness to God when speaking at Lystra: "Nevertheless he left not himself without witness, in that he did good, and gave us rain from heaven, and fruitful seasons, filling our hearts with food and gladness" (Acts 14:17). Here Paul focuses not so much on creation as a past event, but on creation as the present good providence of God. Jesus likewise speaks of the rain falling on the just and the unjust (Matt. 5:45). Paul is challenging nonbelievers, not just on the basis of the creation's witness as a past event, but also on the basis of the witness of a creation that bathes them with sun and bathes their fields with rain and dew. So often Christians argue intellectually for the existence of God, using arguments such as the need for a first cause, and this has value; but the truth is much deeper than this. It isn't just that our world had a first cause, but that we are surrounded with the good things of God. He fills our every human need, and this should be ample testimony to His existence.

Paul clearly states that even though mankind is fallen, man is still a moral and rational being. He is not dehumanized. He still has a conscience (1:19), and he can still appreciate the wonder of creation all around him (1:20). He hasn't become a machine, even though he may choose to think of himself as a machine rather than acknowledge the Creator. A book on the Dutch painter van Gogh points out that from the time he arrived in Paris till the time of his suicide, his self-portraits grew less and less human. But the Fall didn't stop van Gogh or anyone else from being human. Each human is still an image-bearer of

God, and we can speak to him or her of the gospel. He is still a person, though he dehumanizes himself. If the Fall of mankind had resulted in men and women being nothing but machines, they would not be guilty before God. Yet whether in this life or in hell, man continues to be a rational, moral creature. He never becomes a machine.

We marvel at the wonderful things fallen humans can do—in the arts, in creativity, in technology—even while rebelling against God. And yet because they are still human and still rational, they stand condemned under the wrath of God. They could draw a conclusion from the world around them and they don't. That is their condemnation. They are not simply under the *displeasure* of God. There isn't just a fog separating them from God. Rather, they are subject to God's wrath because they are guilty. In the twentieth century our whole concept is that people are estranged from God . . . if there is a God. But Paul's viewpoint is quite different: Because people are guilty, God holds them under His wrath. Therefore, what man needs is a Savior.

Paul will go to great lengths—from 1:18 to 3:20—to explain to the Greeks and Romans, and then to Jews, and then to mankind in general that they are under God's wrath and need to be saved; then he will take just a few verses to tell them how to be saved (3:21-30). After a person knows he needs a Savior, it doesn't take many words to tell him that there *is* a Savior. The problem is for fallen humans, each at the center of his or her own universe, to acknowledge that they need a Savior. They will quickly acknowledge that they need a guide, that they need help, that they need greater technical expertise. But Paul wants them to see that they need a Savior.

Because that, when they knew God, they glorified him not as God, neither were thankful; but became vain in their imaginations, and their foolish heart was darkened. (1:21)

The person without the Bible might then ask, "If all this is true, why are we in the mess we're in? What happened?" From 1:21 to 1:31, Paul explains what happened. He will later speak explicitly of the historical Fall of Adam and Eve (5:12-21), but throughout this section he has in view that first and historic Fall as well as the many "falls" that happen over and over in history, in the lives of individual men and women in every age.

Actually, you can think of the Fall in three different ways. First there was the original Fall of mankind, which ultimately explains why so many people here and abroad do not know the true God. You can also think of the Fall in terms of nations throughout history knowing the truth but then turning from it. If you had stood in Trafalgar Square or Columbus Circle sixty years ago and asked a thousand people what the gospel is, most of them could have told you. Maybe they wouldn't have accepted it, but they could have told you what it is. However, if you stood today in Trafalgar Square, in Columbus Circle, or between the lions in front of the Art Institute in Chicago, and asked a thousand people what the gospel is, you would find very few who could answer. There was a much greater knowledge of Christianity in past generations. We are living in a post-Christian world today.

Thirdly, it is possible for individuals to go through this cycle—to know the truth and then deliberately turn away from it. I'm always amazed at the number of famous people who have come out of missionary or ministerial homes, who have known the gospel, and yet later have deliberately turned away.

So the individual can fall away from the truth. Back of that we see whole cultures falling away. At the beginning stands the original Fall. Paul has all three of these in mind.

So why are we in such a mess? What happened? Paul begins his answer by speaking of a time when mankind "knew God." This was of course absolutely true in the Garden of Eden. Adam and Eve knew God and had communion with Him. Similarly, there was a time when our European and American culture knew God. Applying it to the individual, there are many nonbelievers who were taught about God as children. So when the person without the Bible asks, "Why am I under the wrath of God? How did this happen?" Paul begins by pointing out that either they or someone in their past knew God. Unbelievers are not just a lot of stones scattered out across the world. They all came from someone who knew God and then deliberately turned away—even if in their case that someone was Adam. You don't begin with ignorance. You may find ignorance finally, but you don't begin with ignorance. You begin with men and women who knew God.

Because that, when they knew God, they glorified him not as God, neither were thankful . . . (1:21a)

However, these people who knew God—Adam and Eve, or our closer ancestors, or ourselves—chose not to glorify Him as God, and not to give Him thanks. Non-Christian philosophies don't become popular because of their intellectual appeal, but because people have chosen to rebel against God. They rebel and refuse to glorify and thank God as Creator. Only then do they search for a rationale for their rebellion in the mysteries or promises of other religions.

. . . but became vain in their imaginations, and their foolish heart was darkened. (1:21b)

When people refused to thank God and give Him the glory, their hearts and imaginations became dark and vain. This is not the vanity of a girl spending two hours in front of the mirror combing her hair. It is the vanity of the creature not willing to be the creature, but wanting rather to be the creator at the center of the universe. This vanity causes people to "become fools" (1:22). They become total fools, understanding neither themselves nor the universe they live in. That's why we see so many in the twentieth century who cannot seem to differentiate themselves from machines. They profess to be wise (1:22) in the sense of seeing themselves at the center. This is not the real wisdom of the scientist, the skill of the artist, but a vanity of the fool in the wrong place.

The psalmist says, "The fool has said in his heart there is no God" (Psalm 14:1). This is true in two senses: You would be a fool to say that there is no God; but once you have said such a thing, you become a total fool. The Fall of mankind wasn't just a matter of falling off a curb or something. Humans are in the mess they are in because they have chosen to rebel against God and as a result have become total fools.

On the positive side, we also read in the Psalms of what happens when people choose to *return* to God: "All the ends of the earth shall remember and turn unto the LORD: and all the kindreds of the nations shall worship before thee. . . . . A seed shall serve him; it shall be accounted to the LORD for a generation. They shall come, and shall declare his righteousness unto a people that shall be born" (Psalm 22:27, 30-31). Those who return to God become those who are not fools. They become the humanity of God. They return to the place for which mankind was made in the first place.

Paul touches on the same theme in Ephesians 4:17-18: "This I say therefore, and testify in the Lord, that ye henceforth walk not as other Gentiles walk, in the vanity of their mind, having the understanding darkened, being alienated from the life of God through the ignorance that is in them, because of the blindness [hardness] of their heart." When we accept Christ as our Savior, we return as the seed of God. And here Paul turns to the Christian and says, "Look, you were in this vanity" (the same term he used in Romans), "but now you have become the redeemed portion of humanity, the humanity that is returning to the purpose of its creation. Therefore, don't walk in vanity—don't return to the world's way of looking at things. Don't put yourself again at the center of the universe. Rather, keep God at the center of *His* universe in your thinking and in your life, and find your meaning in reference to Him." You are the "seed" of God on the basis of the finished work of Christ and no longer "fools" about God, the universe itself, or your own purpose.

As those saved from the vanity of this rebellion against God, we have a message for those still in rebellion: "For after that in the wisdom of God the world by wisdom knew not God, it pleased God by the foolishness of preaching to save them that believe. For the Jews require a sign, and the Greeks seek after wisdom: But we preach Christ crucified, unto the Jews a stumblingblock, and unto the Greeks foolishness. But unto them which are called, both Jews and Greeks, Christ the power of God, and the wisdom of God. Because the foolishness of God is wiser than men, and the weakness of God is stronger than men" (1 Cor. 1:21-25). When the world knew of the true and the living God, they deliberately turned aside and became totally vain—the total vanity of being willing to consider themselves as animals, as machines, as a zero rather than acknowledge the Creator, be thankful, and give Him glory.

How do we reach this lost world? Paul warns us that they will in their vanity consider our message foolish. Yet he calls us to take this "foolishness" into their midst. We must stand amid the twentieth century world, with all its pressure, with the total weight of its opposition to the Christian faith, and proclaim the gospel. There is truth to the universe. Man deliberately turned away from it. He is still rational, moral, and has a conscience. We must give him the same message Paul is giving in the first eight chapters of Romans. And while our message may seem foolish to the world that believes that there is no meaning, yet God will use it to speak to some of them. It is the content of that gospel that needs to be given.

Proclaiming this gospel to rebellious mankind can, of course, seem foolish at times. We can be overwhelmed by the difficulty and the size of the task. Yet, thankfully, God has given us only three things to do and then our responsibility is closed. The first is to preach the gospel as clearly as possible, answering all questions as clearly as we can to present the truth about the universe, man, and our dilemma. The second is to pray for each individual who hears it. And the third is, by the grace of God, through faith in the finished work of Christ, to live a life that in some poor fashion will commend the gospel we have preached. When we have done these three things with compassion, amid this world that has turned away from God and is totally dark and vain, some of them will respond.

Professing themselves to be wise, they became fools. (1:22)

Deliberately turning away from God and therefore understanding neither themselves nor the universe, men and women have become absolute fools. They are trying to live in a universe that isn't there in the way they see it—without God, without human beings. And that is total folly. The Bible is drawing the blackness of the world that fallen mankind, in his rebellion, has deliberately chosen. This is what Adam did earlier. He walked away from life and chose death. It is the world our forefathers in the last few generations of northern European and American culture have chosen. This tragic choice is perhaps most clear in the United States, for it has occurred there most recently after about 1890. There are some still living who have witnessed the entire process. It is a blackness of a world man does not understand.

In Deuteronomy, Moses speaks of how God's people can maintain godly wisdom in a world that has rejected God and has therefore become foolish. Speaking of God's laws, Moses charges Israel to "Keep therefore and do [the laws]; for this is your wisdom and your understanding in the sight of the nations" (Deut. 4:6). Several centuries later Jeremiah speaks to an Israel that has forsaken God's law, with the sad result that "The wise men are ashamed, they are dismayed and taken: lo, they have rejected the word of the LORD; and what wisdom is in them?" (Jer. 8:9).

When we reject God's revelation, "what wisdom is in [us]"? What do we know? On what basis do we know anything at all? It is intriguing that this question of how we know plays such a key role in modern philosophy. Having rejected divine revelation, modern philosophers are preoccupied with the study of epistemology, the study of how we know the things we know. And here in the Bible God is asking, "What is your epistemological base, after you have given away my Word?"

And changed [exchanged] the glory of the uncorruptible God into an image made like to corruptible man, and to birds, and fourfooted beasts, and creeping things. (1:23)

A profound emphasis is found in the word "image." Having been made in the image of God (Gen. 1:26), men and women rebel and, wanting to be the center of their universe, they deliberately reverse the process and make God in their image! They were made in God's image—rational, moral, and with significance. But because they have refused to acknowledge themselves as creatures, they have found it necessary to make God in their own image.

Scholars today will talk about people making God in their own image and will think they are rather clever to have made this observation. But Paul observed this in the first century. There is nothing new! It is the same basic problem. Either God exists and made man in His image, or man came out of the fog and made himself a god in his image. The Bible says God was there. The infinite, personal God was there with all His wonderful attributes, and man deliberately exchanged this and made God the corruptible image of mankind or birds or beasts. He exchanged the infinite for the finite. He exchanged great wealth and truth for poverty, for sorrow, and for ignorance.

Remember that Paul is answering the person who asks, "Why are we in the mess we're in?" Paul says this is the reason: Mankind knew the truth but deliberately turned away. Mankind would rather have his ignorance and be at the center of the universe than have the answer and acknowledge God as Creator and himself as creature.

Paul, living in the first century, had the same answer we must give today. There is no difference in the basic questions and answers.

Wherefore God also gave them up to uncleanness through the lusts of their own hearts, to dishonour their own bodies between themselves. (1:24)

Notice the logical sequence: Mankind needs salvation because he is under the wrath of God (1:18). He is under the wrath of God because, in spite of his conscience and in spite of being surrounded by God's wonderful creation, he deliberately sins and turns away from God (1:19-23).

Our situation then is not the result of a mistake but of a real rebellion. The result is sadness, breakdown, man living against his fellow man. Man does not merely need a change of direction, but he is guilty. This understanding lies at the basis of a very different view of sociology, of psychology, and of education for Christians.

And now we see God's response to mankind's rebellion against Him (1:24). He "gave them up." We could picture mankind as a bad dog. He has rebelled and has established his direction. He wants to get away from God, his master. Therefore, God simply lets go of the leash. I remember seeing the Swiss train dogs for border patrols in the mountains. They give these dogs a fearsome, awful character, and when they are unleashed that character determines their direction, and it is a horrible thing to see. This is the picture Paul paints of mankind. It is what happened in our country. People chose to give up the truth, and God gave them up.

Paul restates this awful truth in 1:28: "Even as they did not like to retain God in their knowledge, God gave them over to a reprobate mind, to do those things which are not convenient [becoming]." Mankind had chosen his direction by refusing to acknowledge God. Therefore, God "gave them over"—He let go of the leash—and allowed them to go their own rebellious and immoral way. This is not just a dialectic, but a deliberate rebellion.

God gave mankind up, and they followed their desires into all sorts of immoral behavior. All sins and all human problems flow from our choice not to put God at the center of His universe. As Christians, we should never minimize the efforts of sociologists or criminologists to address social ills. But we must understand that most such efforts are only treating the results, not the disease. There is much legitimate concern today over moral and cultural breakdown, and we are piling on all kinds of supposed cures. These things may help, but don't expect them to cure. They are like powders, salves, cover-ups. If a girl has a bad eruption on her face from eating too many sweets, she may cover it up with powder or she may put on a salve that makes it a little better, but the only cure is quitting the sweets. If the problem with mankind is his rebellion against God, then no amount of treating the result is going to bring any real cure. One must treat the malady directly, which is the rebellion against God. No cosmetic covers will provide the necessary cure.

Who changed the truth of God into a lie, and worshipped and served the creature more than the Creator, who is blessed for ever. (1:25)

Having discussed the cause of mankind's rebellion (1:19-23) and then briefly discussing its results (1:24), Paul now reminds us of the link between the cause (1:25) and the logical results (1:26-31). Mankind "changed the truth of God into a lie." In so doing he lost not only the truth about God's existence, but also the truth about the universe and about himself. When man rebels and steps out of his primary reference to God, a proper relationship to God, everything becomes a lie. Mankind doesn't know who he is. The truth is gone. Not only does he question the existence of God. He questions his own existence as well and everything that flows from the existence of God.

If the rebel against God were totally logical, he would deny all his human aspirations—his aspirations to find truth and all his other aspirations as well. Jeremiah 10:10, in the original Hebrew, says, "The LORD is the God of truth." Mankind has "changed the truth of God into a lie," but "the LORD is the God of truth." There is no other truth or understanding in the universe. When people throw away the God of truth, all truth is gone. All that is left are sets of opinions, and personal gods and pleasures.

. . . and served the creature more than the Creator . . . (1:25b)

The Greek actually says they served the creature "rather than" the Creator—not just more than, but rather than. They turned it all around. Perhaps this was easier to see in Paul's day because they served actual idols, making Venus like a woman and Hercules like a strong man. But nothing has really changed; this creature worship is just more subtle in our own day. Mankind has put himself at the center.

When nonbelievers use the word *God* today, they are usually making their own god in the image of man just as thoroughly as the Greeks did. There are two ways to make a god in the image of man: One is to chisel something out of stone or create something with paint. Another is to sink into your armchair and simply project yourself, the creature, a bit further and say, "This is what God is like!" One doesn't need stone or paint to make a god.

Indeed many of us worship the very creature we know best—ourselves! In Isaiah we read about the tragic results of idolatry, including self-worship. The idolater, says Isaiah, "feedeth on ashes: a deceived heart hath turned him aside, that he cannot deliver his soul, nor say, Is there not a lie in my right hand?" (Isa. 44:20). The people who couldn't recognize a lie in Isaiah's day were the same as the people of Paul's day who had changed God's truth into a lie. And what was the result? They were "feeding on ashes." Likewise today, when we worship and idolize ourselves, we end up feeding on ashes. Mankind says, "I will put myself at the center of the universe," but he ends up feeding on ashes, for that is all that is left: ashes in the realm of morality, ashes in the realm of beauty, ashes in the realm of love, ashes in the realm of meaning.

What is the solution? Isaiah gives it: "Remember this, and show yourselves men" (Isa. 46:8). In other words, "Be rational!" And if you are rational, then you must turn back to God. God has made you rational and moral. If you follow true rationality and true morality so that you are truly human, you will turn back to God. Isaiah's advice is quite the contrary to what people tell us in the twentieth century. They say that faith means taking a jump in the dark. But Isaiah and Paul tell us that a rational pursuit of truth will lead us to God. It would be a turn-around from being man discovering the truth of the universe to knowing God. True rationality will point out that man and God are not dead!

Jeremiah foresees a day when many nonbelievers will, indeed, forsake the lies of idolatry and make a rational choice for God: "O LORD . . . the Gentiles shall come unto thee from the ends of the earth, and shall say, Surely our fathers have inherited lies, vanity, and things wherein there is no profit. Shall a man make gods unto himself, and they are no gods? Therefore, behold, . . . I will cause them to know mine hand and my might; and they shall know that my name is The LORD" (Jer. 16:19-21). Jeremiah, like Paul, speaks of the "lies" of idolatry. Jeremiah, like Paul, emphasizes that these lies are "inherited" from one generation to the next. Fallen men and women reject the truth, but they are still significant human beings and they influence those who follow them. And yet, says Jeremiah, God is always calling people back to Himself.

What has our own generation inherited from our forefathers? They have inherited lies. A young man sat in my class one day and said, "Well, everybody today thinks that there is no God." He just said it flatly. He didn't think about it. He simply repeated the lie he had inherited. He was quite amazed when I suggested that his statement was really an assumption that he needed to examine. Hosea adds (13:2), "They add sin to sin, making idols in their own image." We make them in our verbal distinction about how God is or is not. This is not a variety of religious feeling but a real act of rebellion.

For this cause God gave them up unto vile affections: for even their women did change the natural use into that which is against nature. (1:26)

At this place we can consider the results of mankind's rebellion against God. Paul will speak of homosexuality in 1:27, and that may be the meaning in 1:26 as well, but I think he may be speaking of something else here. Isaiah speaks of women who "are haughty, and walk with stretched forth necks and wanton eyes, walking and mincing as they go, and making a tinkling with their feet" (Isa. 3:16). The Hebrew for "wanton eyes" is actually "deceiving with their eyes." Isaiah seems to be describing women who use their womanliness to deceive, and I think that is what Paul is saying as well. The woman has used what she is as a woman, not as God intended, but to deceive. The lie that mankind has believed (1:25) is such a total lie that everything in life, the most beautiful things of life, are twisted. The things that should give the deepest contact of personality with personality on the human level are destroyed. We have lost contact with the primary reference point, a personal God. When we do this, the next level of contact, of human personality, which should be so beautiful and so wonderful, is also turned into something unwholesome. Man and woman, standing in the presence of God, should be able to relate, personality with personality, in a deep way. But because of mankind's rebellion, that relationship has become a commodity to be traded upon.

And likewise also the men, leaving the natural use of the woman, burned in their lust one toward another; men with men working that which is unseemly, and receiving in themselves that recompense of their error which was meet. (1:27)

With a realism we see throughout the Bible, Paul addresses the issue of male homosexuality. Religious people don't always like to deal with the reality of such things, but the Bible never covers up reality. It deals with humanity just as it is. Paul speaks of the "recompense," the automatic result, of such a way of living. If you minister among people such as this—homosexuals, or women who have made their womanhood a commodity—you will see people who have become absolutely miserable after an initially deceptive attraction. While giving satisfaction on some level of relationship, homosexuality is a total denial of the real world. It creates no continuity and contradicts the identity of the person as a child of a father and a mother. Sad lives end with a handful of ashes strewn to the wind. Of course, sin brings misery at any level, right down the line, but Paul points out here its awful results in these particular areas.

And even as they did not like to retain God in their knowledge, God gave them over to a reprobate mind . . . (1:28a)

"Did not like to retain God in their knowledge" might better be translated, "did not deem it worthy of approval to acknowledge God." Again Paul emphasizes the importance of the intellectual content of what we believe. Because they did not elect to acknowledge God in the realm of knowledge, God gave them over to a "reprobate" mind—a mind void of judgment—in every realm of life. As soon as you turn away from the living God and put something else in the center of the universe, you immediately throw the door open to a mind void of judgment in every area of life. Twentieth-century man has walked this path. Because of it he looks at everything differently. Morality looks different. Marriage looks different. The parent-child relationship looks different. No area of life has been untouched by this mind void of judgment.

God gave them over to a reprobate mind, to do those things which are not convenient. (1:28b)

In more modern language, "to do those things that are not becoming." These rebels did not deem it worthy of approval to acknowledge God. Therefore, God gave them over to a mind void of judgment. And therefore, as a result, they behave in unbecoming ways. Paul enumerates some of those unbecoming behaviors:

Being filled with all unrighteousness, fornication, wickedness, covetousness, maliciousness; full of envy, murder, debate, deceit, malignity; whisperers, backbiters, haters of God, despiteful, proud, boasters, inventors of evil things, disobedient to parents, without understanding, covenant-breakers, without natural affection, implacable, unmerciful. (1:29-31)

Having put himself in God's place at the center of the universe, this is where twentieth-century man is going—and he doesn't know why. America says, "What in the world has happened to our young people? We have given them everything—and look at them!" Crime is spreading throughout all society, not just in situations where we could explain it on the basis of social conditions, but among those who are prosperous and educated. Younger and younger people are choosing this kind of life, and their parents are saying, "What's wrong? What can we do?" But they can't find the cure—the cure that Paul already prescribed in 1:16—because they don't know the nature of the disease.

Who knowing the judgment of God that they which commit such things are worthy of death, not only do the same, but have pleasure in them that do them. Therefore thou art inexcusable, O man,

whosoever thou art that judgest: for wherein thou judgest another, thou condemnest thyself; for thou that judgest doest the same things. (1:32—2:1)

Though this passage includes a chapter break, it really begins a new section. Paul now addresses the reader directly. One can read 1:18-31 with an academic frame of mind, not feeling personally touched by Paul's words. But God never allows doctrinal truths to remain abstractions. They are always brought down to the level of the individual. The truth is always driven home to the individual person. To the person without the Bible who wonders, "How can God hold *me* guilty for the mess the world is in?" or, "Why do I need salvation?" Paul says, "You know that these things are wrong and yet you consent with those who do them . . . and even do them yourself!"

God is just in judging people without the Bible because they, having a conscience (1:19), and being surrounded by the wonders of creation that clearly reveal God (1:20), have rejected God and His moral law. And yet, they judge those who transgress God's law, even while doing the same things themselves (1:32—2:1). We would wonder why God would judge those who have not accepted Christ, if they have never heard of Him, for that judgment would be unjust. But failure to accept Christ is not the basis on which such people will be judged. They have rejected God and the Bible earlier on and inherited lies. Therefore they will be judged on the basis of violating their own conscience.

When those without the Bible appear before God, He will ask them one thing: "Have you kept the moral standards you have used to judge others?" It is as if each of us were born with a small tape recorder around our neck, and that tape recorder records all our moral judgments against others—"he is wrong . . . she is wrong . . . he is wrong . . ."—throughout our whole life. Then, at the final judgment, God simply plays the tape back and we hear in our own voice the moral judgments we have made and God asks, "Have you kept those standards yourself?" Obviously, we would all have to answer no. There have been ample occasions in each of our lives when we have deliberately chosen to do something we knew to be wrong. Even if God erased from the tape all the situations where we could offer a logical excuse for our actions, He would still be justified in judging us for the times we have deliberately done wrong.

Therefore thou art inexcusable, O man, whosoever thou art that judgest: for wherein thou judgest another, thou condemnest thyself; for thou that judgest doest the same things. But we are sure that the judgment of God is according to truth against them which commit such things. And thinkest thou this, O man, that judgest them which do such things, and doest the same, that thou shalt escape the judgment of God? (2:1-3)

When God says, "You are inexcusable," many people will offer one of two objections. They might say, "I may be a sinner, but at least I'm better than most other people." Or they might say, "I may be a sinner, but I'm good enough to get by. Surely God wouldn't condemn me."

Once, while staying at a hotel on the Italian Riviera, I had several conversations about the Lord with two English businessmen, both of whom were atheists. The first insisted that the second had been unfair in his business. One evening he said, "Well, if there is a God He must accept me, because I'm better than others." I said, "What do you mean?" And he said, "Well, look at that man over there. He's just a nasty, dirty businessman. I'm better than he."

About five minutes later I happened to be talking with the other businessman, and he said, "If there is a God, I will be all right." I asked why, and he said, "Well, I'm better than others. I have two sick sisters and I've given my life to taking care of them."

When you talk with nonbelievers about spiritual things, they will often say just this: "I'm better than other people, so I'll get by."

Paul answers these two objections in 2:1-6. God says, "You *won't* get by"; you won't "escape the judgment of God" (2:3). We won't get by because God judges on a standard of perfection. We couldn't get by even by our imperfect human standards, because as we judge others we condemn ourselves, having done "the same things" ourselves. The businessman who accused the other businessman of unfairness had surely made some shady deals of his own.

Each human being has a moral imperative within. Each human being "knows the judgment of God" (1:32). As soon as a child feels the pang of conscience, struggles against it, and sins, he has acknowledged that there is a meaningful moral law in the universe. As soon as he says, "I ought to do this" but then does the opposite instead, he acknowledges a moral law. Numerous modern thinkers—psychologists, anthropologists, sociologists—have tried to explain away this moral imperative. And yet all of them have felt the twinge of their own conscience. Just like a pinched nerve, their conscience has warned them not to do many of the things they have done.

Based on this innate sense of right and wrong, people without the Bible judge others (2:1), and in the process judge themselves as well, because they "do the same things" (2:1). God's judgment against them is totally just, for it is based not on things they don't know but on standards of right and wrong that they know well and that they use to judge others. Parallel to this, in Matthew 12:20 we are also condemned by our spoken words. Revelation 20:12 speaks of the unbelievers' judgment. They will be judged according to their works. The judgment of God is a judgment against the standards of the spoken words. Therefore, it is a judgment on the basis of what a person knows, not on the basis of what he does not know. There is nothing arbitrary.

Or despisest thou the riches of his goodness and forbearance and longsuffering; not knowing that the goodness of God leadeth thee to repentance? But after thy hardness and impenitent heart treasurest up unto thyself wrath against the day of wrath and revelation of the righteous judgment of God; who will render to every man according to his deeds. (2:4-6)

The nonbeliever, when feeling convicted of sin, might say, "I'll get by. I'll make it. After all, I've made it okay so far." But the Lord, with great gentleness, replies, "It is only by My kindness that you have gotten by so far. And yet you despise even that very kindness." While visiting a home for crippled children, I looked at their poor twisted bodies and thought, this is the human race. This is a far more honest view of the human race than the beautiful woman going to the opera, or the athlete in the Olympic stadium. But mankind turns away from such warnings and says, "I'll get by."

It is mankind's nature to deny the sure approach of judgment, as

Peter shows in his second letter (2 Pet. 3:3-4): "Knowing this first, that there shall come in the last days scoffers, walking after their own lusts, and saying, Where is the promise of his coming? For since the fathers fell asleep, all things continue as they were from the beginning of the creation." Just as these latter-day scoffers look at the predictability of nature and refuse to believe that God would ever upset that uniformity of natural causes and bring judgment, so also the man Paul speaks of sees God's kindness all around him and assumes that judgment will never come. God's kindness is meant to lead such people to repentance, but because of their refusal to respond, it will have the opposite result.

But after thy hardness and impenitent heart treasurest up unto thyself wrath against the day of wrath and revelation of the righteous judgment of God . . . (2:5)

What God meant for their good—such things as the witness of creation and the witness of conscience—serves only to deepen these rebels in their rebellion.

This brings us back to 1:16-18. The gospel is God's "power . . . unto salvation" (1:16). Why do we need salvation? Because we are under "the wrath of God" (1:18), and those who despise or take advantage of God's patience are only "treasuring up to themselves" more of His wrath (2:5). Christ speaks of "laying up treasures in heaven" (Matt. 6:19-20). Those who despise God's patience are likewise laying up treasures—the treasures of God's wrath. Both believers and nonbelievers need to realize that everything they do has eternal consequences. Our lives do not just last from our physical birth to our physical death. In everything we say and do, we are making deposits—for good or ill—in the bank of eternity. A young girl may focus forward to the day of her marriage and see nothing beyond that great event. But if she realizes how much her character qualities will affect her marriage, then it will change the way she lives her teenage years. Believers and nonbelievers alike need to be more aware of the supernatural and eternal consequences of their actions. Life does not end when we die. We are either "laying up" good treasures in heaven, or "treasuring up" the horrible treasure of God's wrath.

. . . who will render to every man according to his deeds. (2:6)

This is not talking about salvation by works. Rather, Paul is saying that we will be judged, not on the basis of what we profess to believe, but on the basis of a man's actions. We are dealing with a God who is truly there. Nice little professions of faith don't count with Him. What matters is what we really say and what we really do. We are dealing with a God who is really there and who responds to what we believe in fact.

To them who by patient continuance in well doing seek for glory and honour and immortality, eternal life: But unto them that are contentious, and do not obey the truth, but obey unrighteousness, indignation and wrath . . . (2:7-8)

Here is the word "wrath" again. It is God's wrath against people who all have a conscience, who see creation, who are rational beings, who understand moral principles, and yet who still disbelieve and disobey the truth. As Christians, we should be deeply concerned that the unsaved world is under the wrath of a holy God. We should not be able to think about this without some emotional reaction. Let's get it in our heads: People are lost. If we think of the unsaved world being under the wrath of God merely as an intellectual concept, remaining unstirred emotionally, we have already entered the door of dead orthodoxy. These people are my fellow humans, and they are under the wrath of God.

Try for a moment to think of yourself as a nonbeliever, hearing this for the first time. The Holy Spirit is striving within you and suddenly you realize that you are under the wrath of God. Think how you would be on tip-toe, to see if God was going to do anything about it. Paul's great message, of course, is that God *has* done something about it. It is the theme he began back in 1:16: Mankind is under God's wrath, but there is salvation from that wrath. We'll learn about that salvation beginning in 3:21.

We all need to realize that we are under God's wrath. We all need to listen expectantly to know whether there is an answer to our desperate situation. And we must never forget the wonder of learning that there is an answer. One time someone asked an old evangelist in America, "Why are you so energetic in your preaching?" And he said,

"Well, bless your heart, Son, I never forget the wonder of it." May God have mercy on us if our faith ever becomes a cold, orthodox thing and we forget the wonder of it. Don't forget the wonder of when you individually heard of Christ and believed in Him.

At the same time, however, don't forget that the human race is lost. Even while feeling the wonder of your own salvation, remember that, like Paul, you are a "debtor" to those who are still lost (1:14). May God touch our hearts as Paul continues describing their desperate situation.

. . . tribulation and anguish upon every man that doesth evil; of the Jew first and also of the Gentile. But glory, honor, and peace, to every man that worketh good; to the Jew first, and also to the Gentile: for there is no respect of persons with God. (2:9-11)

God makes no distinction between Jew and Gentile, between barbarian and Greek. All people, equally, must stand up and be counted in the presence of God.

For as many as have sinned without law shall also perish without law: and as many as have sinned in the law shall be judged by the law. (2:12)

All people stand condemned before God on the basis of what they do know. The man without the Bible is condemned on the basis of his moral judgments of others. As we saw in 2:1, he has known and spoken about these moral standards but then has failed to live up to those standards himself.

The man with the Bible, on the other hand, stands condemned on the basis of the Bible he possesses. He "shall be judged by the law" and its moral standards.

For not the hearers of the law are just before God, but the doers of the law shall be justified. (2:13)

What good does it do anyone to have a Bible if they don't believe it? When I was a pastor and would visit people in their homes, I would always read the Bible before I left, and would ask, "Do you have a Bible?" Often they would reply, "Yes, we have a Bible," and then they would start trying to find it. They would look all over their bookshelf and reach around behind it. If there had been a snake hiding there it would have bitten them! Yes, they had a Bible—to record their children's names and press flowers in. But why bother? If they never even read their Bible, why not record their children's names in some other book! There's nothing magic in just owning a Bible if you don't believe and obey it.

(. . . For when the Gentiles, which have not the law, do by nature the things contained in the law, these, having not the law, are a law unto themselves: Which show the work of the law written in their hearts, their consciences also bearing witness, and their thoughts the mean while accusing or else excusing one another;) in the day when God shall judge the secrets of men by Jesus Christ according to my gospel. (2:14-16)

Paul is moving to the next stage of his presentation of God's plan of salvation. He has talked about the non-Jew, the Gentile, the man without the Bible. Now he is preparing to talk about the man who is a Jew—the man with the Bible. Remember again what he said about the Gentiles: "For the wrath of God is revealed . . ." (1:18). And the Gentile listener asks, "Why am I under the wrath of God?" And Paul replies that it is because "that which may be known of God is manifest in them; for God hath shown it unto them" (1:19). Even the man without the Bible has a conscience. This is the first thing that condemns him. Man is still a moral being.

Now Paul says the same thing about the Jews, or, in today's equivalent, about people who have the Bible. They have the Bible (just like the Gentiles, or people without the Bible, still have a conscience), but they don't live up to it. In fact, says Paul, you find many Gentiles (people without the Bible) who live better lives than those who have the Bible. He's not saying these nonbelievers live perfect lives. No human lives a perfect life. All he is saying is that the relatively good example of these nonbelievers condemns those who have the Bible.

Of course, this doesn't excuse the man without the Bible. He is not fully living up to the standard he knows. But it is an additional condemnation of the Jew, the man with the Bible. Paul is simply cutting away every foundation other than grace. You can just feel it. He is cutting away all the arguments people have used down through the ages to say, "I don't need a Savior." You can feel it all being demolished. Someone will say, "Look, here are these heathens over here and they live better lives than people who have the Bible." But as Paul has said, those people's good lives won't save them, because they aren't fully living up to their own standards either.

(. . . their thoughts the mean while accusing or else excusing one another;). (2:15)

This is the experience of all people. We all go through it, like the swing of a pendulum. We excuse ourselves, saying, "I'll get by, I'm better than others," and then, whoosh, we do something really bad and we are plunged into the blackness of self-condemnation and begin "accusing" ourselves. Then, perhaps we take a breath of fresh air or have a good cup of espresso or see someone who seems worse than us, and the pendulum swings back and we begin excusing ourselves again: "I'm not as bad as I thought I was. I'm doing pretty well." Then, all of a sudden, again, into the black. All people experience this swinging of the pendulum—excusing . . . accusing . . . excusing . . . accusing . . . We face our conscience and feel accused; then we explain it away and feel excused.

In the day when God shall judge the secrets of men by Jesus Christ according to my gospel. (2:16)

We are face to face with the fact that there is a day coming in history when the judgment is going to take place. We already saw this in 2:5: ". . . against the day of wrath and revelation of the righteous judgment of God." Paul doesn't allow his message to remain abstract; he brings it down to the most concrete, practical form; and the concrete, unavoidable fact is that there is coming a very real day in space and time, in history, when God is going to judge the world. "In the day"—not necessarily a twenty-four-hour day—"when God shall judge the secrets of men."

"Secrets" should be a fearsome word to us. God will judge not just the open things but the secret things. The man without the Bible says, "That woman is immoral . . . that man is immoral," and then he does the same thing, often in secret. Isn't that the way people think and live? They aren't really trying to be moral, they're just trying to keep things in balance; they point their finger at the person who goes to extremes, even though they are doing the same things in secret. They condemn others for the more open things, the thing that makes the newspaper. But in their own secret lives they are living the same way.

God will judge, not just the things that come out in the newspaper, but all these secret things. All the nice people. All the people who throw the stones. All the people who write the editorials.

Once again, remember the context: People say, "Why am I under the wrath of God? Is God justified in condemning me?" And God says, "Isn't there a good reason for your being under my wrath?" "O, man" (2:1), look for yourself. Isn't it just (2:2-16)?

The judgment will be by God, but it will also be "by Jesus Christ" (2:16). Paul has not mentioned Christ since 1:16 because he has been discussing the problem of sin. But now he mentions Him again, as the Judge of mankind. That may come as a surprise. You have surely encountered people, Jewish and Gentile alike, who say, "I believe in God, I just don't believe in Jesus Christ." But the terrible truth is, when unsaved men and women stand before God for judgment and look Him in the face, they will see only one person of the Trinity as judge, and that will be Jesus Christ. One of the most sobering phrases in the whole Bible is "the wrath of the Lamb" (Rev. 6:16). In Romans Paul talks of the wrath of God, but in Revelation John talks of the wrath of the Lamb. The person of the Trinity who came and suffered so much so that people would not have to be judged, will be their judge. The person who tries to come to God without coming through Jesus Christ, will, at the judgment, come face to face with Jesus Christ. Certainly Jesus was "in all points tempted like as we are, yet without sin" (Heb 4:15); so He understands temptation and He understands our humanity. Yet that does not lessen the awful truth that He will judge us. Jesus, the Savior of the world, will also be its judge. "I am not ashamed of the gospel of Christ," says Paul. But now he adds, Christ is also the judge. Not only is there no way to come to God except through Jesus Christ, as Christ Himself declares (John 14:6), but when one tries to jump this barrier, one cannot, for Jesus Christ stands there as judge. Jesus says, "Come unto me, all ye that labour and are heavy laden, and I will give you rest" (Matt. 11:28). But when someone says, "I'll have nothing to do with you; I'll come to God directly for myself without the mediator, without the suffering Messiah," it is as if he is trying to plow right into heaven, getting by this Jesus Christ. But he can't, because there stands Jesus Christ the judge. No one who ever lived can avoid a relationship with Jesus Christ. It will be one of two possible relationships: It will be the relationship of salvation that Paul describes in 1:16, or else it will be the relationship he describes in 2:16—the relationship of a condemned person to a judge.

The prophet Micah said, "I will bear the indignation of the LORD, because I have sinned against him" (Mic. 7:9). Jesus bore the indignation of our sin on the cross. But if we fail to accept this, there is only the other side of the equation—we must bear the indignation of the Lord for ourselves.

Paul has spoken of Gentiles being under God's wrath (1:18—2:16), and in these last few verses he has begun speaking of Jews being under God's wrath as well (2:9-16). As he prepares now to focus on God's wrath against the Jews (2:17—3:8), we should recall a passage from Zephaniah: "Then I will take away out of the midst of thee them that rejoice in thy pride, and thou shalt no more be haughty because of my holy mountain" (3:11). God, through Zephaniah, told Israel that a day would come when they would no longer be proud simply because His holy mountain, Jerusalem, was in their midst. Those who rejoice for such reasons will be judged, just like everyone else. But this warning doesn't apply just to the Jews or to people in Bible times. Thinking again of our modern-day equivalents—people who have the Bible and people who don't have the Bible—those who have the Bible and the church shouldn't be haughty and look down on those who don't have these things. Even people today who boast that they don't believe in anything may look down on certain other groups and condemn them. But Paul is showing us that sin is universal. We all stand condemned before God. None of us can be haughty because of any "holy mountain" we might claim. Anything that might cause us to be proud is only a reason for greater judgment.

3

THE PERSON WITH
THE BIBLE: GUILTY
(2:17—3:8)

કે

As Paul in 2:17 begins addressing the Jews directly, remember that, in present-day terms, they represent people who have the Bible. We who have the Bible on our shelves, we who have the church in our midst, we who have the culture that grew out of the Reformation: Is this enough for salvation?

Behold, thou art called a Jew, and restest in the law, and makest thy boast of God . . . (2:17)

"Restest in the law" should remind us of what we just read from Zephaniah 3:11. Paul is addressing people who take pride in the fact that God's "holy mountain" (Zeph. 3:11) is in their midst. They "rest" on this fact.

. . . and knowest his will . . . (2:18a)

What do the Jews have? They have the Bible. As Paul will say later, "What advantage then hath the Jew? or what profit is there of circumcision? Much every way: chiefly, because that unto them were committed the oracles of God" (3:1-2). The main advantage the Jews

had over all other people was that they had the Bible. They knew
God's will (2:18). They were resting upon it (2:17). There was a serious problem, however: Having this special blessing had made them
proud. And that's exactly where so many people are today. Look at all
the cathedrals in Europe. People hear the cathedral bells. Isn't that
enough? They have their children baptized, christened, and confirmed.
They have church weddings. Isn't that enough?

You find the same mentality in America. We have a higher per-
centage of people belonging to churches than ever before in history—
more even than in earlier times when people really believed something! Yet God is saying to the Jew back in the first century but also
to many people in our own time that all of this Jewish (or Christian)
heritage doesn't amount to one grain of sand. All it does is condemn
you more!

**Behold, thou art called a Jew, and restest in the law, and makest thy
boast of God, and knowest his will, and approvest the things that are
more excellent, being instructed out of the law; and art confident
that thou thyself art a guide to the blind, a light of them which are in
darkness, an instructor of the foolish, a teacher of babes, which hast
the form of knowledge and of the truth in the law. Thou therefore
which teachest another, teachest thou not thyself? Thou that preach-
est a man should not steal, dost thou steal? Thou that sayest a man
should not commit adultery, dost thou commit adultery? Thou that
abhorrest idols, dost thou commit sacrilege? Thou that makest thy
boast of the law, through breaking the law dishonourest thou God?
For the name of God is blasphemed among the Gentiles through you,
as it is written. (2:17-24)**

How terrible! Here are the Jews, who were supposed to show the
image of the living God before a lost world (2:19-20), and yet they
saw their mission mainly as a basis for pride (2:17, 23). We see the
same problem among Christians today. What would you guess is the
most difficult thing a missionary faces when starting a new work? I
don't know of a single missionary who would disagree that the greatest problem they face is the people who have been there before them
and have been equated in the people's minds with the name Christian.

When Livingston tried to preach the gospel in Africa, he had to deal with the fact that the people associated Christianity with the Portuguese, who had been slave traders in that part of the world. Until recently the biggest problem missionaries faced in Muslim areas was that the Muslims, who were not supposed to drink wine, associated Christianity with the wine merchants who profited by selling a commodity the Muslims could not sell. When people who have the Bible—be they Jew or Christian—behave in such a way, instead of bringing light, they're bringing darkness.

We usually associate the word *missionary* with Christianity, but the Jews of Old Testament times were themselves in a sense called to be missionaries. The book of Jonah is the best illustration of this. When we think of Jonah, of course we think of the great fish, but Jonah's story is important mainly as an example of Israel's failure to proclaim its missionary message. Jonah was told to go and preach to Nineveh, but instead of accepting that missionary call he got on a boat sailing in the opposite direction from Nineveh.

Ezekiel also speaks of Israel's failure in its mission: "Thus saith the LORD God; This is Jerusalem: I have set it in the midst of the nations and countries that are round about her. And she has changed my judgments into wickedness more than the nations, and my statutes more than the countries that are round about her" (Ezek. 5:5-6a). God had put Jerusalem in the midst of the nations for a purpose. Israel's purpose was to speak of God's existence and His character, and to call other nations to God. Jonah is an outstanding example of Israel's failure to do this, but he is not by any means the only example. The Jews were to be a testimony to God, but instead, says Ezekiel, they were quite the opposite. From the time of the Babylonian captivity, the Jews were scattered throughout the known world. Jewish synagogues were established throughout the known world. If only they had stood for God! But as Jonah illustrated and as Ezekiel said and as Paul is saying in 2:17-24, they had done the exact opposite. When Solomon dedicated the temple, he declared that it would become the "house of prayer for all people" (see 2 Chron. 6:32; Isa. 56:7; Matt. 21:13). But it turned out to be quite the opposite.

The temple was to be a testimony to the world that God exists, that

He is really there. The reality of God should have been seen in the righteous lives of the people who worshiped in His house. It should also have been seen in the way God protected His people in battle. This being a fallen world, God's chosen nation from time to time would need His protection in battle, and He intended to give them that protection as a testimony to the nations. But because of their sin, God stopped protecting them, and the other nations could now say, "Their God is just like any other God." Israel's immorality caused other nations to blaspheme God (2:24), and when because of their immorality God stopped protecting them, this caused the other nations to blaspheme God all the more. Israel was to be a living demonstration of the fact that God is there. Instead, because of their sin and consequent string of defeats in battle, the other nations said, "Israel's God is not there."

To apply a New Testament term to Jonah's situation, because of his taking off in the other direction, the gospel was not preached to Nineveh (until after Jonah repented). Because of Israel's frequent sin, God's good character was not exhibited to the world. As Isaiah expressed it, instead of bringing about anything resembling a spiritual birth, Israel had only "brought forth wind" (Isa. 26:18).

Unfortunately, the same can often be said of Christians today. Too often, people of other religions who come in contact with Christians go away disgusted. Almost all the great blasphemous leaders of the world today have been instructed in our universities and have gone away untouched and disgusted. At the same time, God has often withdrawn His hand of protection and allowed people from Christian backgrounds to fall to the influence of ideologies such as atheistic communism or pagan religions of the East. Our situation is exactly parallel to that of the Jews in Bible times. Both Jews back then and Christians today have failed to exhibit to the world the fact that God really exists. Therefore, as Ezekiel goes on to say, "So, it shall be a reproach and a taunt, an instruction and an astonishment unto the nations that are round about thee, when I shall execute judgments in thee in anger and in fury and in furious rebukes. I the LORD have spoken it" (Ezek. 5:15).

What a sad situation. Here are the nations; they are to look toward

Israel and see that God exists. But instead, God has to judge Israel. In fact, He used these same heathen nations to judge Israel. Instead of looking at Israel and learning of God, they destroyed Israel as they blasphemed her God. And that's what Paul is saying here in Romans 2: "In every area of life where you should have been a testimony, instead you have been sinful and proud, and therefore God has had to chasten you. And that in turn has caused other nations to blaspheme your God."

What can we who are a part of twentieth-century Christendom do but put on the sackcloth and ashes and say, "Amen. This is where we are. We're a cause of blasphemy. God can no longer protect us." All of the major "Christian" nations from past history into our day have known the truth and have deliberately turned away from it. Everything that could be said against the Jews of Paul's day can now be said against us. Instead of being missionaries, we have caused nonbelievers to blaspheme. Not only have we not preached the positive message of salvation, we have preached a negative message instead and have caused unbelievers to turn away from a God we no longer honor.

A few chapters later Ezekiel says this to the people of Judah, Israel's southern kingdom: "Neither hath Samaria [Israel's northern kingdom] committed half of thy sins; but thou hast multiplied thine abominations more than they, and hast justified thy sisters [the northern kingdom] in all thine abominations which thou hast done. Thou also, which hast judged thy sisters, bear thine own shame for thy sins that thou hast committed more abominable than they; they are more righteous than thou; yea, be thou confounded also, and bear thy shame, in that thou hast justified thy sisters" (Ezek. 16:51-52). Then, in verse 56: "For thy sister Sodom was not mentioned by thy mouth in the day of thy pride." Then, in verse 61: "Then thou shalt remember thy ways, and be ashamed, when thou shalt receive thy sisters, thine elder and thy younger [Samaria and Sodom]; and I will give them unto thee for daughters." Simply stated, Ezekiel is saying that the Jews of his day were worse even than the notorious Sodomites. Jesus said a similar thing to the Jews of His own day: "If the mighty works, which have been done in thee, had been done in Sodom, it would have remained until this day" (Matt. 11:23).

That's where we stand in our own Christian culture today. I don't like communism, but I believe that communist China is not as bad in God's sight as is our own culture. We who have lived in northern Europe and North America since the Reformation have been greatly blessed by the light of truth. Yet we have deliberately turned away from it. When I hear Paul ask the Jews of his day, "Are you counting on being saved just because you are Jews, when in fact you have been a blasphemy in the face of the nations?" I am certain that God is asking the same question of the so-called Christians of northern Europe and North America today. We are a blasphemy. That doesn't excuse the other side, the people without the Bible; as we have seen (1:18—2:16), they too will be judged. But we can't excuse ourselves. We can't say, "We're the righteous ones. Surely God will protect us." Why should He? We are a blasphemy against Him!

Paul declared both the Gentiles and then the Jews of his day to be under the wrath of God. In 3:9-20 he will say the same thing in broader terms, climaxing with his much-quoted conclusion that "all have sinned, and come short of the glory of God" (3:23), which is another way of saying, "everyone is under the wrath of God." Or as Isaiah said, "All we like sheep have gone astray" (Isa. 53:6). Who needs the Savior? The Gentile has sinned; the Jew has sinned. The man without the Bible has sinned; the man with the Bible has sinned. Who needs the Savior? It's a very simple conclusion, isn't it? All men and women everywhere need the Savior! And if we're going to live in the world as it is, rather than in some make-believe world, we have to live within this circle. When people ask us, "Who needs the Savior?" we must answer, very quietly, very soberly, and with real compassion, "All have sinned and come short of the glory of God."

As we consider what Paul says about all Jews and all Gentiles being sinners in God's sight, it is important that we as Christians today not look down on Paul's first-century readers as though we are somehow above them. As Paul reminds us in Ephesians 2:3, we "were by nature the children of wrath," no less than the worst unredeemed sinner. Each of us has been under the wrath of God. If we have accepted Christ as our Savior, the wrath of God is no longer upon us. But this is not because of anything within ourselves, anything in our race, or in our Christian culture. If we are not under the wrath of God right now, it is only because by His grace Christ has died for us and, also by His grace, we have accepted Him as our Savior. We cannot think of ourselves as being removed by some innate goodness from anyone who is still subject to God's wrath. Whenever we consider God's wrath against a sinful world, it should always be with the attitude that "This is where I myself have been, and this is where I deserve to be except for the finished work of Jesus Christ." It is only in the environment of this humble realization that we dare proceed with our study of Romans.

Looking back a couple of verses, Paul asked his Jewish readers, "Thou that abhorrest idols, dost thou commit sacrilege?" (2:22). The best translation from the Greek would be, "Thou that abhorrest idols, art thou guilty of the greatest irreverences?" Similarly, some years later, John would speak of those who "say they are Jews, and are not, but are the synagogue of Satan" (Rev. 2:9). Here are the Jews, the people with the Bible, who think they are something special. Yet Paul says they are guilty of the greatest irreverence, and John calls them "the synagogue of Satan." Again we must admit, this is surely how God looks at much of Christendom today. Claiming to be under the umbrella of Christendom, claiming to have some sort of special blessing because the bells ring in the cathedrals, because in the United States great numbers of people go to church, and yet we commit blasphemy against God as we turn from the clear teaching of His Word. It is a sober truth and we must face it: If we have the Bible, if we enjoy all the blessings it brings, and yet by our lives bring shame upon God's name, we are guilty of the greatest irreverence.

Then look again at verses 23 and 24: "Thou that makest thy boast of the law, through breaking the law dishonourest thou God? For the name of God is blasphemed among the Gentiles through you." When the man with the Bible treats it as an external thing only, it causes the man without the Bible to dishonor the God of the Bible. Surely, then, the man with the Bible is justifiably under God's wrath.

For circumcision verily profiteth, if thou keep the law: but if thou be a breaker of the law, thy circumcision is made uncircumcision. (2:25)

The external rites of religion are not enough, in and of themselves. To the Jew the crucial external rite was circumcision; to the man with the Bible in our own generation it is baptism or confirmation or church membership. But such things, says Paul, are not helpful. In fact, they are harmful; they are no more than "uncircumcision" unless there is a reality behind them.

Therefore if the uncircumcision keep the righteousness of the law, shall not his uncircumcision be counted for circumcision? And shall not uncircumcision which is by nature, if it fulfill the law, judge thee, who by the letter and circumcision dost transgress the law? (2:26-27)

That last phrase could better be translated, "who with the advantage of the letter and circumcision dost transgress the law." As we noted before, Paul is not for a moment saying that the person without the Bible is justified. Indeed, because these Gentiles do not keep their own standards, they too stand condemned in God's sight (2:1). Paul is simply saying, to the Jews of his day and to professing Christians today, "Shame on you! There are people without the Bible, people without all the advantages you have, who live better lives than you live."

This doesn't excuse the man without the Bible, but oh how it condemns the man with the Bible! There stands the Jew, saying, "I'm a Jew. I have the circumcision. I have all these other things." And God is saying to him, "Yes, but look, with all the advantages you have, time after time it can be pointed out that the people without the Bible, the surrounding world that does not believe, live better lives than you do. And therefore you cause the living God to be blasphemed. This doubly condemns you. It doesn't excuse the others, but it doubly condemns you!"

For he is not a Jew, which is one outwardly; neither is that circumcision, which is outward in the flesh: but he is a Jew, which is one inwardly; and circumcision is that of the heart, in the spirit, and not in the letter; whose praise is not of men, but of God. (2:28-29)

External rites, whether those of Judaism or of Christendom, are meaningless unless there is a circumcision of the heart, unless God has touched the person's heart and there is a reality to his or her faith. To live under the umbrella of Christendom, whether Roman Catholic Christendom or Protestant Christendom, and then to live lives that are a scandal in the sight of nonbelievers, to profess a faith that means nothing in our inward parts, this surely places us under God's wrath. If Christianity is for us merely a blessing not taken advantage of, then surely God can say to us, just as He said to the Gentile world in 2:1, "Therefore thou art inexcusable, O man."

As we move into the third chapter, Paul says with great insistence that his Jewish readers need the Savior because they are under the wrath of God even though they have had great spiritual advantages. Spiritual blessing, says Paul, is not an automatic result of one's race or of one's external adherence to a religious tradition. Any spiritual blessing we are to experience must come from a much deeper reality. Paul is parading all mankind before us—first Gentiles, then Jews—trusting that as we look at them we will also see ourselves and realize that nothing we are, in and of ourselves, can save us from God's justifiable wrath.

What advantage then hath the Jew? Or what profit is there of circumcision? (3:1)

Paul knew of course that his Jewish readers would ask this question, no less than a Jewish person reading his words today would ask it. If Jews, just like Gentiles, are under the wrath of God, then what advantage is there in being one of God's "chosen" people? Paul answers his own question, very strongly.

Much every way: chiefly, because that unto them were committed the oracles of God. (3:2)

"Oracles of God" refers, of course, to what we know today as the Old Testament. The Jews' chief advantage over the Gentiles was that they had God's Word. They could know! In chapters 9—11 of Romans Paul will deal with the Jews in great detail. In 10:19 he will ask, "Did not Israel know?" And throughout the tenth chapter he shows exactly how Israel knew of God: They knew about God because divinely inspired people like Moses (10:5, 19) and Isaiah (10:16, 20) told them about Him. In other words, they knew because they had the oracles of God, the Old Testament.

So the question is not whether Israel knew about God. Israel did know. They knew about God in a way that people without the Bible did not know. But did this knowledge of God solve their spiritual problem? Did this mean they didn't need a Savior? "Not at all," says God, "because, even though you knew, you didn't believe." And because they didn't believe, all their knowledge of God didn't help them; quite to the contrary, it condemned them all the more.

Paul has approached the question of the standing of the Jewish nation before God from three different angles: Their lives are worse than those of all the people around them who don't have the Bible, therefore they are condemned (2:17-24); they observe the external rites as God directed, but it is not from the heart, therefore they are condemned (2:25-29); they knew about God, they had the Old Testament, but they didn't believe it, therefore they are condemned (3:1-2).

For what if some did not believe? shall their unbelief make the faith of God without effect? God forbid: yea, let God be true, but every man a liar; as it is written, That thou mightest be justified in thy sayings, and mightest overcome when thou art judged. (3:3-4)

Does the unbelief of God's chosen people, in spite of all their advantages, suggest that God is faithless, or that He has broken His covenant promises to Israel? "God forbid!" says Paul. "Not at all." God has kept every one of His covenant promises. The fault lies entirely with those who failed to believe those promises.

But if our unrighteousness commend the righteousness of God, what shall we say? Is God unrighteous who taketh vengeance? (I speak as a man) God forbid: for then how shall God judge the world? For if the truth of God hath more abounded through my lie unto his glory; why yet am I also judged as a sinner? And not rather, (as we be slanderously reported, and as some affirm that we say,) Let us do evil, that good may come? whose damnation is just. (3:5-8)

Paul anticipates that some of his readers might say, "If our sin makes God's righteousness more conspicuous by contrast, is it really fair for Him to judge us?" To which Paul replies, in essence, "Yes, but this doesn't change the matter. It's still your own unbelief. God is still justified in condemning you, because you've had all this light in the Old Testament revelation. You knew about God! You knew! You had the advantage. And yet you didn't believe." And once again we must ask, if this is what God says about the Jews in Paul's day, about their having the Old Testament Scriptures and yet being guilty before Him—indeed being especially under His wrath because of all the advantages they had—if this was true of the Jewish world of Paul's day, what would God say to the world of Christendom today?

Think of the advantages we have had in northern Europe and North America. With our whole culture built on the Reformation. With the ability to buy a Bible in any 5 and 10 cent store. With our literature full of Bible quotations. If the Jews were condemned because they didn't believe despite their advantages, what must God say to our "Christian" nations today? If the Jews had an advantage, we certainly have more! If God condemned the Jews for their lack of response, may He have mercy on us!

We who have the Bible today stand more condemned than people today who don't have the Bible—who have only the witness of their conscience. But we also stand more condemned than those who had the Bible in Paul's day. To have these advantages and not believe, to have these advantages and turn away from God, to have these advantages and yet to cause the name of the living God to be blasphemed. What excuse can we make? How do we expect to get away with it? When young people from all over the world come to a country like the United States to study in our universities, only to return home cynical and atheistic, should we be surprised when God looks at us and says, "You are under My wrath!"

If any people in all of history needed the Savior, it is us in present-day Western Christendom.

4

THE WHOLE WORLD: GUILTY
(3:9-20)

Paul has talked about Gentiles being condemned before God (1:18—2:16); he has talked about Jews being condemned before God (2:17—3:8). Now he draws them both together, and shows that all people everywhere stand in the same place in God's sight:

What then? are we better than they? No, in no wise: for we have before proved both Jews and Gentiles, that they are all under sin. (3:9)

For Paul to equate Jews and Gentiles in his day would perhaps be equivalent to equating professing Christians and atheists today. Many times when I've talked about this passage people have responded, "What do you mean? Are you saying that a member of a Christian church is just as guilty in God's sight as that awful Communist or atheist over there?" And God is saying through Paul, "Yes, he is!"

We can get so riled up with righteous indignation against people who openly deny God's existence. It isn't hard for us to agree that they desperately need salvation and to feel very virtuous about recognizing their sin. But when Paul swings around and says that, in the sight of God, we need salvation too, then our emotional response might be very different. Certainly Paul's Jewish readers would have responded strongly against Paul's assertion that Jews are no better than Gentiles in God's sight. Paul anticipates their strong reaction and finishes the matter by quoting from their Bible, the Old Testament.

As it is written, There is none righteous, no, not one: There is none that understandeth, there is none that seeketh after God. They are all gone out of the way, they are together become unprofitable; there is none that doeth good, no, not one. (3:10-12)

It isn't just Paul who says that all humans are sinners. Quoting from Psalms 14:1-3 and 53:1-3, he shows that the Old Testament, the Bible of his Jewish readers, says it too. And as we saw earlier, Isaiah says it too: "All we like sheep have gone astray; we have turned every one to his own way" (Isa. 53:6). The person without the Bible hasn't kept his own standards perfectly, so he deserves the wrath of God. But those of us who have the Bible, who have had even higher moral standards, haven't kept our standards either. This is not a theological abstraction, coming from a metaphysical mood. Moral corruption is the result of individual immoral desires. Paul describes a concrete tragedy of sinful desires, not a human state or definition.

This understanding of sin's universality is the truest and greatest "leveler" of humanity. Jesus emphasized this over and over again. People would point to someone and say, "Look at that sinner," but Jesus would always show them that all people are equally sinners. All stand on the same level before God.

Paul's words are concrete, and they are also very personal. We saw him earlier become very personal when he said, "Therefore thou art inexcusable, O man" (2:1). But his words in 3:10-12 are just as personal. For if there are "none righteous," then *I'm* not righteous. If there are "none that understandeth, . . . none that seeketh after God" in the way that God should be sought after, then I don't understand and I don't seek after God as I should. If "they are all gone out of the way," then that includes me—I have gone out of the way. If there are none who do absolute good, "no, not one," then I don't do absolute good either. If all humans, without exception, are morally corrupt, then I am morally corrupt too, no matter how good I may think I am.

Even those of us who have accepted Christ as our Savior should never think of sin as an abstraction. All people are morally corrupt. We're not in a position to think of sin in terms of other people. As we saw in Ephesians, we were all "by nature the children of wrath" (Eph. 2:3). This is where each one of us has lived. This is the pit out of which we have been dug. This is what we are.

Christians sometimes speak of being "shocked" by this or that kind of behavior. We should certainly never hesitate to say that something is wrong, if it is wrong. But how can we be "shocked" or surprised about the sins of others when we are morally corrupt ourselves in God's sight? If we truly understand how sinful each of us is in God's sight, then we will understand that we are on the same level with everyone else. In terms of our sin nature, we have all been cut down to the same size.

Paul makes this matter of human sinfulness personal by including himself in the discussion. He doesn't say, "Are the Jews better than the Gentiles?" Rather, he says, "Are we better than they?" (3:9). He identifies himself with his fellow Jews. "Am I, are we, better than they?" he asks. And the answer is, "No. We, and I, are no better than they."

Paul's quoting from the Old Testament surely would have been devastating to his Jewish readers—and by extension to Christian readers today. How can anyone feel that he or she is in a good position before the holy God merely because of having the Bible, when the Bible itself says that none are righteous? For the self-righteous person, after verse 12 there is nothing but rubble. No one is safe just by being under the umbrella of Judaism, and no one is safe just by being under the umbrella of Christendom. None are righteous, "no, not one."

Does this mean we are all without hope? If each one of us is so morally corrupt in God's sight, is there any hope for us? Remember that at this point in his letter to the Romans, Paul is still preaching the "first half of the gospel"; he is still trying to show that all people need to be saved. Don't forget the context: "I am not ashamed of the gospel of Christ: for it is the power of God unto salvation" (1:16).

"But why do I need salvation?"

"Because you are under the wrath of God."

"And just why am I under the wrath of God?"

Paul is answering that question in this first half of his gospel presentation (1:18—3:20), and he continues in 3:13 with a terrible picture of the human race.

Their throat is an open sepulchre; with their tongues they have used deceit; the poison of asps is under their lips: whose mouth is full of cursing and bitterness: their feet are swift to shed blood: destruction and misery are in their ways: and the way of peace have they not known: there is no fear of God before their eyes. (3:13-18)

What an awful picture Paul paints of mankind in his own day. And can we really claim that mankind today is any better? Has mankind "progressed" in terms of morality, as so many would like to believe? God's Word would surely say, "No, not one!" We may be progressing in this way or that, but not in our moral standing before God. We dare not make an abstraction out of Paul's horrible portrayal of us. This is the way we humans are, and this is the way a holy God sees us.

Now we know that what things soever the law saith, it saith to them who are under the law: that every mouth may be stopped, and all the world may become [may be shown to be] guilty before God. Therefore by the deeds of the law there shall no flesh be justified in his sight: for by the law is the knowledge of sin. (3:19-20)

Paul is now drawing to a conclusion his case against the Jews; but, as he has since verse 9, he is broadening his analysis to include all mankind. Since no one, whether Jew or Gentile, is perfectly keeping the law, the only possible conclusion is that all humanity is guilty before God and subject to his proper judgment. "Therefore by the deeds of the law . . ." Here Paul has in view not just the Law of Moses, but good works of any kind. "Therefore by the deeds of the law [by good works] there shall no flesh be justified in his sight." The sense of the original Greek is even stronger: "No flesh shall ever be . . . no flesh can ever be justified." The person who doesn't have the Bible is judged by the perfect standard of God on the basis of his or her own condemnation of others, as we saw in 2:1. No one can ever say, "I have perfectly kept the standard by which I have judged others." But then along comes the Jew, saying, "Yes, but we have the Bible." And God says, "Yes, and you haven't kept it either." So, the conclusion now is all blackness. "Therefore by the deeds of the law there shall no flesh [ever] be justified in [God's] sight: for by the law is the knowledge of sin."

We have come to the end of Paul's presentation of the "first half of the gospel." Paul has taken most of the first chapter, all of the second chapter, and a lot of the third chapter to show us that we need salvation. He hasn't yet told us how to be saved. The word *salvation* has occurred only once, in the theme verse: "I am not ashamed of the gospel of Christ: for it is the power of God unto salvation" (1:16). And you can just hear the cry, whether it's in the humanistic Greek and Roman world of Paul's day, or whether it's in the humanistic twentieth century: "Why do I need salvation?" People may have all kinds of opinions about whether God exists or what He is like if He does exist, but when they are told that God says they must be saved, they will usually raise objections.

It is interesting that people don't object to existentialism the way they object to Christianity. The existentialist says all people are lost. The existentialist says everyone is damned. The existentialist say it's all hopeless. Cynics and nihilists of all kinds say it's a hopeless life, it's a black life, it's an impossible life, man is a zero. But this is where Christianity differs radically from existentialism, and this is why people react so strongly to Christianity but not to existentialism. Existentialism says man is a zero and he is hopelessly damned. Christianity says man is damned, not because of what he is but because of what he has freely chosen to do. If a man is damned because of what he is, you can't say that he's wrong—he's just pathetic. But Christianity says that man is not pathetic. In fact, man is a marvelous creation of God. But he is also a rebel against God, and as such deserves God's wrath. Man is not pathetic, man is a rebel. It is not as if man were hopelessly caught in a net from which he can't escape; he is caught in a net, all right, but he is there by choice. And if men and women are caught in this net by choice, says the Bible, then there is something more involved: They must accept the responsibility, the guilt, for being there.

And that brings us to the second half of the gospel.

5

JUSTIFICATION AFTER
THE CROSS
(3:21-30)

In 3:21, Paul begins to explain the solution to mankind's need of salvation. But before we go on we must note once again the amount of space Paul has devoted to what we have called the "first half of the gospel"—the fact that human beings desperately need salvation. We are guilty, we are without excuse, we need salvation; and none of us can be saved on the basis of any good works we have done. And just why, someone might ask, is our situation so hopeless? Why is it so impossible for us, on our own, to find the cure? Our sin is incurable because of whom we have sinned against. We have deliberately sinned against a holy God, and therefore our situation is hopeless.

People have said to me over and over again, "But how can someone be eternally condemned for what he or she did in just seventy years, even if it was seventy years of wickedness?" The problem is not how little or how much we have sinned, but against whom we have sinned. We have sinned against an infinitely holy God who really exists. And in sinning against an infinitely holy God who really exists, our sin is infinite.

It is as though there were, opening at our feet, an infinite chasm of guilt. Suppose we brought our little buckets of righteousness (if we could even find any little buckets of righteousness!): How many finite buckets of righteousness would it take to dump into an infinite chasm of infinite guilt? It's impossible! Having once sinned against an infinite God, the chasm is infinite and nothing we can dump in this chasm can fill it up.

So, is it hopeless? At this point in Paul's presentation of the gospel, yes, it is hopeless. Whenever we are presenting the gospel to anyone, at this point we must say, "Yes, for you it is hopeless." There must be no deviation from this stark reality. There must be not a hair's breadth left of humanism or egotism. There must be no hope in anything, positively or negatively, internally or externally, religious good works or moral good works. There must be left not one single shred of hope, or we're not presenting what the Bible teaches. People need salvation because they are totally under the wrath of a holy God. There is nothing for any individual human being to dump into his or her personal chasm of guilt. It's nothing but an endlessly deep hole.

At this particular place Christianity and modern existentialism meet. The modern existentialist says, "Man is damned," and the Bible says, "Man is damned." The only difference is, with the existentialist's damnation there truly is no hope; but thank God the Bible now goes on and, from 3:21 through 4:25 says, "Yes, there is overwhelming hope! There is a solution!"

Let's recall again our theme verse: "For I am not ashamed of the gospel of Christ: for it is the power of God unto salvation to every one that believeth; to the Jew first, and also to the Greek" (1:16). Having shown the universal need for salvation, Paul will now show where that salvation can be found. In 3:21-30 Paul will explain how those who have lived from the time of Christ on can find salvation. In 3:31—4:22 he will show how the people living before Christ found salvation. Then, in 4:23-25, he will bring these two eras of humanity together. Just as he showed the guilt of the Gentiles (1:18—2:16), then of the Jews (2:17—3:8), and then drew them together to show that all mankind is under the wrath of God (3:9-20), so will he now show the way of salvation for those living after Christ (3:21-30) and then for those living before Christ (3:31—4:22). Then he will again draw the two groups together (4:23-25). It's a logical sequence.

Let's begin with 3:21: If all mankind is damned, if all are under the wrath of God, if there are no little buckets of righteousness to be poured into the infinite chasm of guilt, then how can anyone be justified?

The answer is simple and wonderful.

But now the righteousness of God without the law . . . (3:21a)

As soon as Paul begins giving his answer, we see the clear contrast with the previous verse: "Therefore by the deeds of the law there shall no flesh be justified in [God's] sight. . . . But now the righteousness of God without the law . . ." Do you see the sharp line that's drawn here? Here is a way to be justified with God in spite of the fact that all of us are morally corrupt. Here is a way to be justified with God in spite of the fact that we all have been rebels. Here is a way to be justified with God whether we've been the man without the Bible or the man with the Bible. Even though our hearts condemn us. Even though we have nothing good to bring.

But now the righteousness of God without the law is manifested, being witnessed by the law and the prophets. (3:21)

Remember how Paul began, in 1:2, by showing that his teaching is not unique to him or to the New Testament but is in the Old Testament too? And how in 3:10-12 he showed, once again, the continuity between his teaching and that of the Old Testament? Paul now quotes the Old Testament again. The Old Testament, just like the New, shows both the lostness of mankind and the means of salvation for mankind. There is no line to be drawn between the basic teaching of the Old and the New Testaments. The Bible is a total unity.

This is why we can rightly speak of the "Judeo-Christian tradition." This terminology is entirely proper. We don't believe just the New Testament. We believe the Old Testament too. A true Bible-believing Christian is just as interested in reading the Old Testament as the New. The two comprise one message, one complete unity. There are not two religions, the Old Testament and the New Testament religion; there is only one. Just as the Old Testament along with the New insists that all people, in and of themselves, are morally corrupt, so also both the Old Testament and the New Testament tell us that there is a "righteousness of God without the law."

Even the righteousness of God which is by faith of [in] Jesus Christ. (3:22a)

This, says Paul, is the answer. He will show the way for wicked men and women to be justified with God. Justification comes to sinful men and women when God declares that their guilt is paid for on the basis of the finished work of Jesus Christ. Because of Christ's sacrifice of Himself on the cross, God declares that we are righteous.

Notice I said that God "declares" that our guilt is gone. The word *declares* is of utmost importance. It will come up again and again in our study of justification in 3:21—4:25. God does not "infuse" us with righteousness. It's not something that's pumped into you. God makes a legal declaration. Our guilt before God is a legal matter. When an unsaved person comes before God at the judgment, God will judge that person and say, "You are guilty." It will be a judicial declaration. Likewise, justification is a judicial act. How thankful we should be that there's the possibility of this prior judicial act before we must face God at the judgment. We have earned the declaration from God that we are guilty and therefore deserve His wrath. But on the basis of the finished work of Christ, God can declare us to be justified. He can declare that our guilt is gone.

What occurs when you accept Jesus as your Savior, first and foremost, is that God makes a declaration; and the declaration is, "Francis Schaeffer [or your own name], I declare you justified. You are properly, justly guilty on the basis of breaking your own moral standards. But on the basis of the work of Jesus Christ, your guilt is gone. The price is paid."

Salvation is first and foremost a legal matter, since it has to do with our guilt before God. Later, in Romans 5—7, we will discover that salvation has other aspects in this present life. Then in chapter 8 we'll learn of the wonderful future aspects of salvation. But the first great thing we learn is that salvation removes our guilt. God declares, "Your guilt is gone."

Upon what basis does God declare us to be righteous, or free of guilt? It is only upon the basis of the finished work of Jesus Christ. God remains a God of justice. He doesn't say, "I won't bother with your sin," or, "I'll overlook your sin." That kind of attitude would make Him less than a perfect God. He would be acting in an arbitrary, relativistic way. But because Jesus bore the penalty for our sin, God can declare us justified.

Even the righteousness of God which is by faith [in] Jesus Christ unto all and upon all them that believe . . . (3:22a)

This should remind us of something we saw in our theme verse: ". . . the gospel . . . is the power of God unto salvation to every one that believeth" (1:16). The gospel, as we noted, is universal; it is not just for Israel, but for the Gentile world as well. There is, however, a limiting factor: It is only for those who believe. This righteousness of God, available because of Christ, is available only "unto all and upon all them that believe."

. . . for there is no difference: For all have sinned . . . (3:22b-23a)

In the midst of what would seem to be a climactic point in his presentation of the gospel, Paul returns to the crucial "first half" of his message—for he realizes that the gospel is meaningless unless a person really understands the depth of his guilt before God. There's no use in asking someone, "Don't you want to be saved?" unless that person knows how desperately he or she needs salvation. Without that deep sense of need, a gospel presentation is just a waste of time. If the Jew or the nominal Christian comes to an evangelistic meeting convinced that God will accept him as long as he does the best he can; if a Christian Scientist comes thinking he will be accepted just by thinking good thoughts; if the Roman Catholic comes thinking he can find his way to God by his own suffering in purgatory . . . no one who has such a mentality is going to accept Christ as Savior.

So Paul, at the very height of his gospel proclamation, returns again to the theme of sin. We might say to him, "Paul, you covered all this at the end of the first chapter, in the second chapter, and through most of the third chapter. Why don't you move on?" But Paul, moved by the Holy Spirit, knows that unless people understand how truly guilty they are before God, they will never consider accepting what Jesus Christ did for them.

For all have sinned, and come short of the glory of God. (3:23)

The verb tenses in this verse cover both past and present. In the past, all have sinned; in the present, all are coming short. Suppose that God would say, "All right, I will judge you on the basis of what you have done in your life up to now." We would have to respond, "But I've sinned throughout my life." And we would stand condemned. Suppose that God would then say, "All right, I'll just forget the past and I'll begin judging you from this day onward." Surely, none of us is so foolish as to think that, from today onward, we could live sinless lives. Surely our hearts tell us that, even on the basis of our present and future life, we would still be condemned. "For all have sinned, and are coming short of the glory of God." Paul leaves no room for human egoism. In the past we have sinned, in the present we are sinning, and in the future we will continue to sin. Salvation by works is impossible in all directions.

That is why our only hope is that God will find some way to justify us gratis, freely, without the need for a single iota of merit on our part.

Being justified freely by his grace through the redemption that is in Christ Jesus. (3:24)

That is exactly what God has done for us, through Christ! He has justified us "freely by his grace through the redemption" that is available to us because of Christ's death on the cross.

This "redemption" Paul now talks about is just what we need. Nothing less will do. We don't need a spiritual guide. We don't need just some vague unity between Christ and ourselves. What we need is redemption, because what we are is guilty. On the basis of our personal moral code or on the basis of the law, we are guilty (1:18—3:20). But now, on the basis of "the redemption that is in Christ Jesus," we can stand justified in God's sight.

God's grace, His redemption, is free to us. But it isn't free in the sense that nobody paid for it. The reason it is free to us is because Jesus has paid the price. In one sense God never really forgives anyone's sin. He can't. If God forgave a single sin in the sense of just closing His eyes to it, we would no longer live in a moral universe. God Himself would no longer be moral. So He doesn't forgive a single sin; every sin is punished. Yet, because Jesus paid the price for our sin, the matter is settled. It has been settled, not within the context of the absolute moral law by which God rules the universe, but outside of that law, or as Paul says in 3:21, "without the law."

Throughout the Old Testament we learn of God's perfect standard of justice. For instance, in Deuteronomy 25:1 we read, "If there be a controversy between men, and they come unto judgment, that the judges may judge them; then they shall justify the righteous, and condemn the wicked." What does justice mean? It means that the wicked will be condemned. By that standard, each one of us stands condemned before a God who by His own moral law must condemn us. Yet, because Christ paid the price for all our sin, "all them that believe" in Him (3:22) stand justified in God's sight. This justification is given "freely" (3:24), without the addition of one iota of good works on our part—without our adding one hair's breadth to the scale of divine justice.

Whom God hath set forth to be a propitiation through faith in his blood, to declare his righteousness for the remission of sins that are past, through the forbearance of God. (3:25)

God "set forth" Christ; that is, He presented Him to the world, to be a "propitiation." A propitiation is a covering. Under the law in the Old Testament, the "mercy seat" covered the Ark of the Covenant. Now, Christ's death on the cross covers our sins, just like the little boy being covered by his father's overcoat. But Christ's death doesn't cover the sins of just anyone, only the sins of "all them that believe." There are always these two elements: There is the work, which was entirely done on the cross by Jesus Christ; and there is the faith, the believing, the accepting of Christ's work for our salvation. Christ's death brings about "the remission of sins." Nothing else, no additional work on our part, needs to be added. Christ's death is a complete propitiation. It covers everything.

To declare, I say, at this time his righteousness: that he might be just, and the justifier of him which believeth in Jesus. (3:26)

A better translation, to capture the sense of the Greek, would be, "that he might be just *and yet* the justifier of him which believeth in Jesus." In a way, this phrase and the verses that surround it constitute the center of the whole Bible, for they answer the most profound of all questions: How can God remain the absolutely just ruler of the universe, and yet justify me, an ungodly sinner?

Note, first of all, that God *must* remain absolutely just, or we have no real basis for moral standards. It is impossible to have moral standards without there being a moral absolute. Without an absolute, we are left with either hedonism or some sort of relative standard such as "whatever is best for society." Words like *right* and *wrong* cease to have any real meaning. There must be an absolute, and the Bible provides the only adequate answer to this need for a moral absolute: The moral absolute is the perfectly "just" character of God Himself.

That's why 3:26 is such a key verse. Because Jesus has borne our guilt on the cross, God can remain "just." The moral basis of our universe can be upheld. Yet at the same time He can be the "justifier" of all those who believe in and accept Christ's payment for their sin.

Whether I have been among those with the Bible, or those without the Bible, I have been numbered among the ungodly. Whether I've been a Jew or a Gentile, I've been under the wrath of God. So how can God justify me? As soon as God would justify me by overlooking my sin, He's no longer just. And as soon as He is no longer just, we no longer live in a moral universe. And if we no longer live in a moral universe, everything collapses. But there is a way in which God can deal with my sin and your sin, and yet remain just. There is a way in which God, remaining just and therefore not deviating one iota from His holiness, not letting down the bars one tenth of one percent, can justify you and me. He can do this because Jesus Christ, His Son, took the full punishment for our sin.

God's love is seen, not in forgiving sin, for in a sense no sin can ever be forgiven or we would cease to live in a moral universe. God's love is seen, rather, in sending His only Son, Jesus Christ, to pay the price, to be the covering for all our sin. God maintains His holiness. He doesn't deviate from His total justice. And yet, without abandoning His moral law, He can fully justify anyone who believes in Jesus and accepts His perfect sacrifice for sin.

So, who is eligible for this covering of sin? Anyone? Everyone? Unlike many modern philosophers, God does not view us as just so many faceless masks. He doesn't deal with us as if we were mere machines. He treats us as individuals. He deals with us on the level on which He created us—as moral and rational beings. Therefore, even though Christ's death is a sufficient covering for all sins, there is a condition on who will receive this covering. This covering of sin, this justification, applies only to "every one that believeth" (1:16), to "all them that believe" (3:22), to "him which believeth" (3:26).

Which individuals does God justify? He justifies those who through faith accept what Christ has done for them, those who are united to the work of Jesus Christ with the instrument of faith.

There are two factors in salvation: the basis and the instrument. The basis of our salvation is the finished work of Jesus Christ, without a hair's breadth of any human good works added to the scale. The instrument by which we share in this salvation is our faith, our believing God. Our faith does not have saving value. We're not saved on the basis of our faith. We're saved only on the basis of the finished work of Jesus Christ. But the instrument by which we share in this is our faith. Our faith links us to the salvation Christ provides. Our faith is the empty hands that accept the gift of salvation.

Our faith has no saving value. Our religious good works, our moral good works, have no saving value because they're not perfect. Our suffering has no saving value. We would have to suffer infinitely, because we have sinned against an infinite God; and we, being finite, cannot suffer infinitely. The only thing in all of God's moral universe that has the power to save is the finished work of Jesus Christ. Our faith merely accepts the gift. And God justifies all those who believe in Jesus (3:26).

If all this is true, then verse 27 is certainly an understatement:

Where is boasting then? It is excluded. By what law? of works? Nay: but by the law of faith. (3:27)

By modern-day humanist standards, the gospel is decidedly "unhumanist." If my faith has saving value, if my suffering has saving value, if my religious works have saving value, if my moral works have saving value, I could boast before God on that basis. As Paul will express it in 4:4, I could consider God to be in my debt and could say to Him, "You owe it to me." But as we have seen up to this point in Romans, we humans are all in a decidedly unhumanist situation. We have all sinned. We have all rebelled. And since we have sinned and rebelled against an infinite God, we are infinitely guilty. There is only one hope for us—the grace of God. Not the grace of God in closing His eyes against sin, but the grace of God in sending the Redeemer, the propitiation, the one who shed His blood. This is our only hope. There is no room for boasting.

Therefore we conclude that a man is justified by faith without the deeds of the law. (3:28)

This is Paul's great conclusion, and this verse was so very crucial to Martin Luther's understanding of the gospel. Considering that Luther lived after hundreds of years of a Roman Catholic emphasis on works, and during a time of increasing humanism, you can just see why this verse became his great cry. This was Luther's verse, and it should be ours as well. It should fill us with thankfulness as we recall that we have been "children of wrath, even as the others" (Eph. 2:3), but have been saved eternally by grace through faith. This should smash any cold orthodoxy just like a dish being smashed on the floor. How can we be cold about this great truth? "Therefore we conclude that a man is justified by faith without the deeds of the law."

Is he the God of the Jews only? Is he not also of the Gentiles? Yes, of the Gentiles also: seeing it is one God which shall justify the circumcision by faith, and uncircumcision through faith. (3:29-30)

Paul has brought it all together. Why do we need salvation? Because we're guilty. Why do we need salvation? Because we're under the wrath of God. The man without the Bible, the Gentile, is under the wrath of God (1:18—2:16). The man with the Bible, the Jew, is under the wrath of God (2:17—3:8). Then Paul draws them all together, declaring everyone to be under God's wrath (3:9-20). Then he tells us this marvelous way of salvation that God has provided through the finished work of Jesus Christ (3:21-28). And then he draws all mankind together again, declaring that God is the same God toward all people; and all people—Jews and Gentiles alike—must be justified in exactly the same way (3:29-30).

6

JUSTIFICATION BEFORE
THE CROSS
(3:31—4:25)

৵৶

Paul now anticipates a question his Jewish readers might ask, and this question introduces chapter 4:

Do we then make void the law through faith? God forbid: yea, we establish the law. (3:31)

In chapter 10, Paul will show clearly that the Old Testament Jews were justified by faith, just as God's people have always been. Here in chapter 4 he will illustrate this truth by the example of faithful Abraham. He introduces his discussion of Abraham by saying that his (Paul's) message of salvation through faith actually establishes the law.

Just how does salvation through faith "establish" the law? It establishes the law because salvation through faith was the purpose of the law. As Paul explains in Galatians, the law was intended to be a "schoolmaster" to bring people to Christ (Gal. 3:24). John the Baptist, born just before Christ, was actually the last Old Testament prophet, and his message of repentance was the same as that of all the Old

Testament prophets. John's purpose, like that of the law and of all the other Old Testament prophets, was to prepare people for Christ. The law was a schoolmaster to bring us to Christ. Paul says he isn't trying to destroy the Old Testament, he isn't ceasing to be Jewish. For the gospel he is proclaiming is the very purpose of the Old Testament law. When we relate to people from a Jewish background, we must live before them and present the gospel to them in the light of Paul's perspective. We must try to show that the Old and New Testaments are not two separate revelations from God, but are in fact one. They may not readily accept our message, but this must be our approach.

Having concluded that Jews and Gentiles alike can be justified only by faith (3:28-30), Paul will strengthen this in chapter 4 by reminding us of Abraham, the father of the Jewish people. Salvation by faith alone is nothing new. It applies to those living on both sides of the cross. The Old and New Testaments are of one piece in proclaiming this message. As Paul said at the very beginning of Romans, the gospel was "promised afore by his prophets in the holy scriptures" (1:2). All people are sinners, and the purpose of the law is to make us all understand that we are sinners. Just like the label we have applied to Romans 1:18—3:20, the law is the "first half of the gospel." When we finally understand that we haven't kept the law and are therefore under God's wrath, then we are ready to listen to the second half of the gospel, the good news of redemption through the blood of Christ.

Take note again of where we are in our study: Having shown us our need for salvation (1:18—3:20), Paul is now explaining the wonderful truth that we can be justified in God's sight through faith alone (3:21—4:25). From 3:21-30 he has spoken of justification for those living this side of the cross; from 3:31—4:22 he will explain that those who lived before the cross were also eligible to be justified by faith. Then, in 4:23-25, he will draw together those who lived before Christ and those who have lived after Christ—just as he drew together the Jews and Gentiles in 3:9-20 and again in 3:29-30—and will show once again the unity in God's plan of salvation on both sides of the cross.

Reformed theologians view the history of God's dealings with mankind in terms of a succession of covenants. They speak first of all of the covenant of works, which was in operation from creation until the Fall of man. Adam and Eve could have had perfect fellowship with God on the basis of their own works, for there is nothing intrinsically wrong with man as man. There's nothing wrong with humans being finite. There's nothing wrong with their having physical bodies. There's nothing wrong with their being sexual creatures. I mention these three areas—man's finiteness, his physical nature, and his sexuality—because many people find the basic problem of man in one of these three areas. But the Bible insists that there is nothing wrong with any of these three, because this is the way God has made us. And prior to the Fall, although they were limited, finite beings, although they had physical bodies, and although they were sexual creatures, Adam and Eve could come before God on the basis of their own works.

Then, of course, sin entered the world, at the time of the historical Fall of Adam and Eve. This was not just some sort of mythical notion of a Fall, but an actual, historical Fall when Adam and Eve deliberately disobeyed God and therefore sinned. As soon as they sinned, as soon they fell, they could no longer come before God on the basis of the covenant of works. But as soon as this happened, the covenant of grace came into effect. In fact, we read in Genesis that, within twenty-four hours after mankind's first act of disobedience, God had promised that the Savior would someday come (Gen. 3:15).

Actually, it is not entirely correct to speak of the "covenant of works" and the "covenant of grace," for in a sense both of these are covenants of works. The first is a covenant of works that humans, before the Fall, were able to keep. The second is not a covenant of grace in that God no longer requires works; rather, it is a covenant of works that Christ has kept on our behalf. For Christ, the gospel is a covenant of works; thankfully, however, for us it is a covenant of grace.

The covenant of grace extends from the Fall of mankind in Genesis, to the last human being who will ever be saved. It includes the people who lived before the cross as well as those of us who live after the cross. There are some differences in the way God dealt with people before the cross and how He deals with people since the cross, but all of this—before and after the cross—falls under the covenant of grace. There is a marvelous unity in God's dealing with us humans throughout history. From the Fall of man to the last person saved, it is a covenant of grace to mankind, based upon a covenant of works perfectly kept by Christ. That's the basis upon which the promise of salvation was first made to Adam and Eve (Gen. 3:15), and that's the basis upon which it has been repeated in various ways to all humans who have ever lived or will ever live.

Our discussion at this point may seem rather cold and theological, but it ceases to be cold and theological when you realize your own part in it. If, after Adam and Eve fell, God had continued to deal with us humans only on the basis of our works, all of us would be lost. But God immediately made the promise. There is a covenant of grace. It has been in effect since Genesis 3:15: It is the same promise, the same covenant of grace, on both sides of the cross.

In chapter 4 Paul will show how this broader covenant of grace can be seen in God's particular covenant with Abraham. God's covenant with Abraham can be divided into two specific parts: the national portion, in which the promise is given to the Jews as Jews (in chapters 9—11 Paul will show that this covenant is still in effect); and the spiritual portion, which is available to all people on both sides of the cross.

People on both sides of the cross are saved on the same basis: Christ's finished work on the cross. God told Abraham that the covenant blessing would come through his seed (Gen. 13:15; 22:18). Paul points out that this word "seed" is not plural but singular, and that it refers to Christ (Gal. 3:16). Christ Himself would bring about the blessing God promised to Abraham 2,000 years before Christ's day.

On the Mount of Transfiguration, Moses and Elijah came and talked with Jesus, and only one subject of conversation was great enough for such a moment: As Luke tells us, Moses and Elijah were talking with Christ about His approaching death (Luke 9:30-31). Why was this the topic of their conversation? Because Moses and Elijah, who had lived many centuries before Christ, needed Him to die so that they could be saved.

Having established that those living before the cross could be saved only by what happened on the cross, one might wonder whether or not they understood this. The Bible does not answer this question for us concerning each person we read about in the Old Testament. Abraham, for one, probably had a good understanding of the basis of his salvation. But in the fourth chapter Paul will insist that, whether the people of Old Testament times knew a little or a lot about it, they did in fact have available to them the same means of justification as we have today.

How are we justified? Paul will say in 4:3 that Abraham was justified because he "believed God." An evangelist will say that we are justified by believing on Christ as Savior, and that is exactly right. It is perfectly proper to say it this way. Yet there is something that must happen before a person believes on Christ as Savior: They must first "believe God" just as Abraham believed Him.

Notice I didn't say that we must first "believe in God"; rather, I said we must "believe God." Is this a distinction worth making? Various forms of the phrase "believe in God" occur throughout Scripture, even here in Romans. And of course the very first step in faith is believing in God in the sense of believing that He is there, that He exists. But then the next step is simply to "believe God." We must believe Him in the sense of believing that He will keep His promises, starting with Genesis 3:15 and throughout Scripture.

Believing God is something more than just the neoorthodox "leap of faith" promoted by Kierkegaard and others. The only faith that is of value is the faith that believes God. This is very important to understand, because our whole twentieth-century emphasis is that faith has value as a thing in and of itself. The greater the distance you step out, according to this non-Christian view, the greater the value of your faith. To this modern notion of faith, the Bible says absolutely no! Whether we are thinking of the faith that we who live after the cross place in Christ as Savior, or the faith of those who could only look forward to Christ's coming, the important thing is not the faith itself but the object of the faith: the God who is there.

So we come to Abraham, living approximately 2,000 years before Christ, during the time of Hammurabi. God made a covenant with him—the same covenant He had made with Adam and Eve as soon as they committed the first sin. God told Abraham that all nations of mankind were going to be blessed through his seed. People throughout the Old Testament—on the other side of the cross from us—probably understood the significance of this covenant to varying degrees. But however little or however much they understood it, what was involved in each case was believing God. And in chapter 4, Paul tells us of the act of faith wherein Abraham demonstrated that he did in fact believe God.

What shall we say then that Abraham our father, as pertaining to the flesh, hath found? (4:1)

Paul has asserted that faith, rather than making the law void, actually fulfills it (3:31). How better could Paul illustrate this than to show that Abraham, the father of the Jews, understood this and was justified in this way!

For if Abraham were justified by works, he hath whereof to glory; but not before God. For what saith the Scripture? Abraham believed God, and it was counted unto him for righteousness. (4:2-3)

As we have noted, people try in various ways to be justified on the basis of works. For instance, many Roman Catholics believe that they will be able to stand before God on the basis of their good works in this life, with any deficiency being made up either by their suffering in this life or by their suffering in purgatory. Let's say, for the sake of illustration, that a person of this doctrinal persuasion suffers for one million years in purgatory. Even after that much suffering, that person would not be able to stand before God and say, "I've done it. I've merited the merit of Christ." Even a million years of suffering would not fill up that person's infinite chasm of guilt. Likewise, even if a Hindu were able to pass through a million reincarnations, he or she still could not stand before God and say, "I've done it."

Whatever one's religious beliefs, and whether one lives after the cross or before the cross, no one who has ever lived—not even faithful Abraham—has been able to stand before God and demand eternal salvation on the basis of his or her good deeds. Salvation comes only through the covenant of grace. There is no place for works and no room for pride or boasting. As humans, we don't like this. It hurts our pride to have to come before God with nothing in our hands. But there is no other way to come, according to the Bible.

As we have seen, this issue of salvation by works versus salvation by grace involves the whole question of whether or not we live in a moral universe. How does God remain holy and yet justify someone who has sinned against Him? The answer is, our justification is based entirely on the finished work of Christ and not on anything that any of us can do. Therefore, God can accept us and yet remain completely holy. Because of what Christ did on the cross, we can live in a moral, orderly universe and yet not be condemned.

If, after Adam had sinned, he could still have brought some good work to justify himself before God, then we would have to conclude that God had lowered His standards, that He had accepted something less than perfection. And if God had lowered His standards, then our universe would have been in some sense a less moral, less orderly place. It is so very important, then, that Paul establishes that not even Abraham could be justified by works. This is a key part of the Christian answer to the intellectual questions of life. We understand where sin came from: There was a historical Fall, whereby "judgment came upon all men," as Paul will later explain (5:18). But we also understand that, because of the finished work of Christ, we are not all condemned to eternal death.

Now, however, the question has to be asked, How did Abraham find justification before God? Paul answers that question in verse 3, where he quotes from Genesis 15:6.

For what saith the Scripture? Abraham believed God, and it was counted unto him for righteousness. (4:3)

Abraham was justified, he was considered righteous in God's sight, because he "believed God." We will learn in verse 21 that Abraham's belief in God was not just some sort of vague or general faith, but belief in a specific promise of God: "[Abraham] being fully persuaded that, what [God] had promised, he was able also to perform." No faith in God is really valid unless it involves faith in a specific revelation or promise of God. God had made a specific promise to Abraham, and Abraham believed that God could and would keep that specific promise.

The verses leading up to 4:21 give clues as to the specific promise God made to Abraham, but to learn exactly what that promise was, we must read Genesis 15:1-6: "After these things the word of the Lord GOD came unto Abram in a vision saying, Fear not, Abram: I am thy shield, and thy exceeding great reward. And Abram said, what wilt thou give me, seeing I go childless, and the steward of my house is this Eliezer of Damascus? And Abram said, Behold, to me thou hast given no seed; and, lo, one born in my house is mine heir. And, behold, the word of the LORD came unto him, saying, This shall not be thine heir; but he that shall come forth out of thine own bowels shall be thine heir. And he brought him forth abroad, and said, Look now toward heaven, and tell the stars, if thou be able to number them: and he said unto him, So shall thy seed be. And he believed in the LORD; and he counted it to him for righteousness."

This is a specific promise. God promised Abraham that he and Sarah would have a child even though, because of their advanced age, this was humanly impossible. Chapter 11 of Hebrews, the great faith chapter, describes Abraham's faith in God, and notes that his wife Sarah also believed God's promise that they would have a son: "By faith Abraham, when he was called to go out into a place which he should after receive for an inheritance, obeyed; and he went out, not knowing whither he went. . . . Through faith also Sarah herself received strength to conceive seed, and was delivered of a child when she was past age, because she judged him faithful who had promised. Therefore sprang there even of one, and him as good as dead, so many as the stars of the sky in multitude, and as the sand which is by the sea shore innumerable" (Heb. 11:8, 11-12).

The writer of Hebrews then describes how Abraham's faith in God's specific promise of a son was put to the ultimate test: "By faith Abraham, when he was tried, offered up Isaac: and he that had received the promises offered up his only begotten son, of whom it was said, that in Isaac shall thy seed be called: Accounting that God was able to raise him up, even from the dead; from whence also he received him in a figure" (Heb. 11:17-19).

Each time he was tested, Abraham believed God's promise. Even before we picked up the story in Genesis 15, God had promised Abraham that he was going to have descendants as innumerable as the sand of the sea and the stars of the heavens (Gen. 12:2; 13:14-17). But if Abraham was ever going to have descendants so numerous, he first had to have *one*. It's all very nice to talk about having a million descendants, but if you're ever going to have a million descendants you've got to first have one. Abraham didn't have one. And both he and his wife were too old for procreation. Yet God continued to say that Abraham was going to have a child, and the whole world was going to be blessed through his posterity. In this impossible situation, Abraham believed God; and this, the Bible tells us, was his act of faith.

Christian faith, like Abraham's faith, is never a vague thing; it is always an acting upon the specific promises of God. Whenever I sense that someone is ready to accept Christ as Savior, I deal with that person on the basis of a specific promise of God. I do this very carefully because I think this is where it all hangs. You can choose various promises, but the one I like is John 3:36: "He that believeth on the Son hath everlasting life." This is the whole point. Do I or do I not believe that God can and will fulfill this promise to give me everlasting life? God has said, "If Francis Schaeffer [or your name] believes on Christ, he that believes on the Son has everlasting life." God thunders it down through the centuries, or whispers it softly, however you wish to think of it: "If [your name] believes on the Son, he has everlasting life." Either you believe this promise from God, or you don't believe it. Either you "believe God" (Rom. 4:3), or you don't believe Him.

This focus on a specific promise helps people understand that belief in Christ is not just some sort of generalized faith. It isn't a vague thing. It isn't an emotion. It isn't a "leap of faith." It is choosing to believe a specific promise of God. It may be the promise of John 3:36, or a promise such as, "Come unto me, all ye that labor and are heavy laden, and I will give you rest" (Matt. 11:28), or, "Behold, I stand at the door, and knock: if any man hear my voice, and open the door, I will come in" (Rev. 3:20). The important thing is that, in each case, the person responds in faith to a specific promise made by God

Himself. Saving faith is not a blind leap; it is our response to the specific, dependable promises of God.

Abraham, living 2,000 years before Christ, responded in faith to a
specific promise of God, and Paul repeats what the Old Testament
already says, that this was "counted unto him for righteousness" (Gen.
15:6; Rom. 4:3). Now Paul shows us once again that, if we try in any
way to include works in our salvation, the whole gospel message falls
to the ground.

**Now to him that worketh is the reward not reckoned of grace, but of
debt. (4:4)**

If anyone, instead of coming to God under the covenant of grace,
is somehow able to find salvation on the basis of works, this means
that God must owe him something. As we shall see, however, all God
"owes" us is the "wages" of our sins against Him, which is "death"
(6:23). Our only hope of salvation is grace. The basis of salvation by
grace is the finished work of Jesus Christ. The instrument is our faith.
Nothing else is allowed.

**But to him that worketh not, but believeth on him that justifieth the
ungodly, his faith is counted for righteousness. (4:5)**

Whom does God justify? He justifies the ungodly. If God were to
set a limit of, say, 80 percent, and declare that all who are at least 80
percent righteous can be saved, then He wouldn't be justifying the
ungodly—He would be justifying the godly on the basis of an 80 percent standard. But God never justifies the godly; there aren't any,
because God maintains a 100 percent standard. Those who are justified are always sinners. When Jesus said, "I am not come to call the
righteous, but sinners to repentance" (Matt. 9:13), He didn't mean
there are some who are righteous; He meant there are some who *think*
they are righteous. A person can never find salvation until he knows
that he is a sinner. We're all sinners, but not all of us know we're sinners. That's why, when someone expresses a desire to be saved, I
never let the person say, "I accept Christ as Savior" until first of all he
or she has said, "I acknowledge that I deserve the wrath of God." I
think that a lot of people put up their hands in evangelistic meetings

and say they've accepted Christ as their Savior, but they haven't really because they don't realize that they are among the ungodly. They don't see that they are deservedly damned. If I don't see that I am deservedly damned, then I can never accept Christ as my Savior. I may say the words, I may join the church, I may be baptized, but I'm not saved.

For a person to accept Christ as Savior, he must first of all know he is a sinner. He must know that he cannot earn his way into the presence of a holy God. He must understand he is justly under the wrath of God. Then, he must believe the God who has promised, "He that believeth on the Son hath everlasting life."

This whole issue of salvation involves our creature-Creator relationship with God. God made us to love Him, to believe Him, to have fellowship with Him. When did Eve sin? Eve sinned when she chose not to believe God. God had made a negative promise to Adam and Eve. He extended a warning to them: If they ate of the forbidden tree, they would "surely die" (Gen. 2:17). Eve became a sinner when she ceased to believe that negative promise. God said, "Thou shalt surely die." Then Satan came and contradicted what God had said. Satan, who had already put himself at the center of the universe in wanting to be equal with God (Isa. 14:12-15), said to Eve, "No, in the day you eat, you will not die; you will become like God" (Gen. 3:4-5).

What was Eve's sin? Very simply, Eve believed Satan and disbelieved God. God's command not to eat of the tree was not just some arbitrary command. It was an important part of the creature-Creator relationship. Adam and Eve rejected that relationship, and thus we have the Fall. As you and I are confronted with God and His promises, we are in a sense in the place of Eve. God makes us a promise, and either we believe Him or we don't believe Him. We either take our place as a creature before Him, and believe Him; or like Satan we try to put ourselves, instead of God, at the center of the universe.

Notice how Paul is developing his thought. He has concluded ". . . that a man is justified by faith without the deeds of the law" (3:28), and now he is presenting Abraham as an example of someone who was, in fact, justified in God's sight without performing the deeds of the law. To understand this better, let's look ahead again to the end of chapter 6: "The wages of sin is death; but the gift of God is eternal life through Jesus Christ our Lord" (6:23). As we have noted, if God were to deal with us on the basis of wages, there would be only one thing He could ever pay us and that is death.

Think of it this way: Here is the paymaster's window, and we come up to it one by one and say, "Pay me what you owe me," and in justice the paymaster must pay each of us our proper wages. But now suppose that the paymaster is God. We each come up to the window and say to God, "Pay me what you owe me." And God hands out identical pay envelopes to each of us. There is only one payment possible from a holy God to creatures who have deliberately sinned against Him, and that pay envelope is marked with one terrible word: death.

Many today who have no knowledge of the Bible experience this death as they search in vain for their purpose in life. The more logical such a person is, the more he sees this—that he can't find anything in life, he can't get hold of anything, the whole thing slips through his fingers. Well, the Bible tells us the reason for this. The reason simply is that since man sinned, since the historical Fall, the only thing man can earn in this life is death. But the good news, of course, is that true life, eternal life, is possible as a "gift of God . . . through Jesus Christ our Lord."

Even in Old Testament times God showed His people in various ways that salvation was by grace through faith and not by works. As soon as God had given Israel the Ten Commandments (Ex. 20:1-20), He commanded them to build an altar (Ex. 20:21-26), whereupon they would offer sacrifices to atone for their inability to keep the law. We see this combination of the law and the altar again in chapter 24: "And Moses wrote all the words of the LORD, and rose up early in the morning, and builded an altar" (Ex. 24:4). The text goes on to emphasize the need for the shedding of blood to atone for Israel's inability to keep the law: "And Moses took the blood, and sprinkled it on the people, and said, Behold the blood of the covenant, which the LORD hath made with you concerning all these words" (Ex. 24:8). The very covenant itself was sealed by the shedding of blood. There had to be the blood. Why? Because no one would be able to keep the law. Even back then, they understood.

Indeed, the very method and materials used to build the altar were symbolic of Israel's inability to come to God on the basis of works. The altar was to be built using a minimal amount of human labor: "And if thou wilt make me an altar of stone, thou shall not build it of hewn stone: for if thou lift up thy tool upon it, thou hast polluted it" (Ex. 20:25). Before the Jews had any opportunity of thinking they could in any way earn salvation, God made it clear to them that they could really do nothing at all to that end, not even so much as taking a chisel and smoothing the stone of the altar.

These instructions about not hewing the stones for the altar came at the original giving of the law, a pivotal time in Israel's history. The instructions were repeated at a second pivotal time, when they entered Canaan. As they again recorded the law, this time in plaster on Mount Ebal, once again they heard the special instructions regarding the altar: "And there shalt thou build an altar unto the LORD thy God, an altar of stones: thou shalt not lift up any iron tool upon them. Thou shalt build the altar of the LORD thy God of whole stones" (Deut. 27:5-6). Both when they first heard the law at Sinai, and when they heard it again in Canaan, Israel was made to understand that you can't be saved by human effort.

The book of Romans, with its tremendous message of grace, is only reiterating what the Old Testament taught in various other ways. That's why Paul can say so strongly that, rather than "making void" the law through his message of grace, he is in fact "establishing" it (3:31). That's why he can say in Galatians that the law is a "schoolmaster to bring us to Christ" (Gal. 3:24). The message is the same, from the giving of the law, to the entering of the Promised Land, to the preaching of John the Baptist, to the teaching of Paul. When John called people to repent, he was calling them to honestly face the law and to realize that they hadn't kept it, and therefore needed the "Lamb of God, which taketh away the sin of the world" (John 1:29). The only way we can fail to see this continuity is to misunderstand the law. Indeed, as Paul will show in chapters 9—11, many Jews did misunderstand the law, seeking to establish their own righteousness and failing to understand that salvation is by faith.

Paul has shown that Abraham was saved by faith rather than

works (4:1-5). He now anticipates another possible objection: Someone might say, "Salvation by faith alone is fine for Abraham, who lived 500 years before the law was given. But after the law was given, didn't it all change?" Of course we have just seen that the law itself actually taught salvation by faith. But let's forget that for a moment and put ourselves in the position of Paul's typical Jewish reader—the ones he describes in chapters 9—11 as having misunderstood the law. "Didn't it all change after the giving of the law?" they might now have asked.

To answer that anticipated question, Paul introduces David, who lived some 500 years *after* the giving of the law!

Even as David also describeth the blessedness of the man, unto whom God imputeth righteousness without works, saying, Blessed are they whose iniquities are forgiven, and whose sins are covered. (4:6-7)

Paul is quoting from Psalm 32:1-2. If someone would say, "Well, justification by faith is okay for Abraham, but after the law there's a difference," the answer is, There's no difference at all. It was the same on both sides of the law. Not only did Abraham understand that justification is through faith, but David, living 500 years after the giving of the law, understood it too.

Not only did Abraham and David, before and after the law, understand that salvation is by grace through faith, but Paul will show in the first few verses of chapter 10 what we have already learned from Exodus and Deuteronomy: Moses himself, the giver of the law, also understood that salvation is by grace through faith. Paul says, "For Moses describeth the righteousness which is of the law, That the man which doeth those things shall live by them" (Rom. 10:5). If you're going to be saved by the law, you must keep it. But then Paul quickly adds, "But the righteousness which is of faith speaketh on this wise, Say not in thine heart, Who shall ascend into heaven?" (Rom. 10:6a). Here Paul is quoting the words of Moses in Deuteronomy 30:12, and he adds a parenthetical word of explanation: "(that is to bring Christ down from above)" (Rom. 10:6b). He then says the same thing in another way, paraphrasing Moses from Deuteronomy 30:13: "Or, who shall descend into the deep? (that is, to bring up Christ again from the dead)" (Rom. 10:7). Paul then climaxes his argument by building on the words of Moses in Deuteronomy 30:14: "But what saith it? The word is nigh thee, even in thy mouth, and in thy heart: that is, the word of faith, which we preach" (10:8). Abraham understood. David understood. And Moses understood!

There is a tremendous unity throughout the Bible as it presents the covenant of grace. Certainly, there are differences in how this was expressed before and after the cross. Nonetheless, the basic message is the same. Salvation is always the same, before the cross and after the cross, before Moses and after Moses. No matter how many subdivisions you might visualize in trying to understand the Bible on either side of the cross, the unity is there, the unity of the covenant of grace. Salvation is always on the basis of the finished work of Christ, and the instrument is always faith. This was always the purpose of the law. "Therefore we are not nullifying the law; we are establishing the law." That is Paul's point.

Even as David also describeth the blessedness of the man, unto whom God imputeth righteousness without works. (4:6)

God "imputes" righteousness to us, without the need of any works on our part. What does "impute" mean? Let me explain it by telling about something that happened in my family. When we lived in Champéry, Switzerland, one of my daughters, in an effort to be magnanimous, gathered up the village children and went to the grocery store, where we had an account. She bought lots of candy and with great care distributed it to all the children. Word of this got around, and each day more and more children went with her to the store to get candy. Then one day the storekeeper suddenly got worried. He thought this looked a little strange, to have half the village children in a little parade after our child, coming to his store to get candy. So, he called us and said, "Do you know what your daughter is doing?" And of course we were totally surprised by his report of her generous deeds!

So what was the storekeeper to do? He was stuck. He realized he probably shouldn't have let her take all that candy. But what could he do? Well, he could have demanded that our daughter pay him. After all, she was the one who owed the money. Of course, this would have been impossible, because the amount she owed was way beyond her ability to pay.

So how was the situation resolved? Well, we said, "Put it on our account." The total bill would have been a tremendous amount to our child, and she couldn't have paid it. On our account, it didn't make much difference.

Now actually we could have used the word "impute." We could have said to the storekeeper, "Impute her debt to us." That's exactly where we stand before God, and that's what imputation means. We have sinned, and because we are finite and have committed infinite sin against an infinite God, we could never adequately pay for our sin. But Christ can pay, does pay, and says, "All right, put this on My account." This is imputation. When we accept Christ as our Savior, all of our sin is put on His account. Because He suffered infinitely on the cross, He can infinitely pay our infinite debt!

The Bible makes it clear that Abraham did understand and that David did understand how salvation was to be received. Let's look at Genesis 22, where Abraham is tested when God tells him to offer up his son Isaac. We know the story. The angel stopped Abraham's hand just as he was about to kill Isaac, and there appeared a ram, caught in a thicket, and Abraham offered the ram "in the stead of his son" (Gen. 22:13). Abraham realized that the Lord had provided the ram as a substitute for his son. Then we read in verse 14 that "Abraham called the name of that place Jehovah-jireh: as it is said to this day, In the mount of the LORD, it shall be seen." Jehovah-jireh means "the Lord will provide." A better translation of the latter part of the verse would be, "In the mount of the LORD, it shall be provided."

Of course, when we think of the ram being the substitute for Isaac, we think of Christ's substitutionary death in our place. (Remember that we noted, at Romans 1:18, that "substitution" is a concept unique to Christianity.) The most striking thing about the account of Abraham and Isaac is that the substitutionary sacrifice took place on Mount Moriah (Gen. 22:2). Mount Moriah was a long three days' journey from Abraham's home, and Abraham was an old man. Why did God require Abraham to make that strenuous three days' journey to this mountain? Why didn't He let this poor old man offer the sacrifice near his own home?

Remember, after Abraham had sacrificed the substitutionary ram, he said, "This is Jehovah-jireh and in this place the LORD will provide." Did he perhaps know that there was something special about that particular piece of geography? As it turns out, this could have been the very place where Jesus—our substitutionary lamb—would later be crucified, for we learn in 2 Chronicles 3:1 that the temple was built on Mount Moriah. Abraham, living 2,000 years before Christ and 1,000 years before even the building of the temple, said, "It's going to happen here!"

The Bible makes it even more clear that David understood the plan of salvation. Peter, preaching at Pentecost, quoted from David's words in Psalm 16:8-11: "For David speaketh concerning him, I foresaw the LORD always before my face, for he is on my right hand, that I should not be moved: Therefore did my heart rejoice, and my tongue was glad; moreover also my flesh shall rest in hope: Because thou wilt not leave my soul in hell, neither wilt thou suffer thy Holy One to see corruption. Thou hast made known to me the ways of life; thou shalt make me full of joy with thy countenance" (Acts 2:25-28).

Peter then explained the significance of David's words: "Men and brethren, let me freely speak unto you of the patriarch David, that he is both dead and buried, and his sepulchre is with us unto this day" (Acts 2:29). In other words, when David spoke of "not seeing corruption," he wasn't talking about himself. Rather, ". . . being a prophet, and knowing that God had sworn with an oath to him, that of the fruit of his loins, according to the flesh, he would raise up Christ to sit on his throne; he seeing this before spake of the resurrection of Christ, that his soul was not left in hell, neither his flesh did see corruption" (Acts 2:30-31). Peter is saying that David was a prophet, and that when he wrote Psalm 16 he knew it referred to Jesus Christ!

David understood! He understood the principle of faith, and he understood that the basis of that faith was the death and resurrection of the coming Messiah, Jesus Christ. It seems clear from Genesis 22 that Abraham understood. And to anyone who will accept the New

Testament's word as authority, it seems clear beyond all doubt that David understood.

The book of Hebrews makes an interesting statement relating to this matter of whether the people before Christ understood the plan of salvation. Having spoken of the disobedience and rebelliousness of the Israelites (Heb. 3:7-19), the writer of Hebrews warns his Jewish readers of the *Diaspora* not to follow their example (Heb. 4:1). Then he says, "For unto us was the gospel preached, as well as unto them; but the word preached did not profit them, not being mixed with faith in them that heard it" (Heb. 4:2). The gospel was proclaimed "unto them," long before the coming of Christ! And then, as now, many failed to respond in faith. The Old and New Testaments are a unity: The basis of salvation is the gospel, the finished work of Jesus Christ; and the instrument of salvation is faith.

Coming back to Romans 4, remember that Paul has asked, "Does the idea of salvation by grace through faith negate the law?" And he says, "God forbid!" The gospel, far from negating the law, actually "establishes" it (3:31). Then he has presented Abraham and David as people who lived under the law but also understood the gospel. In verse 8, he continues to quote David from Psalm 32.

Blessed is the man to whom the Lord will not impute sin. (4:8)

In the Greek it is stronger: "Blessed is the man to whom the Lord will by no means impute sin." This repeats the thought of verses 6 and 7, and again we must remind ourselves: Abraham, living roughly 500 years before the law, understood that he was justified by faith. David, living about 500 years after the law, had the same understanding. As far as salvation is concerned, the law changed nothing. The idea of salvation by grace does not nullify the law, for this was the purpose of the law—to show us that we need God's grace. There is a unity to the covenant of grace. People who were lost in Old Testament times and people who are lost in New Testament times and people who are lost today are all saved on the same basis: The basis is grace, and the instrument is faith.

Cometh this declaration of blessedness then upon the circumcision

only, or upon the uncircumcision also? for we say that faith was reckoned to Abraham for righteousness. (4:9)

The word "declaration" should be familiar. We saw earlier that justification is a declarative act of God. It is a legal matter. God doesn't somehow infuse us with righteousness. Rather, because of Christ's death, God declares us to be righteous.

But the question at hand is this: You say that Abraham was justified by faith. Does that mean justification is only for the Jews? Abraham was saved by faith, but what about the Gentiles? Paul answers that question in verse 10.

How was it then reckoned? when he was in circumcision, or in uncircumcision? Not in circumcision, but in uncircumcision. (4:10)

Was Abraham "reckoned" (declared) to be righteous before or after he was circumcised? It was at least seventeen years and perhaps as many as twenty-five years before he was circumcised. If being a Jew, for a male, means being circumcised, then Abraham hadn't even become a Jew at the time of his justification by faith! There were no Jews at the time of Abraham's justification by faith.

And he received the sign of circumcision, a seal of the righteousness of the faith which he had yet being uncircumcised: that he might be the father of all them that believe, though they be not circumcised; that righteousness might be imputed unto them also. (4:11)

Abraham didn't "receive the sign of circumcision" until many years after God had declared him to be justified. It wasn't a matter of his believing and being justified one day and then being circumcised the next. It was a very long time between the two events, possibly up to twenty-five years. Circumcision was only a "sign" and a "seal" of the "righteousness" that Abraham already possessed long before being circumcised. And because he possessed this righteousness before being circumcised, he is to be considered "the father of all them that believe," uncircumcised Gentiles as well as circumcised Jews. Abraham was a Gentile when he believed and became a Jew later with the sign of circumcision.

As Christians, Abraham is our spiritual father. Occasionally you find Christians expressing anti-Semitic feelings, but this is ridiculous from the biblical viewpoint, as well as being very sinful. According to the Bible, when we accept Christ as our Savior, we become spiritual Jews. For a Christian, to have an anti-Semitic feeling is therefore to have a feeling against oneself in a certain sense. Later in Romans, Paul will explain how Gentiles who believe in Christ become a part of spiritual Israel. As we have seen, there were two halves to the Abrahamic covenant. There were the promises to Israel as a nation past, present, and yet to come, and Paul will discuss these in chapters 9—11. But the Abrahamic covenant has a spiritual half as well, based on the work of Jesus Christ. When anyone accepts Christ as Savior, he or she is "grafted into" the spiritual half of the Abrahamic covenant (11:17-24).

Many Christians seem to think of Christianity as a Gentile religion and find it very unusual when a Jewish person becomes a Christian. But we must constantly remind ourselves that most of the first Christians were Jewish. Indeed, every author of New Testament books, with the possible exception of Luke, was Jewish. Paul, the apostle to the Gentiles, was Jewish. The whole fabric of the early church was Jewish. And, as Paul is now reminding us in verse 11, when anyone, Jew or Gentile, becomes a Christian, Abraham becomes that person's spiritual father. He carries this theme on into verse 12.

And the father of circumcision to them who are not of the circumcision only, but who also walk in the steps of that faith of our father Abraham, which he had being yet uncircumcised. (4:12)

All who accept Christ as Savior can claim Abraham as their spiritual father. They can enjoy the blessings of the spiritual half of God's covenant with Abraham. And who are these that enter into this place of blessedness? Who are these that enter into the gospel promises? As we noted in discussing chapter 3, it is all those who by their faith are linked to the saving work of Christ. We could think of the promises of God as a solid ring. If I stand beside this ring, I become a second solid ring, with no place for the two rings to be joined together. How am I, as this second, separate ring, to enter into the ring of God's promises? The answer is that I need a third ring to link my ring with the ring of God's promises, and this third ring is faith. In Hebrews 4:2 we read of people who failed to benefit from the gospel because they were not linked to it by faith. Here in Romans 4:12 we see the positive side: We are told of those who *are* linked to the gospel; it is those "who also walk in the steps of that faith of our father Abraham." And what was Abraham's faith? "Abraham believed God, and it was counted unto him for righteousness" (4:3). Saving faith is always the same: believing the God who is there. This is what Abraham did, and this is what each of us must do. There is no other way. God has made a promise, and we must believe Him.

Paul says this over and over again, so that it almost becomes repetitious. Way back in the first chapter, in our theme verses: "For I am not ashamed of the gospel of Christ, for it is the power of God unto salvation to every one that believeth; to the Jew first, and also to the Greek" (1:16). Then throughout these first eight chapters of Romans, Paul expounds that theme over and over again. The gospel is universal, in that it is available to all, Jew and Gentile alike. But it is also highly exclusive, in that only those who believe God do have it. It's as wide as the world but as narrow as those who truly believe God and enter into it through the finished work of Jesus Christ. Here in 4:12, Paul is simply restating this theme. The gospel is universal, "not of the circumcision only," but it is also exclusive, being only for those "who also walk in the steps of that faith of our father Abraham." Abraham is the father of all believers. See also Galatians 3:2 for a statement of the same relationship. And all this takes us back to the promise in Jeremiah 3:17 to both Jews and Gentiles. The covenant of grace is to all who believe Romans 4 and Galatians 3:7, 14, 29.

For the promise, that he should be the heir of the world, was not to Abraham, or to his seed, through the law, but through the righteousness of faith. (4:13)

There are two common ways of looking at this verse, both of which are helpful. Paul may be saying that the promise didn't come through the Law of Moses, since the law was not given till about 500 years after Abraham. Or he may simply be saying that one is saved by faith rather than by works. Both of these ideas are undoubtedly involved. As we have seen, as soon as the Ten Commandments were given, the altar was given. The altar was given before the Israelites had a chance to sin. And it was to be an altar of whole stones, built with minimal human effort and no tool marks on the stones. From the beginning, it was made clear that no one could expect to become a child of God simply by keeping the law. In addition to the law, there had to be an altar.

. . . not . . . through the law, but through the righteousness of faith. (4:13)

"The righteousness of faith" is an important phrase. It doesn't mean that faith makes you righteous. This would be contrary to the entire teaching of Paul, indeed the entire teaching of the Bible. Rather, righteousness comes as you are linked—as we saw in the illustration of the three rings—to the promises of God that have been fulfilled through Jesus Christ. By faith, you are entered into this righteousness. It is not an infused righteousness. Rather, it is always a declared thing. It is a legal matter between God and us. Legally, we stand guilty before God. But on the basis of the finished work of Jesus Christ, God declares us to be justified. This, and only this, is the "righteousness of faith."

A little girl was asked, "Do you know what justification means?" And she answered, "Yes, when I accept Christ as my Savior, it's just as though I had never sinned." Justification; just as though I had never sinned. This is a beautiful truth. We are sinners. We deserve the justice of God. But when I believe God and believe on Christ as my Savior, on the basis of His finished work, it is just as though I had never sinned. My guilt is completely covered, it is quite finished. My guilt is gone.

We must be so careful never to let faith become a work. Faith has no value in and of itself. Faith is the act whereby you raise your empty hands, believe God's promise, and accept the finished work of Jesus Christ on your behalf, whereupon God declares you justified. In legal terms, your sin has ended.

This, as we have seen, is why we can be forgiven of all our sins and yet still live in a moral universe, a universe where moral absolutes are still intact. This is the answer to the problem of a moral universe that no other religion can offer. When He forgives us, God doesn't give up His justice. His perfectly holy character is still the moral absolute that holds our world together. But when we believe God, our guilt is placed upon Jesus Christ. His death covers it. While remaining "just," He becomes our "justifier" (3:26). And He declares that the legal problem of our sin is resolved for all eternity.

As we will learn in the final chapter of this study, the Bible makes it very plain that Christians will never stand in judgment before God concerning the legal aspects of their sin, for that has been dealt with at the cross. Believers will go through a judgment, but it will not involve the possibility of being declared lost. When you accept Christ as your Savior you are declared justified on the basis of the finished work of Jesus Christ. The legal aspects of your guilt are finished forever. This should be the Christian's joy. We should be happy people in the presence of a just and moral God, in a moral universe, knowing that the legal aspect, the guilt of our sin, is all in the past—and will remain in the past forever.

For if they which are of the law be heirs, faith is made void, and the promise made of none effect. (4:14)

Paul is simply stating in another way what he said in verse 4: "Now to him that worketh is the reward not reckoned of grace, but of debt." If I can earn something toward my eternal salvation, God owes me something. But this is not the case. I can earn nothing toward salvation and therefore God owes me nothing.

Because the law worketh wrath: for where no law is, there is no transgression. (4:15)

Paul is not saying that you wouldn't be saved if you kept the law perfectly. Adam did not need a Savior if he had stayed obedient. He did not need a Savior just because he had a body, because he was finite, because he was a sexual person. The need for a Savior arose only after he disobeyed.

If you kept the law perfectly, you *would* be saved! But nobody does keep the law perfectly. Therefore, "the law worketh wrath." While the law brings about wrath, however, it also helps us understand that we need the Savior. It is a schoolmaster to bring us to Christ. You will never lead anyone to the Savior until that person knows that he or she is a sinner. This is the mistake of much evangelistic work—the mistake of thinking that people will accept Christ as their Savior without knowing their need of the Savior. This just won't happen. Somehow or other, on some level, the law must be preached. People must understand that, because they don't keep the law, they need the Savior. Then they are ready to hear the gospel. That's why Paul has tried to show, over and over in these chapters, that no one keeps all the law, whether that be the law of conscience or the Law of Moses.

Because the law worketh wrath: for where no law is, there is no transgression. (4:15)

Does this mean that, before the Law of Moses was given, no one was lost? That is certainly what it might seem to say. Paul actually answers this question in the next chapter: "For until the law, sin was in the world: but sin is not imputed when there is no law. Nevertheless death reigned from Adam to Moses, even over them that had not sinned after the similitude of Adam's transgression, who is the figure of him that was to come" (5:13-14). We could paraphrase Paul in this way: "Yes, there is no judgment until there is the law; nevertheless, those between Adam and Moses had the seal of death upon them. Why? Because they were sinning against another law. They did not have the revelation of the Law of Moses, but they did have a law."

Of course, we know from chapter 2 what that other law was. The people who lived before the giving of the law, just like people without the Bible throughout history, will be judged against what they do know about right and wrong. And as Paul declared in 2:1, none of these people without the Bible perfectly keeps their own moral code of conduct. It is true that, "Where no law is, there is no transgression." It is also true that no one was judged on the specific basis of the Law of Moses before that law was given. But the overriding reality is that, from the time of Adam on, all humans have sinned against one law or another.

This is a very important part of the Christian position, because it would be unjust to judge people on the basis of a law they don't have.

In fact, however, people are going to be judged upon the basis of the law they do have. Never mind whether they have the Law of Moses or not. People without the Bible are going to be judged on the basis of the law they do have. "Because that which may be known of God is manifest in them; for God hath shown it unto them" (1:19). "Which show the work of the law written in their hearts, their conscience also bearing witness, and their thoughts the mean while accusing or else excusing one another" (2:15). When Adam fell, and all mankind with him, he did not fall from being a free, moral creature, able to choose between right and wrong. Even as a fallen creature, man is still man, and is therefore morally responsible before God.

Many people feel that all "sincere" people will be saved, whatever they may believe concerning God. But the Bible just doesn't say this. A nonbeliever could be saved by works if he or she perfectly followed the law or perfectly followed his or her moral beliefs. But the Bible says (3:10-12), and personal experience confirms, that no one does this.

Therefore it is of faith, that it might be by grace; to the end the promise might be sure to all the seed; not to that only which is of the law, but to that also which is of the faith of Abraham; who is the father of us all. (4:16)

Abraham is the father of us all. He is the father of the circumcised who believe; the father of the uncircumcised who believe; the father of those who lived on the other side of the cross who believed; the father of those who live on this side of the cross who believe. Abraham is the father of us all.

(As it is written, I have made thee a father of many nations,) before him whom he believed, even God, who quickeneth the dead, and calleth those things which be not as though they were. (4:17)

When we read in the first chapter that "The just shall live by faith" (1:17), I said that the words *life* and *death* are going to become key words as we go on. From here through the end of chapter 8, the words *life* and *death* will be pitted one against the other constantly. Paul will finish his discussion of justification at the end of chapter 4, then will move on to sanctification (5:1—8:17), and from there on to glorification (8:18-39), and this theme of death and life will be like two nails upon which all these themes are woven.

God can and does quicken the dead. The promise that Abraham believed, resulting in his being declared righteous, was that God would bring back to life Sarah's ability to have children. He believed this despite how hopeless it seemed from a human point of view.

Who against hope believed in hope, that he might become the father of many nations, according to that which was spoken, So shall thy seed be. (4:18)

"Against hope" could better be translated "beyond all possible hope." This is a marvelous expression. Faith in God is not a blind step into the dark. It always involves believing a specific promise of God. In Abraham's case, this meant believing a promise that defied every logical human basis for hope. Humanly speaking, it was ridiculous for Abraham to think that he and Sarah could have a child when she was more than ninety years old. Yet he believed, beyond all possible hope, because he believed in God's power to keep His promise. God had created the world from nothing, so he could certainly create a child from older parents!

As if to emphasize that Abraham's faith was not just "faith in faith," Paul spells out the specific promise of God that Abraham believed: "So shall they seed be."

And being not weak in faith, he considered not his own body now dead, when he was about an hundred years old, neither yet the deadness of Sarah's womb. (4:19)

Actually, in the best Greek text, there is no negative after "considered." Rather, it would read, "And being not weak in faith, he considered his own body now dead . . ." Abraham considered, or took into account, the fact that his own ability to father a child was dead. And he took into account that, as far as childbearing was concerned, Sarah's body was also dead. In China, a woman who is past childbearing age is sometimes referred to as a "coffin." This is certainly not a very gentle expression, but for a husband and wife in that situation it declares a stark truth. Sarah may have been very much alive in other ways, but as far as reproduction was concerned, she might as well have been dead.

Nonetheless, taking all of this into account, Abraham believed.

What did Abraham believe? He believed that God could "quicken the dead" (4:17). He didn't believe this as a theory or a theological abstraction; he actually believed. Even after taking into account the deadness of his and Sarah's childbearing potential, Abraham believed that God could fulfill His promise to give them a son. As Paul continues describing Abraham's very specific faith in God's very specific promise, the force is just like a hammer.

He staggered not at the promise of God through unbelief; but was strong in faith, giving glory to God; and being fully persuaded that, what he had promised, he was able also to perform. (4:20-21)

Please don't pass by these continued emphases on belief versus unbelief. Belief, for the Christian, is never a blind step of faith. Belief, for the Christian, is always believing God, believing He exists and believing His promises. So here we find that Abraham "staggered not at the promise of God." Now, God's specific promise to give Abraham a son was certainly something to stagger about. Far from staggering, however, Abraham "was strong in faith." We could also translate this, "was made strong by faith." His faith laid hold of God. His faith believed. This was his strength. "Giving glory to God; and being fully persuaded that, what he had promised, he was able also to perform."

This faith of Abraham is surely the death of Kierkegaard's shallow and contorted concept of faith. Abraham's faith was a titanic step, but it didn't involve stepping out in 50,000 fathoms of anything. It was stepping out onto the rock-solid promise of God. He believed God, and he believed God could do a specific thing. What he believed specifically was that God could quicken the dead, to bring forth life out of that which was a coffin, that which was truly dead. This is what Abraham believed.

The writer of Hebrews declares that "Without faith it is impossible to please him: for he that cometh to God must believe that he is, and that he is a rewarder of them that diligently seek him" (Heb. 11:6).

He goes on to describe various examples of faith, including Abraham's and Sarah's faith regarding their having a child. Faith in God must always be a personal thing. There is no other way to come to God. And that is exactly what Abraham did. Abraham believed that God existed. He believed that God was personal, a real person. And he believed that God would keep the very personal promise He had made to Abraham.

And therefore it was imputed to him for righteousness. (4:22)

God imputed righteousness to Abraham because Abraham believed God's promises. Paul is simply repeating the wonderful truth he stated in 4:3 as he quoted Genesis 15:6: Abraham's faith was "counted" or "imputed" to him as righteousness. Because of his faith alone, not because of any good works he had done, Abraham was declared by God to be righteous.

Paul now begins drawing things together again, showing how these truths about salvation through faith apply not just to Abraham, but to all people—Jew and Gentile alike—for all time.

Now it was not written for his sake alone, that it was imputed to him; but for us also, to whom it shall be imputed, if we believe on him that raised up Jesus our Lord from the dead; who was delivered for our offenses, and was raised again for our justification. (4:23-25)

God imputed righteousness to Abraham because Abraham believed God's promises. And He will impute this righteousness to us as well, if we believe His promises. Abraham was dead and Sarah was dead, as far as reproduction is concerned. God made a promise. Abraham believed that God could quicken the dead—and the child was born. There was life from death. Likewise, Jesus was dead, but we are called to believe that God did in fact raise Him from the dead.

As we noted earlier, in most evangelistic preaching the emphasis, rightly, is on "accepting Christ as our Savior." In the context of his discussion of Abraham, however, Paul seems to emphasize the role of God the Father in salvation. He says that we must believe on "him who raised Jesus from the dead." In so doing, we're believing the same God that Abraham believed.

Several other passages in the New Testament similarly underscore the role of God the Father in salvation. Elsewhere in Romans, we read: "Therefore we are buried with him by baptism into death, that as Christ was raised up from the dead by the glory of the Father . . ." (6.4). And again: "But if the Spirit of him that raised up Jesus from the dead dwell in you . . ." (8:11). And yet again: "If thou shalt confess with thy mouth the Lord Jesus, and shalt believe in thine heart that God raised him from the dead, thou shalt be saved" (10:9). Peter likewise urges his readers to "believe in God, who raised him up from the dead" (1 Pet. 1:21). Jesus Himself stressed the role of God the Father in salvation, and the importance of believing on Him: "Verily, verily, I say unto you, He that heareth my word, and believeth on him that sent me, hath everlasting life" (John 5:24). Throughout the New Testament, then, you find this emphasis on "believing on him that raised Jesus," or "believing on him that sent me."

Abraham believed God, and the child was born. We are now called on to believe the same God. And what has He done for us? He has raised Jesus from the dead. We are in a sense presented with the same call to faith that came to Abraham. The calls come at two different times in history, but the two are in essence the same call. Who is a Christian? At the rock-bottom level a Christian is simply a person who believes God. We're back in Hebrews again. We must believe that God "is, and that he is a rewarder of those who diligently seek him."

I am making such a strong point of the historical continuity of our faith with the faith of Abraham because of what I see as a lack of a sense of history in our time. I've already discussed the uselessness of presenting the gospel without sufficiently explaining the fact that people are lost. But I also fear that some people "accept Christ as their Savior" while not even believing in the historical reality of the biblical account. One young man who came to L'Abri was very disturbed because some friends at the Christian university he had attended in the United States had encouraged him to confirm his faith on the basis of what has come to be known as Pascal's wager. The philosopher Blaise Pascal suggested that belief in God was a good bet, because if it isn't true, you haven't lost anything, and if it is true, you go to heaven. But if this is all you believe, you don't go to heaven. Christian faith is not a wager or a magic formula or saying the right words. It isn't like wearing a rabbit's foot around your neck. Christian faith is believing the God who really exists.

Suppose that Abraham had had some serious mental reservations and had said, "Oh well, I don't know if God will fulfill His promise or not, but just as an escape, I'll say, 'Yes, I believe.' After all, what's there to lose?" If Abraham had said that, he and Sarah would never have had a child. Abraham had to truly believe the reality of the fact that God existed and that He would keep His promise. Then, there came forth life from the dead.

It must be the same for us. What are we called upon to do? We're called upon to "believe on him that raised Jesus our Lord from the dead" (4:24). The moment that we do believe on Him who raised Jesus from the dead, we are believing exactly what Abraham believed when he believed that God could bring forth life from death. And when we believe Him and believe on Christ as our Savior, we who are dead become alive. "For therein is the righteousness of God revealed from faith to faith as it is written "The just shall live by faith" (1:17)!

This concept of living by faith is not just an idea, it isn't just a word, it's a reality. Before we believe God, we are truly dead. But when we believe God, and believe what He has done and therefore take Christ as our Savior, we who were dead are made alive. We were dead, just as dead as Sarah's womb. As far as the possibility of reproduction was concerned, Sarah was completely dead. As far as the possibility of eternal life is concerned, we were completely dead, under the wrath of God, separated from God, without purpose. Sarah's dead womb couldn't produce anything, and the unsaved individual can't really produce anything with significance. It's just a turning of wheels that will pass away with the passing of time. But Abraham believed God, and out from that dead womb there came the child. Isaac's birth was a real historical event. It wasn't just a nice story. It occurred in space, in time, in the hard stuff of history—in a specific geographic place at a specific hour of a specific day. Abraham was justified because he believed the God who is there, and he believed the promises of the God who is there.

Jesus has come. Jesus has died. Jesus has risen. Throughout Scripture, God promised that this would happen. Will we believe

God? Will we believe that He raised Jesus from the dead? It is an event that, like Isaac's birth, was made of the hard stuff of real history. As soon as we believe this, we, who like Abraham and Sarah have been dead, will be made alive. Just as Sarah and Abraham could now produce a child, we now can begin to produce that which has meaning in life.

Salvation is not just making a wager with our eternal destiny, or repeating a magic phrase. Salvation begins with the fact that God exists, and that man has rebelled against Him. Then there comes a point when each of us must decide: Will we believe God, or will we continue to rebel against Him?

Paul has shown us exactly what justification by faith means for us today (3:21-30). Then he has shown that people in Old Testament times were saved in exactly the same way as we are saved today (3:31—4:22). Then he has turned it around and said, "This is how Abraham was justified, and we can be justified in exactly the same way" (4:23-25). We, like Abraham, can be justified by believing that God is there, and believing that He has raised Christ from the dead, just as He promised to do.

If we believe God, if we are no longer dead but are bringing forth life, we're ready to go on into chapter 5, where Paul talks about how to begin living the Christian life. As Sarah's womb brought forth a child, so, when we believe the same God and His promises and therefore pass from death to life, we can begin to bring forth (on the basis of the finished work of Jesus Christ) that which is living instead of that which is dead. Chapter 5 will tell us what this means.

PART TWO

SANCTIFICATION

(5:1—8:17)

7

THE RESULT OF JUSTIFICATION: PEACE WITH GOD

(5:1-11)

Having discussed justification (1:18—4:25), Paul now turns his attention to sanctification (5:1—8:17). In 5:1-11, he will talk about the peace we have with God as a result of justification. In 5:12-21, in a sort of parenthetical section, he will explain the origin of sin. Then, for the remainder of this section (6:1—8:17), he will deal with the sad reality that, even after being eternally justified and forgiven by God, we continue to see all too much sin in our lives.

As we begin this new section, we must remember again that Paul is not writing some sort of theological textbook, but is writing to ordinary men and women. Romans probably represents the customary content of the messages Paul gave whenever he arrived in a new city on his missionary journeys. Since he had never been to Rome, he was probably presenting to them, by way of this letter, the same material with which he began his ministry in each new location. We can just imagine Paul preaching in some new location. As he goes through the things we have read in Romans 1—4, by the end of chapter 4 he has seen several people respond and therefore pass from death to life. So, while in the first four chapters Paul has written as though his readers were still lost, beginning with chapter 5 he is writing as though they are already Christians.

If we had only the first four chapters of Romans, we would have enough information to be saved. All the big intellectual questions of life are answered in these four chapters; whether you're a simple person or a complex person, a person of the first-century Greek world or a citizen of the twentieth century, there's more than enough in these first four chapters to bring you from death to life. So, from now on, Paul will talk to us as though we have now accepted Christ as our Savior.

As we have noted, of course, that doesn't mean there is any discontinuity between chapters 1—4 and chapters 5—8. We were dead (1—4) and now we're alive (5—8). Having been dead and now being alive, just as Sarah was able to bring forth a child, we can begin to bring forth that which is life and not death. So, Paul begins this next section:

Therefore being justified by faith, we have peace with God through our Lord Jesus Christ. (5:1)

Verb tenses will be very important in our study of this section. Let's start right off by noting the verb tenses in this opening statement: "Therefore being justified by faith [in the past], we have [in the present] peace with God through our Lord Jesus Christ." The Greek makes this past tense very plain. Based upon Christ's finished work on the cross about 2,000 years ago, and based upon the past specific moment in space and time when we individually accepted Christ as our Savior—whether five minutes of five years ago—based upon what transpired in these two moments in the past, we find ourselves in a certain situation in the present.

This question of historical sequence is a very important distinction and must be kept in mind. There is a constant danger in our culture of thinking of Christianity as merely a sort of a progression, without understanding that there must be a moment of justification, a moment of birth. Just as in a marriage there must have been a moment somewhere in the past at which we came into a contractual marriage relationship with the other person, so also there must have been a moment in the past when by grace we accepted Christ as our Savior and were therefore declared justified by God.

Having accepted Christ as our Savior, "we have peace with God." The first and most important aspect of this peace with God is not the peace in our own hearts but the fact that God is at peace with us. Though we were separated from God by the guilt of our sin, on the basis of Christ's finished work God has declared us justified. On the basis of Christ's finished work, He is at peace with us.

Because God is at peace with us, because He has declared us justified, because we have returned to the purpose of our creation, we can in the present have a relationship with God and can have true peace in our own hearts. People struggle like mad to have peace in their hearts. They try all kinds of psychological methods to find some point of integration. But all such efforts lead only to disappointment unless it involves the relationship and the purpose for which we were created. The only way we can return to that purpose and to that relationship is by having our guilt before God removed on the basis of Christ's finished work. Once we have thus had our guilt removed, there can be a peace in our hearts that is not false, a peace that, as we shall see in verse 5, will never disappoint us.

Therefore being justified by faith, we have peace with God through our Lord Jesus Christ: by whom also we have access by faith into this grace wherein we stand, and rejoice in hope of the glory of God. (5:1-2)

Our peace with God gives us "access" to certain things in this present life. It is not just a future hope. There is a future aspect of our salvation, and Paul will talk about this more in 8:18-39. But right now he is talking about a peace with God that, for the Christian, is a present reality. This is not just to be an ideal, it is to be something that we experience right now. We are to "rejoice in hope of the glory of God." This is to be a present experience, because it is a reality. We have returned to the purpose of our creation. This peace can be a present experience because it is true in the framework of the universe as it is. We stand justified in the very presence of the infinite God Himself.

God is at peace with us, therefore we should have peace in all aspects of our lives.

Our English translation says we can "rejoice" in hope of the "glory" of God. A more literal translation would be that we can "glory in hope of the glory of God." We will see the same thought repeated in verses 3 and 11. We "rejoice [glory] in hope of the glory . . ." (verse 2). We "glory in tribulations" (verse 3, where the KJV actually uses the word *glory*). And we "joy [glory] in God" (verse 11). This glory, this joy, this rejoicing, is what we who have found salvation should have in the present moment, on the basis of the past work of the Lord Jesus and the past moment when individually we passed from death to life by accepting Him as Savior.

Do those of us who have made a profession of faith in Christ experience the reality of this peace with God? God promises this peace, and God never made an empty promise. He never meant for our Christian life to be just an ideal, with no reality to it. He meant for each of us who has confessed faith in Him to experience this "glory in hope of the glory of God." God has given us commands that, in our own human power, we cannot fulfill. He commands us to "be perfect" (Matt. 5:48), and this is our standard, even though in this life we can never fulfill it. God can command no less than perfection, for He is perfect (Matt. 5:48). Yet in pursuing this standard of perfection, we are comforted to know that God will never give us a promise that He cannot fulfill, and He has promised us that we can be at peace with Him.

Christians throughout history have sought this peace in various ways. In earlier church history some sought it in monasticism or even in ascetic pursuits such as pillar-sitting. Pillar-sitting isn't much in vogue today, but we see a similar mentality in some things Christians do. When they go to some sort of retreat or Bible conference, even to a place like L'Abri, thinking that here they can find a peace they couldn't find in their day-to-day Christian life, they escape to their own form of pillar-sitting or mountaintop monasticism. Surely the peace with God that Paul describes is something more than just a weekend retreat experience. As we go on in this chapter, we'll see that it is very practical in its description of what our Christian life should be. We all know Christians who, very soon after making a profession of faith, seemingly have no joy in their life and have ceased to be a vital part of church life. Perhaps we have been in that situation ourselves. How can the Christian life be a reality, not just a theoretical thing, for us and for our fellow Christians?

The key to answering this question about sanctification is given in these first two verses of chapter 5: "Therefore being justified by faith [in the past], we have peace with God [in the present] through our Lord Jesus Christ: by whom also we [in the present] have access by faith into this grace wherein we stand." We are justified by faith. That's something that has already happened, in the past. But now, in the present, by this same faith, we have access to God's grace. Once you see that, you have the key to the Christian life.

Salvation, as we have seen, is not only justification. Salvation *includes* justification, when we accept Jesus as our Savior and therefore become free of our guilt before God. But salvation also includes certain ongoing realities in our present life. Salvation actually takes place in three tenses. In the past tense, it was salvation from the *guilt* of our sin, which happened when we accepted Jesus as our Savior. In the present tense, it is salvation from the *power* of sin, which is what the word "sanctification" basically means. The power of sin in its outward appearance and inward ideas is to be broken. Then, in the future tense, in our glorified state in heaven, it will be salvation from the very *presence* of sin.

How were we justified in the past tense? We were justified by faith. How do we go on now, in the present tense, and enjoy "access" to the wonderful realities that the Bible promises in the present life? We do this "by faith" as well. We "have access by faith into this grace wherein we stand" (verse 2). We know that our justification rested completely upon the finished work of the Lord Jesus, and not in any way upon our own abilities or goodness. What about our sanctification? It, like our justification, rests completely upon Christ's work, not on ours.

The basis of our sanctification is a major theme in Paul's letter to the Galatians. He asks, "Having begun in the Spirit, are ye now by faith and not by works going on by works?" (Gal. 3:3). The answer, of course, is a resounding no. Both our beginning as Christians and our perfection as Christians is by *faith*, not by our own human efforts. When Paul said, in his theme verses (Rom. 1:16-17), that the gospel is "the power of God unto salvation," he was including salvation in all three of its aspects. For salvation is a running stream, not static. The gospel is the power of God for our salvation from our guilt in justification. But it is also the salvation in our present battles for our sanctification and for our salvation in the redemption of our bodies in glorification. There is a tendency for Christians to talk a great deal about the need to develop Christian character, as though, having accepted Christ as our Savior, we can now begin operating on the basis of our own qualities of character. But if we are expecting to become strong enough on our own to win the battle, we're never going to win the battle. It's too much for us.

We need to read our theme passage again, in its entirety: "For I am not ashamed of the gospel of Christ: for it is the power of God unto salvation to every one that believeth; to the Jew first, and also to the Greek. For therein is the righteousness of God revealed from faith to faith: as it is written, The just shall *live* by faith" (1:16-17). We are justified by faith, and then, "the just shall live by faith"! Since salvation includes sanctification, we could actually read verse 16 as: "For I am not ashamed of the gospel of Christ: for it is the power of God unto sanctification to everyone that believes." Whether we are talking about the past, present, or future aspect of salvation, the basis is always the finished work of Christ, and the instrument whereby we lay hold of Christ's finished work is always faith.

It was a tremendous blessing to my own heart when I began to understand this. You don't accept Christ as your Savior and then just wait around to go to heaven. There is a present aspect to salvation. Many people have asked me, "But how do I find that reality? I believe all this, but how do I get ahold of it?" And I always emphasize that, somehow or another, we must "jump the fence" from merely giving our mental assent to this idea of sanctification and get hold of it as a reality that we practice day by day. And how do we do this? How do we get hold of the reality of sanctification in our Christian life? We start by remembering how we became Christians in the first place.

Perhaps as we do this it would be helpful to look at justification and sanctification as taking place in three similar steps. There are two necessary steps for a person to accept Christ as Savior, and there's a third step that is not necessary but that from my own experience is very helpful. The first necessary step in finding salvation is to know and admit that you are a sinner. Nobody accepts Christ as their Savior until he or she knows he or she is a sinner. The second step is, by faith, to actually accept Christ as your Savior by coming under His blood. At that point, your salvation is a finished matter. There are only these two necessary steps.

But my experience is that there's a third step, one that is not necessary but that is most helpful. The third step, which I have encouraged in my work with the people who come to L'Abri, is to say thank you to God for your salvation. For so many of these new Christians, that's when the emotion comes. That's when they experience the reality of it. Of course, someone can be saved without saying thank you, but for many people in our ministry, that's when the reality has hit home. That's when they have realized that it's really done, that they have really laid hold of the finished work of Christ. They have said thank you to God for something that's total and accomplished. Then comes the peace (5:1).

The same thing applies to sanctification. When you come up against sin in your life, or when you are facing temptation, there are still the two steps that are necessary and the third step that is not necessary but is most helpful. First, you must acknowledge the sin to be sin, just as in justification you had to acknowledge yourself to be a sinner. You will not make real progress in your Christian life unless, whenever you face temptation or whenever you have already given in to temptation, you are quite frank before God and call the sin sin. As long as you just go along and call it all kinds of fancy names and excuse it away, you will never make any progress toward sanctification.

The next step in sanctification, as in justification, is by faith to lay hold of the finished work of Jesus Christ. This is true whether you are facing temptation or after you have already given in to it. First, you admit that you are greatly tempted or that you have already sinned. Then you bring this individual sin under the blood of Christ. "Bringing the sin under Christ's blood" means that, as soon as you admit your sin, you can have the assurance that your sin is covered by Christ's blood, just as the little boy in our illustration was completely covered by his father's overcoat. When God looks at us, He sees only the overcoat; He sees only Christ's righteousness, only the blood Christ has shed on our behalf. When we bring our sins under the blood of Christ, we are simply claiming the reality of the covering Christ has provided for our sin. And, as with our initial justification, once we have brought each individual sin under Christ's blood, the matter is finished.

But then, as with justification, there is that third step—a step that is not necessary but that I have found is very helpful. Having admitted your sin and having brought it under the blood of Christ, say thank you. And I think you'll find that, as soon as you say thank you, the certainty of your forgiveness will come and you will have peace of mind. We Christians tend to put the emphasis on overcoming before we sin, and this is fine. But when we do sin, let's be first willing to call it sin and then to bring it under the blood of Christ. Then let's say thank you to God on the basis of His promise that Christ's blood has covered our sin and that our fellowship with Him is now restored.

I served for many years as a pastor, knowing all the while that there was a vacuum in my preaching. I could tell people how to accept Christ as Savior, we could talk about being in heaven after Jesus came back, but I had very little to tell them about the *present* aspect of salvation. If we don't know something of the reality of salvation in our present life, it doesn't mean that we are lost, but it means that the whole thing takes on an air of unreality. After all, you can talk about being in heaven when you die, but you aren't in heaven yet. Somehow or other there must be a reality, not in the area of where we are not, but in the area of where we are. Without it our talking becomes just argumentation and unreal to us individually. We have got to get a grasp on how our faith relates to where we are right now.

I can recall times at Thanksgiving services when I would ask a person who had been a Christian for twenty or thirty years to tell the congregation what they were thankful for, and all they could think of was their initial experience of salvation twenty or thirty years ago.

That is, of course, something to thank the Lord for; but I would some-times wonder, don't we have anything else to add? Don't we have something to thank the Lord for yesterday, or today? If we don't, then we have surely fallen into mere orthodoxy, with no reality to it at all.

Many people seem to view the Christian life as though, well, you accept Christ as your Savior, and then you just kind of pull yourself together. "Where's your Christian character?" they say. "Just be strong." New Christians may even become involved in witnessing or other kinds of ministry while their own personal lives just kind of die down to a low simmer.

Paul's answer to this problem of a stagnant Christian life is that, just as faith was the instrument of our receiving justification, so also faith is to be the instrument of our present Christian living. Something he says at the very end of Romans can help us see this: "Now the God of hope fill you with all joy and peace in believing, that ye may abound in hope, through the power of the Holy Ghost" (15:13). Without the believing, without the faith, you are not going to abound in hope through the power of the Spirit. There is nothing mechanical about this, but a personal choice to believe. And the Person of the Holy Spirit then will give believers that hope, joy, and peace.

The biblical view is a complete system. Contrary to the twentieth-century view of an impersonal world, the Bible gives us a personal world. There is nothing mechanical about the Christian walk, no way to quantify spiritual reality. It is always a person to person relationship in which we believe God.

Something the apostle John says in his first letter is also helpful. I'll begin with a verse that I went for years without preaching on: "For this is the love of God, that we keep his commandments: and his commandments are not grievous" (1 John 5:3). John says God's com-mandments "are not grievous," but for many years I found them griev-ous, and the more grievous I found them, the less I preached on this verse. My difficulty in dealing with this verse was that I was separat-ing it from the next verse: "For whatsoever is born of God overcometh the world: and this is the victory that overcometh the world, our faith" (1 John 5:4).

This is the same thing that Paul is saying in Romans 5:1-2, and we'll see it is really what he is saying from 5:1 all the way through 8:17. The key to not finding God's commandments "grievous" is in the victory we experience through our faith. The key is in believing God. The key is in understanding that "the just shall live by faith." The key is in not trying to live in our own strength, but finding our strength through laying hold of God, through believing God on the basis of the shed blood of the Lord Jesus.

In my own life, there are some sins that seem to crop up again and again. In despair I'll say, "I've done it again!" So what do I do then? I acknowledge the sin. I lay hold of the work of Jesus Christ. I bring that individual sin under the covering of His blood. If, after doing so, my conscience continues to bother me, it is because I am minimizing the validity and the power of Christ's blood.

Sometimes, in these situations, I have pictured my conscience as a big black dog, jumping up on me with its muddy paws. If I have brought the individual sin under Christ's blood, and the big black dog of my conscience still jumps up on me with its muddy paws, I must in faith say, "Get down!" I must remind myself of the infinite value of Christ's blood to cleanse me of all sin. "This is the victory that overcometh the world, even our faith in relation to temptation before our sin after we fall." Or as Paul is telling us in 5:1-2, justification comes by faith, and the resulting peace with God also comes by faith.

We find another helpful thought on this matter in Paul's letter to the Ephesians: "Above all, taking the shield of faith, wherewith ye shall be able to quench all the fiery darts of the wicked" (6:16). The Greek is actually "of the wicked one," referring to Satan. What can shield us from Satan's "fiery darts"? The shield of faith. And what is this faith? It is the same faith that was involved in our justification. It is believing God on the basis of the shed blood of the Lord Jesus. How dare we who have been so marked with sin stand and say, "Now I am a child of God"? We can dare to say this, not through any merit of our own, but because of the saving value of Christ's blood. As we lay hold of this truth, it is like a giant shield. The first man of ancient times who had a lightweight shield that couldn't be punched through by arrows had a tremendous advantage in warfare. Likewise, we who are trusting not in ourselves but in Christ have a tremendous advantage in our battle against sin and temptation with this shield of faith.

Look also at Colossians 2:6-7: "As ye have therefore received Christ Jesus the Lord, so walk ye in him: rooted and built up in him, and stablished in (by) the faith." How are we going to be rooted and built up in Christ? How are we going to be established in Christ? We do this "in the faith," or "by faith."

Paul tells Timothy that his knowledge of "the holy scriptures" can make him "wise [in the present] unto salvation through faith which is in Christ Jesus" (2 Tim. 3:15). If we look to ourselves for sanctification, there can be nothing but sorrow. But we don't have to look to ourselves. Rather, we look to Scripture and to the Christ revealed therein.

Again, in Hebrews: "For unto us was the gospel preached, as well as unto them: but the word preached did not profit them, not being mixed with faith in them that heard it" (Heb. 4:2). We looked at this verse once before in relation to justification, but it applies to sanctification as well. God has promised such things as peace and joy to those who have believed Him, but unless we are united to these promises on the basis of Christ's finished work through faith, they're not real to us. Faith links us to the promises of God for the present life, just as it did for our initial salvation.

Coming back to Romans 5:1: Having been justified, in the past, we are now, in the present, able to have peace in our hearts. How? By faith. We need to help each other know the reality of this present aspect of salvation. Our peace with God is not just some introspective thing. It is a peace based upon God's promise that Christ's atoning death is enough to meet all our present failures. When I became a Christian, I realized that Christ's blood was enough to cover my past sin. By the same token, I can also know that it is enough to cover the sins I have committed since I awoke this morning. From time to time I do something so bad that I realize that, if it depended on me, I would surely be lost again. When those times come, I must realize that I can bring those things under the shed blood of the Lord Jesus, and that His blood is enough to cleanse me. Then I can simply say thank you. This is the source of peace in the Christian's heart. It isn't just an emotional experience. It doesn't require sitting on a pillar or going to a Bible retreat every other weekend. It's the objective reality of the finished work of the Lord Jesus Christ, applied to our present necessity in day by day, moment by moment cleansing.

Someone might ask, "How often can we do this? How often can we claim forgiveness for these endless daily sins?" We can do so as often as we need to. When Peter asked Christ, "How often shall I forgive my brother?" Christ said, "Not seven times, but seventy times seven" (Matt. 18:22). If we humans are supposed to forgive each other that often, surely God's forgiveness of us is infinitely greater. How often should we ask His forgiveness? As often as we need to!

Someone might object: Doesn't this do discredit to the work of the Lord Jesus, to fall into temptation and an hour later to fall into the same temptation—and both times to "bring it under the blood of Jesus?" Doesn't this trivialize Christ's work? Quite the contrary, there is really only one thing that can minimize Christ's saving work, and that is our failing to lay hold of it.

I'm convinced from watching other Christians and reading about Christians through the centuries, and through personal experience, that this is when we begin to make our forward steps as Christians: When I know through experience that I can lay hold of Christ's blood by faith to cover my sins this morning, and then to cover my sins this afternoon, even if they're the same sins—when I know this, the preciousness of Christ's blood becomes a tremendous reality. I begin to live in the light of His presence and in the light of His work—not just in the past or in the future, but in the present. I begin to live in the reality of the supernatural world.

Some would teach that once a person is truly a Christian he is perfect in this life, but the Bible doesn't teach this. A true Christian is not someone who is in any sense approaching moral perfection; rather, a true Christian is that person who knows, by experience, the ever-present wonder of being able to lay hold of the blood of Jesus and then being able to say thank you, knowing that his or her fellowship with God is completely restored.

Look at Hebrews 13:21 where the writer tells us that we are made perfect through Jesus Christ, not in our own strength. Our conscious side is to act through faith in the victory of Jesus Christ. Peter also echoes Paul's teaching concerning the place of faith in the believer's life. He speaks of those "who are kept by the power of God through faith unto salvation ready to be revealed in the last time" (1 Pet. 1:5). Peter seems to be focusing on the future aspect of salvation, but he has in view its present aspect as well, as he agrees with Paul that it is God's power that "keeps" us, and that we appropriate that power "through faith."

Look also at the very striking language of John in Revelation 12: "And I heard a loud voice saying in heaven, Now is come salvation, and strength, and the kingdom of our God, and the power of his Christ: for the accuser of our brethren [Satan] is cast down, which accused them before our God day and night. And they overcame him by the blood of the Lamb" (Rev. 12:10-11a). This isn't just a pretty story, and it wasn't just put in the Bible to fill space. It is our present reality as Christians. Whenever the devil accuses us, we overcome him by the blood of the Lamb. There's only one way to keep from giving in to temptation, and that is by the blood of the Lamb. Or as we heard John say elsewhere, "This is the victory that overcometh the world, even our faith" (1 John 5:4).

We are born again through faith, but our faith shouldn't stop there. In a sense, every moment of our lives is to be lived at the point of our spiritual birth. When we were born again, God removed our guilt once and for all on the basis of the finished work of the Lord Jesus, when by faith we believed God. Faith does not have value; it is the instrument. The value lies only in the finished work of Jesus. As we go on in the Christian life, in a sense we are to keep on experiencing that initial moment of forgiveness. We believed God in the moment of salvation; let's keep right on believing Him. We trusted in the finished work of the Lord Jesus in that moment; let's keep right on trusting in it. This is not mechanical in any way. God deals with us as moral, rational creatures, who must believe and trust God.

Therefore being justified [in the past] by faith, we have [in the present] peace with God through our Lord Jesus Christ: by whom also

we have access by faith into this grace wherein we [in the present] stand, and rejoice in hope of the glory of God. (5:1-2)

Have we looked at these two verses long enough? Is it time to move on? In a way, as Christians, we never move beyond these two verses. From now until Jesus comes back again or we die, this is where we live. In a broader sense, this is true of all of Romans 5:1—8:17. From the time we accept Christ as our Savior until we die or until Christ comes back, we live in this part of Romans.

Some Christians teach what they call the "second blessing," or the "baptism of the Holy Spirit," which they say takes place subsequent to the time when you accept Jesus as your Savior. They teach correctly that you are justified when you accept Christ as your Savior; but they say that, at some subsequent time, you can experience a second work of grace. The Bible doesn't teach any such thing. The Bible says that when you have accepted Christ as your Savior, you are indwelt by the Holy Spirit. No "second work of grace" is needed. Sadly, however, many Christians go a lifetime and never learn the reality of the principle I am talking about. Many Christians who could tell you that salvation is only on the basis of Christ's finished work, nevertheless try to live their lives in their own strength. They don't seem to know that there is also a life on that same basis.

I have known many Christians who for twenty years or more have carried the weight of some terrible sin. They have worried about it every day of their life. They have become hamstrung in their Christian living by the weight of one sin. But this isn't the way it is supposed to be. When I have sinned, I am to be sorry for it. Then I bring it under the blood of Christ. And then I can say, "Thank You that it is forgiven." If that terrible sin involved injury to someone else, we should go back and try to pick up the pieces. We should make restitution as best we can. That should not, however, prevent us from claiming the full forgiveness available to us through Christ. Suppose you have committed some terrible sin, and it comes to your mind many times a day, and each time it does you thank God again for your forgiveness. Saying thank you many times is a lot better than bearing the burden. And saying thank you is the only correct response, if we truly believe that the finished work of Christ has justified us and can also sanctify us.

In this constant attitude of thanksgiving for our continual cleansing from sin, we can truly begin to experience the moment-by-moment reality of our faith. A key to knowing this reality is in becoming increasingly sensitive to our sin and then quickly bringing it under Christ's blood. For a certain period of my own life I did something that I found very helpful: I carried a piece of paper in my pocket, and as soon as I did something I knew to be wrong, I wrote it on this piece of paper. Then I thanked God for His forgiveness. Then, in a column on the right-hand side of the paper, I put a check mark, in the knowledge that that particular sin was gone. I don't know if that method would help you, but it was a great blessing to my own soul to see those check marks come on down the page in a day or a week, because this is where a Christian ought to be living.

As Christians, we should be living in sensitivity to the sins in our lives, but we shouldn't be carrying the burden of those sins for fifteen or twenty years after we have confessed them. Ideally, as Christians, we should have nothing on our conscience because, as soon as we sin, we bring that sin under Christ's blood. We shouldn't wait around for an hour, and we shouldn't wait around for a week. We shouldn't play with our sin, nor should we bear it in agony. As soon as we sin, we should quickly bring it under Christ's blood. And after we have done that, the sin is gone.

Someone might say, "Won't this just cause you to sin more?" I can say for myself that, through the years, this process of confession of sin and then thanksgiving for forgiveness has helped me to move slightly in the other direction. Only slightly, I'm sure, but at least slightly. What leads us to sin more is becoming hard and insensitive to the sin. Confessing each sin, and thanking God for our forgiveness, leads in the opposite direction—away from sin.

And not only so, but we glory in tribulations also: knowing that tribulation worketh patience. (5:3)

Paul has just talked about "rejoicing in hope of the glory of God." That may be easy enough to do when things are going well in our Christian lives or while we are enjoying fellowship with other Christians; but then we leave the circle of fellowship and hit a wall and bruise our nose. At that point we must ask ourselves, Was this all just a pep talk, or is it the truth? Is Christianity just a psychological thing, or is it real? If Christianity is dealing with truth, it has to deal with truth not just in the first glow of new faith, but in the everyday problems of my life after I've become a Christian. If the Christian faith is more than just a pep talk, it has to relate somehow to the particular rough-and-tumble of each Christian's life. Remember that "shield of faith" we read about in Ephesians? The question before us is, can each of us, individually, be confident that our shield of faith won't be punctured by the latest variety of arrow the enemy throws at us? Do these shields of faith work only when we're in a safe place with other Christians, or do they work out there in the rough-and-tumble of everyday life?

In 5:3, Paul says our faith does work out there in the rough-and-tumble: "Not only so, but we glory in tribulations also." "Tribulations" is that rough-and-tumble of life. It doesn't refer only to physical persecution. As it happens, however, the Christians Paul was writing to in Rome were in fact facing real physical persecutions. What was the secret of their strength? It was what we've been talking about. It was faith: what they believed about God, history, and their own situation before God. Can you imagine the Roman Christians as they were being led to the Coliseum, simply slapping each other on the shoulder and saying, "Courage, man! Courage!" That's pretty poor stuff when you're facing a lion.

Our faith is not just a theoretical thing. It is faith amid temptation. It is faith amid tribulation. It is faith amid the rough-and-tumble of life. What is the rough-and-tumble of your life? What challenges do you face? Whatever they are, whether they include eventual martyrdom or whether they involve something more "prosaic" such as bearing the scorn of nonbelieving friends and relatives, whatever your particular challenges are, your faith in Christ is sufficient to meet them. "And not only so, but we glory in tribulations also," because we walk by faith.

. . . knowing that tribulation worketh patience. (5:3b)

In one of his psalms, David writes, "I waited patiently for the

LORD" (Ps. 40:1). The Hebrew is stronger: "In waiting I waited for the LORD." There are two ways to wait. You can "wait waiting," or you can wait not waiting. You can wait with an attitude of waiting on and trusting in the Lord, or you can wait impatiently. I'll have to admit that a lot of my own waiting is of this second sort, either waiting impatiently or else waiting with a fatalistic attitude of, "Well, that's just the way life is." But Paul tells us that if we learn to trust the Lord, we can learn true patience; we can learn how to wait waiting.

. . . knowing that tribulation worketh patience; and patience, experience; and experience, hope: and hope maketh not ashamed. (5:3b-5a)

This "hope maketh not ashamed" takes us all the way back to our theme verses, where Paul says that he is "not ashamed of the gospel of Christ" (1:16). There, as we noted, Paul is saying that he is not ashamed of the gospel as a belief system that he then lays out. He is not ashamed of it amid the Greek intellectual world or amid Rome's imperial might. Here in 5:5, however, he is saying that he is not disappointed in the past nor in the present tribulation. He is proud of the gospel because of the great hope it has given him; it is a hope that has not disappointed him, and therefore a hope of which he need never be ashamed.

Just how did it come about that Paul's hope did not disappoint him or make him ashamed?

And hope maketh not ashamed; because the love of God is shed abroad in our hearts by the Holy Ghost which is given unto us. (5:5b)

Our present state of not being ashamed or disappointed is based upon two past objective facts: the fact that Christ died for us; the fact that the Holy Spirit has come to live within us. Christ has died. The price for our sins is paid. And now God Himself, in the form of the Holy Spirit, indwells us. These two things are not just subjective ideas, they are objectively true. They are as objectively true as when the moon comes out at night. The death of Jesus is objectively real, and our being indwelt by the Holy Spirit is objectively real. Both realities are the work of God, not the result or goal of our own efforts. Amid tribulation, this reality is there, but you've got to lay hold of it by faith.

And Paul wants to assure you that, just as you need never be ashamed of the gospel as a belief system (1:16), you also need never be ashamed of or disappointed in your practice of living by faith. This was Paul's message, and this is to be our calling as twentieth-century Christians. We are to proclaim the system clearly and without shame (1:16), and we are also to be living demonstrations that these things are real (5:5). No matter how perfect the system, unless there's some demonstration that it is real, we can't expect people to believe it. Our goal should be that people won't just hear our message and say, "Yes, that's the way it should be," but that they will see the peace of God in our hearts and say, "Yes, that's the way it is!" The peace of God is not a mystical thing on top of a pillar or at a Bible conference, but the reality of the finished work of Jesus in the midst of history.

This is the first time since 1:4 that Paul has mentioned the Holy Spirit. He will mention Him again in 7:6, and then in chapter 8 he will have a great deal to say about the power of the Holy Spirit in the life of the believer. The giving of the Holy Spirit is just as real and objective as the death of Christ for our salvation.

For when we were yet without strength, in due time Christ died for the ungodly. (5:6)

"In due time [in the past] Christ died for the ungodly." Paul is continuing to call us to understand our present reality as Christians in the light of the past reality of Christ's finished work. In so doing he is once again beginning to develop the theme of death versus life, which we saw in 1:17 and again in 4:17. Christ died for the ungodly.

For scarcely for a righteous man will one die: yet peradventure for a good man some would even dare to die. But God commendeth his love toward us, in that, while we were yet sinners, Christ died for us. (5:7-8)

People often say, "But what can Christ do for me? I'm such a sinner." Or, "What can Christ do for me? I've sinned again." Paul answers that question: When did Christ die for us? When we were still sinners! All of us, no matter how long we have been Christians, need to be reminded of this. I certainly need to be reminded of it. When I've fallen again, when I've sinned again, when I've done something wrong and think, "Surely, as long as I've been a Christian, I shouldn't have done that" . . . at such times, I need help. And my help at such times comes from remembering the basis upon which my salvation rests. Who was this Francis Schaeffer for whom Jesus died? When I honestly answer that question, and remember the kind of person I was when Jesus died for me, surely I won't continue to be discouraged or to think that He will abandon me now.

Someone might be reading Romans and say, Paul has lost his outline! He already explained justification in the earlier chapters. Why is he bringing it up now? But Paul hasn't lost his outline at all, for the present reality of our peace with God (5:1-11) is based entirely upon the finished work of Christ on our behalf (3:21—4:25). Whenever I sin, whenever I lose my sense of peace with God, what is the one thing that can comfort me? The one comforting and overwhelming fact is that, when I was totally a sinner, without strength and without one good thing to commend me to God, it was then that Jesus died for me.

"For scarcely for a righteous man will one die." You can find a few cases where people died for nice people, but who dies for the awful scoundrel? Who dies for the enemy? Well, who was the enemy? I was! I was the enemy of God. I was stamping through God's universe, shaking my fist in His face. And in the very moment when I was shaking my fist in God's face and tramping through the Creator's universe, muddying all His streams, that's when Jesus died for me. And if this is when Jesus died for me, what hope it gives me now! Now, even when I fall, the blood of Jesus is enough. He didn't save me because I was strong; He saved me when I was weak. He didn't save me when I was a pretty thing; He saved me when I was a mess. On the basis of this reality, I can have comfort.

When we as Christians sin, we can react in one of three ways: 1) We can become hardened to our sin. 2) We can sink into utter despair and say, "It's all over." And as I've said, I've known Christians who have spent twenty years despairing over one sin. But neither of these reactions is right. The only right course of action for us as Christians is to 3) become increasingly sensitive to our sin, but also increasingly to know the forgiveness that is ours on the basis of the blood of

Christ—to have the assurance that, if Jesus died for me as I was before my salvation, how much He must love me now!

Much more then, being now justified by his blood, we shall be saved from wrath through him. (5:9)

Justification is our reality in the present tense, based on the fact that, at some particular time in the past tense, Jesus died for us and we accepted His death on our behalf and therefore we became justified. Paul is giving us a complete picture of salvation. On the basis of this past and present reality we will, in the future, "be saved from wrath through him."

For if, when we were yet enemies . . . (5:10a)

"While we were yet sinners . . ." (verse 8), and now, "When we were yet enemies." How strong do we want Paul to make it? Hasn't he emphasized this enough already? But do you see why he is stressing this? He is anticipating how some of his readers will react. He isn't dealing with theoretical arguments; he's dealing with living flesh-and-blood people just like you and me. He has said, "Therefore, being justified by faith, we have peace with God," and he knows many of his readers will become very exhilarated about this. But then they will go down the stairs and, bam! they fall into sin again and are plunged into the darkest despair. Paul knows that he isn't dealing with ideal people. He's dealing with us! The church at Rome had the same experiences we have. Paul doesn't just want to offer us good psychology. He wants us to understand that our Christian faith has reality for our everyday personal lives. The gospel isn't for ideal people. Ideal people don't exist. The gospel is for people like us.

For if, when were enemies, we were reconciled to God by the death of his Son . . . (5:10a)

Once again, note the tenses. Everything turns on the tenses. In the past tense, in real history, Jesus died. In the past tense, we accepted Him as our Savior and thus were reconciled to God and became indwelt by the Holy Spirit. On the basis of those events in the past tense, we can have hope in the present tense.

For if, when we were enemies, we were reconciled to God by the death of his Son, much more, being reconciled, we shall be saved by his life. (5:10)

Verses 9 and 10 are very similar: "Much more then, being now justified by his blood, we shall be saved from wrath through him" (verse 9). "Much more, being reconciled, we shall be saved by his life" (verse 10). But notice the new element in verse 10: Paul has been talking about Christ's death, but now, at the end of verse 10, he reminds us that Christ isn't dead—He's alive! If, when we were enemies, Jesus died for us, what will this living Christ do for us now!

We were dead, but now we're alive. Abraham believed that God could bring life out of the dead (4:20-21). We believe that God raised Jesus from the dead (4:23-25). On the basis of Christ's work on our behalf, and through our faith in His work, we're alive (chapters 5—8). And Jesus is alive (5:10). If Jesus died for us while we were enemies and now He's alive, what will He do for us now! We're dealing with a living Christ. He is there. The physical resurrection of Jesus is a historical fact. We're not just dealing with an idea. Jesus is the ascended, living Christ.

Paul carries this life and death theme throughout the chapter. We "shall reign in life by one, Jesus Christ" (5:17); God's grace will "reign through righteousness unto eternal life by Jesus Christ our Lord" (5:21). Jesus died for us; it is a finished work. He died for us while we were yet sinners, while we were God's enemies. "How much more," then, in the present life, having accepted Christ as our Savior, and having a living Savior . . . how much more can we expect to have everything we need for our present life!

And not only so, but we also joy in God through our Lord Jesus Christ, by whom we have now received the atonement. (5:11)

At this present moment of time, "we glory in God through our Lord Jesus Christ," and this is on the basis of something we acquired in the past: ". . . by whom we have now received the atonement." This always reminds me of the Twenty-third Psalm, where in verses 5 and 6 David carries us from the present to the future: "Thou preparest a table before me in the presence of mine enemies: thou anointest my head with oil; my cup runneth over." David had great joy, even on the battlefields of the present; and this great joy was based on his certain hope for the future: "Surely goodness and mercy shall follow me all the days of my life: and I will dwell in the house of the LORD for ever." Our faith in Christ brings blessings not just in the past and future, but in this present life as well. It brings the oil of gladness amid the battles of life. Our justification was on the basis of Christ's finished work, and our present life is to be lived on the same basis. We have a right to lay hold upon the things of God on the basis of Christ's work on Calvary. We can do so with overwhelming confidence. Christ has paid the price. We have a living Savior. Christ has finished the work. Through His finished work there is the possibility of glorying in God amid life's struggles. Each of us has our individual temptations; each of us falls. But the cleansing is always there. We need never, never be afraid that we have fallen to the place where God will turn away from us. Through Christ, forgiveness always awaits us if we confess our sin and bring it under the covering of His shed blood. Through Jesus Christ our Lord, amid the rough-and-tumble, we can have strength.

People often say to me, "I don't know if I would have the strength to be a martyr." Of course we don't have such strength at this moment; but at the moment of the martyrdom, whether it is physical death or the little deaths of being scoffed at and turned away from by our family and loved ones—even amid these little deaths, on the basis of Christ's finished work and through the means of our faith, we can glory in God.

Paul is emphasizing over and over again the two steps, and they're not to be confused: There is the past step that was once for all accomplished in the death of Jesus and then in our individually accepting Him as Savior, leading to our justification. Then there is this present step of coming to know the power and joy of God in our lives, and it is on the same basis as our initial salvation: "through our Lord Jesus Christ" (5:11).

8

DEAD IN ADAM,
ALIVE IN CHRIST
(5:12-21)

℞

Paul now comes, in Romans 5:12-21, to what we could think of as a parenthesis. This will be the first time in Romans that Paul has talked about the entrance of sin into the world through the Fall of Adam. Perhaps the most interesting thing about this is the place where it appears. Remember that Paul has already explained why mankind needs salvation (1:18—3:20), yet he did so without even mentioning Adam and Eve. Could it be that even the order in which Paul explains is a guide for us in presenting the gospel? As Paul explains mankind's need for salvation, the emphasis is on how individual humans have turned away from God. He talks about people knowing the truth and deliberately turning away from it in culture after culture; serving the creature rather than the Creator; sinning against their own moral standards. Now, in chapter 5, he will give the root explanation for all of this. The bottom-line reason that all people are sinners, Paul now shows, is because of the historical Fall of mankind in Adam. And when one denies the historicity of Adam, one throws away the authority of Paul. But the intriguing thing is that Paul discusses Adam at this place, where he is talking to Christians and not to non-Christians.

I think that Paul does this purposely and with care. If we begin presenting the gospel by discussing things like the Fall of mankind or the inspiration of the Bible, we can easily get bogged down and never get beyond such issues. Of course, if the person with whom you are talking asks about the origin of sin, you should explain it. But it is interesting that Paul, in his natural flow of presenting the gospel, doesn't begin at that point. It isn't that he's ashamed of it, because when he does get to the subject, he is very emphatic about it. Yet he doesn't begin there. Rather, he begins his discussion of mankind's need for salvation by showing that individual people, down through the centuries, have turned away from God and have deliberately sinned against their own moral standards.

Now, as Paul does begin explaining how sin entered the world, he insists very strenuously that Adam was a real historical person.

Wherefore, as by one man sin entered into the world, and death by sin; and so death passed upon all men, for that all have sinned: (For until the law sin was in the world: but sin is not imputed when there is no law. Nevertheless death reigned from Adam to Moses, even over them that had not sinned after the similitude of Adam's transgression, who is the figure of him that was to come. (5:12-14)

Paul's straightforward statement that "by one man sin entered into the world" shows he clearly believed that the account of Adam and Eve in Genesis 1—3 was real history. We see this in other places as well. In 16:20, Paul says that "the God of peace shall bruise Satan under your feet shortly," undoubtedly a reference to what we have seen to be the first promise of the Savior, in Genesis 3:15. As Paul in 1 Corinthians speaks of the coming resurrection of believers, he assumes the historicity of Adam: "For as in Adam all die, even so in Christ shall all be made alive" (1 Cor. 15:22). We could look also at 1 Timothy 2:13-14, where again Paul speaks of Adam and Eve as though they were real historical people.

Jesus also believed in the historicity of the first few chapters of Genesis. We see this in Matthew 19:4-5, where He quotes Genesis

2:24, assuming it to be historical fact, to explain His opposition to divorce. There is a tendency in our day to view the first three chapters of Genesis as merely myth or parable, an idea or an allegory. But considering that both Paul and Christ accepted those chapters as real history, if we reject them we are rejecting the authority not only of Paul but even of Christ Himself. Seeing, however, that both Christ and Paul *did* believe in the historicity of Adam and Eve, we can be confident and unapologetic in presenting Genesis 3 as the sufficient explanation of sin's entrance into the world.

Paul says that "death reigned from Adam to Moses"; that is, death reigned even before the law came. As we saw in 2:1, those who lived from the time of Adam until the giving of the law will not be judged by the Law of Moses, but on the basis of what they knew, apart from the law, about right and wrong. They will not be judged by what they didn't have (the law), but by what they did have (their own conscience and moral standards). So all come under condemnation, for even before the Law of Moses all were guilty.

There was a historical Fall, bringing death to all people, even those who lived before the giving of the law. But then there was also the equally historical coming of the Redeemer.

But not as the offence, so also is the free gift. For if through the offence of one many be dead, much more the grace of God, and the gift by grace, which is by one man, Jesus Christ, hath abounded unto many. (5:15)

There were two historical acts: the historical act of Adam, wherein all mankind became sinners; and, parallel to this, the historical act of Jesus, who came to raise up what had been lost. There is an interesting Old Testament parallel to this, in the Jewish custom of the brother raising up a seed for a brother who had died: "If brethren dwell together, and one of them die, and have no child, the wife of the dead shall not marry without unto a stranger: her husband's brother shall go in unto her, and take her to him to wife, and perform the duty of an husband's brother unto her. And it shall be, that the firstborn which she beareth shall succeed in the name of his brother which is dead, that his name be not put out of Israel" (Deut. 25:5-6).

Simply stated, if a man died with no heir, his brother was to take his wife, and the child who was born would carry on the name of the dead brother. The book of Ruth centers in just such a situation. When Ruth lies down at the feet of Boaz (chapter 3), she is not suggesting some sort of immoral act. Rather, since her husband has died, she is asking Boaz her kinsman to do for her exactly what the passage in Deuteronomy says should be done. She is asking that Boaz marry her so that a child may be born to raise up an heir for her dead husband.

With this in mind, let's look at Isaiah 53, a chapter of tremendous importance concerning the work of Christ. In 53:10 we read, "Yet it pleased the LORD to bruise him; he hath put him to grief: when thou shalt make his soul an offering for sin, he shall see his seed." Note the phrase, "He shall see his seed." Although He was never married, Jesus is going to have a seed; He is going to have children. This refers, of course, to all of those who by God's grace have accepted or will in the future accept Christ as our Savior. We who have done so are Christ's children.

In Romans 5, Paul is explaining that the human race fell through Adam's sin, but a second man came and raised up this fallen humanity. Just as in the Old Testament a brother raised up seed to his brother who had died childless, so, with humanity having died in the sin of Adam, Christ came to raise up a real, living humanity. The man who raised up seed for his dead brother under the Old Testament law was called a kinsman redeemer. Christ is the true kinsman redeemer. He has raised up a seed to God.

Some people in our own time say that "God is dead," but whether people overtly say such a thing or simply choose to live as though God doesn't exist, they themselves in fact become dead, because their unbelief has destroyed the purpose of their existence. They can no longer find themselves as real humans. But because Christ has come and has died, those who do believe in Him can become a true and living humanity.

Some other cross-references should help us understand the drive of this fifth chapter concerning Adam and Christ. Look at Isaiah 9:6: "For unto us a child is born, unto us a son is given: and the government shall be upon his shoulder: and his name shall be called

Wonderful, Counselor, The mighty God, The everlasting Father, The Prince of Peace." A child is to be born who shall be called "the everlasting Father." Is this a confusion between God the Father and God the Son? I don't think so at all. I think this relates to what we saw in Isaiah 53:10: Jesus, by His death on the cross, raised up a seed that is the true humanity, and in this sense He is indeed the everlasting Father. We can think of Jesus in various ways. The book of Hebrews emphasizes that He is our brother. But He has raised up this seed, this true humanity, and if we have accepted Christ and He is our Savior, in this sense we are also His children and He is our everlasting Father. Even in Hebrews we see Christ portrayed as our Father as He says, "Behold I and the children which God hath given me" (Heb. 2:13). Just before this, in verses 11 and 12, we are called Christ's brothers. Christ is our brother, in the sense that He became one of the human race. But while we're His brothers and sisters, we are also His children.

This has a profound implication for our view of humanity. Because it has fallen, humanity is far less than God meant it to be. But since Christ has become the second Adam, there is now a humanity raised up that is humanity indeed—a humanity that is fulfilling the purpose of its existence, which is to love God. God told Adam that if he ate the forbidden fruit he would die. When Adam ate the fruit, he didn't die physically right away, but he was dead for all intents and purposes. He had rejected the purpose of his existence and so he was dead—and with him, all humanity has died (5:12; 1 Cor. 15:22). What we see of humanity today is less than human. When a man like van Gogh paints himself as less than human, he is portraying what mankind really is. Van Gogh understood. We look out across the human race, with all its longings, all its possibilities, all its potentiality, all its creativity, all its motions toward morality, all its motions toward significance, and we realize that unredeemed humanity is dead. We must have tremendous compassion. The story of fallen mankind is indeed a great tragedy.

Thankfully, of course, this is not the end of the story. Christ has come, and through His substitutionary death on the cross He has made it possible for a seed to be raised up that will be the true humanity. As Christians, our whole life must be consumed by a sorrow for fallen humanity, but also by the joyful proclamation of the true humanity made possible through Christ.

Mankind is dead, but Christ has come, the second Adam has come, and the second Adam, Christ, has finished the work. Therefore, you are not dead. You are alive. You are the real humanity. You are not a corpse. Once you begin to feel this, you begin to understand the deep call to the Christian life, which is the larger context of Paul's discussion of Adam.

You remember we pointed out the unity between chapters 4 and 5. Abraham understood that his and Sarah's bodies were dead as far as reproduction was concerned. But they both believed the promise of God, and out of this death there came a living faith. Prior to this there was nothing but death, but now that he had believed God, there was that which is living, a son of promise. So when we come to the fifth chapter of Romans, Paul says to us, "You are living. Humanity has died. It has sinned. It has no purpose of existence. But if you have accepted Christ as your Savior, even though you have been dead, you are now alive. And because you are alive you can begin to live within the framework in which the human race was meant to live from the very beginning." The world is dead because it is Adam's seed, but we are alive because we are Christ's seed. In light of this, how should we live? Paul's discussion of Adam is therefore not just something thrown in illogically; it fits very much into the whole emphasis on sanctification in 5:1—8:17.

Keep in mind also the theme of life versus death. We were dead, now we're alive. We were dead because we are Adam's children, but when we accepted Christ as Savior we became Christ's children. This ties into the whole New Testament emphasis on being born again. We were born naturally as the children of Adam, and therefore we are dead. But when through the preaching of the word of God we accepted Christ as our Savior, we were born again and we became alive because we became the children of Christ.

Thinking again of the place of this discussion in Romans—in the section on sanctification—we see that we have been born again, we are alive, and therefore we can bear the fruit of a sanctified Christian life.

We were dead, but now we're alive. Now we're to live this way.

We are to be Christ's seed in practice. How? In our own strength? No. We are to be His seed on the basis of His finished work. There are two lines of humanity. The humanity that is born naturally as the children of Adam is dead. We "have been the children of wrath, even as the others" (Eph. 2:3); but now we have accepted Christ as our Savior. We are His seed, and laying hold through faith of this great reality, on the basis of Christ's finished work, we are to live a Christian life now.

Because Jesus has come and has died, He has created something new. He has children. We who have believed in Him are His children. We are the living human race, and the rest are dead. Far from making us proud or exclusive in any way, this should lay a great compassion on us, for we still share the basic human nature of those who are still lost. The angels surely look down with compassion on the lost world, but we should have more compassion. For we, unlike the angels, share the human nature of those who are still lost. Not only do we have their nature, but we also were, in the past, in the desperate situation that they are still in. We have been children of wrath; they are still children of wrath. We have been dead; they are still dead. Surely, then, we must have compassion.

Of course this notion of two humanities is completely contrary to the twentieth-century mentality, with its emphasis on the unity of the human race. This has been expressed theologically in the liberal concept of the "fatherhood of God and the brotherhood of man." The biblical viewpoint is that there are two human races, the human race that stands in the place of Adam and is condemned, and the human race that stands as the seed of Christ, which He has purchased with His blood.

Once again, please note that Paul has not just stuffed this discussion of sin's origin in here inadvertently. He is reminding us who we are. There is lost humanity, and then there is a seed of Christ, which is redeemed humanity. This should give us great compassion for those who are still lost, but it should also make us see the great importance of how we live as Christians. We must realize that it is a terrible thing to bring a bad name on the Christ who died for us. Children who go bad bring discredit on their parents. But when you and I do not live as we should as Christians, we are bringing discredit on the very one who died for us and whose children we are.

Paul has explained the reason why mankind is dead (5:12-14), but he is also now beginning to focus on the wonderful reality of being alive through Christ.

But not as the offense, so also is the free gift. For if through the offense of one many be dead, much more the grace of God, and the gift by grace, which is by one man, Jesus Christ, hath abounded unto many. And not as it was by one that sinned, so is the gift: for the judgment was by one to condemnation, but the free gift is of many offenses unto justification. For if by one man's offense death reigned by one; much more they which receive abundance of grace and of the gift of righteousness shall reign in life by one, Jesus Christ.) (5:15-17)

Paul doesn't want to dwell too long on the negative side, explaining why mankind is dead. His real emphasis is on the positive side: "All right, you were dead, but now you're alive!" Beginning in 6:1, he will go on to say, "Now that you are alive in Christ, be alive! Don't go on living as though you were still dead." Christ died for us while we were sinners (5:10), but now He is alive. Adam sinned, and therefore all mankind is dead (5:12-14), but Jesus, the second Adam, has come. Jesus has died, and now Jesus is alive. There is the possibility of true life in the rough-and-tumble of life, in the midst of tribulation.

"We shall be saved by his life" (verse 10); we "shall reign in life by one, Jesus Christ" (verse 17). We could think of "shall reign" as a future thing. But surely the fact that Paul says this here means that there is a sense in which we can "reign" with Christ even in this present life. We are now the children of God, and as such we are to reign. We have stepped out from the seed of Adam, this humanity that has revolted and is dead. By the grace of God we have become the humanity that is redeemed. We are the seed of Jesus Christ. Well then (Paul will say beginning in 6:1), let's live this way! Paul's explanation of sin's origin is not just an academic exercise. It's a call to life! It's a call to live as the children of God—as the descendants of Jesus Christ. The lost world is in the parade of Adam, but we are to follow in the way of Jesus Christ. Paul's emphasis is not primarily on the death of humanity, but on the reality that now, as the seed of Christ the second Adam, we are to be alive.

Therefore as by the offence of one judgment came upon all men to condemnation; even so by the righteousness of one the free gift came upon all men unto justification of life. (5:18)

A more accurate reading of the Greek would be, "Therefore as by the one offense . . ." and "by the one righteousness," thus putting the focus on Adam's first sin, and on Christ's specific righteous act of redemption.

Some have interpreted this verse to mean that just as all humans came under judgment because of Adam's sin, all will be saved by Christ's act of righteousness, regardless of their personal belief or disbelief. But this universalism simply cannot be reconciled with Paul's emphasis, throughout Romans, on the importance of the human response of faith. Rather, when Paul speaks of "all men," he means that there is no other way to be saved. There was one historical Fall, and there was one historical act of redemption.

For as by one man's disobedience many were made sinners, so by the obedience of one shall many be made righteous. (5:19)

"Made" righteous is better understood as "declared" righteous, as we have noted throughout this study. Salvation is the declarative act of God. We have sinned and have been declared to be guilty. When we accept Jesus as our Savior, we are justified and declared to be free of guilt. "For as by one man's disobedience many were declared sinners, so by the obedience of one shall many be declared righteous."

Moreover the law entered, that the offence might abound. (5:20a)

This is better translated, "the law entered, in addition, that the offense might abound." The people who lived between Adam and the Law of Moses didn't have the Law of Moses, but they were sinners nonetheless because they had the law of their own moral standards and they had violated that standard (2:1; 5:14). Then, *in addition* to this moral standard that all humanity has had from the beginning, God gave the law through Moses, and this made it possible "that the offence might abound." In other words, the law made it abundantly plain that all people were sinners. The law didn't make them sinners, it simply made it very plain that they were sinners. As we have seen, this was an act of grace on God's part; He gave us the law as a schoolmaster to show us our need for salvation (Gal. 3:24).

But where sin abounded, grace did much more abound: that as sin hath reigned unto death, even so might grace reign through righteousness unto eternal life by Jesus Christ our Lord. (5:20b-21)

As he concludes his explanation of sin's entrance into the world through Adam, Paul's emphasis is not on death but on life. It is actually an emphasis that flows from verse 10, "shall be saved by his life," through verse 17, "shall reign in life by one, Jesus Christ," to here in verse 21: God's "grace [shall] reign through righteousness unto eternal life by Jesus Christ our Lord." Rather than simply explaining that all humanity died in Adam, Paul emphasizes the other side. All humans either have been or still are dead in Adam, but those who have accepted Christ as their Savior are not still dead but are alive. And if we are alive, if we are the redeemed humanity, and at such a cost, how important it is that we show this in our everyday lives.

That will be Paul's theme in chapter 6.

9

THE CHRISTIAN'S STRUGGLE
WITH SIN: I
(6:1-23)

&

Paul showed us that we need justification (1:18—3:20). Then he showed us how to be justified (3:21—4:25). He has begun to describe the wonderful results of justification (5:1-11), and has explained the entrance into the world of both sin and salvation (5:12-21). He will now, in chapters 6 and 7, speak of the tragic reality that, even though we are alive in Christ, all too often we live as though we were still dead.

Sarah's dead womb couldn't produce life, but through her faith and Abraham's faith there came life (4:1-22). We have been dead, but now that we have believed in Christ we have become alive out of the dead womb of humanity (4:23—5:21). Those of the human race who still follow in the parade of Adam are still dead, but those of us who have taken Christ as our Savior are the living humanity. Christ is the living vine, and we are connected as branches to that vine. How marvelous this is! But how we must weep when we feel the thrust of God speaking in chapters 6 and 7 and see ourselves in what he is saying—when we see that all too often we who are in the live stream of humanity live as though we were dead.

Paul introduces this theme immediately:

What shall we say then? Shall we continue in sin, that grace may abound? God forbid. How shall we, that are dead to sin, live any longer therein? (6:1-2)

Here again Paul speaks of death and life. We have been reconciled to God by Christ's death, and we shall be saved by His life (5:10). We were dead, but now we're alive. Adam sinned, and humanity died; but then Christ died, and because He died, we who have believed on Him are now alive. There is a living humanity. We are dead to sin but alive to Christ. But "How," Paul asks, "shall we, that are dead to sin, live any longer therein?" Surely Paul must have been weeping as he asked this, and we should weep too. If we're alive to Christ, we should be dead to sin. Yet tragically we often live as though we were dead to Christ and alive to sin.

Remember we have seen that, just as we were justified on the basis of Christ's shed blood, we can claim cleansing on that same basis whenever we sin. God doesn't expect us to be some kind of Nietzschean superman. He knows that we will still sin. But why can't we, after becoming Christians, learn to walk on the same principle of faith by which we were saved? Why can't we keep drawing on the finished work of Christ through faith so that we do live as living people instead of on the other side of the ledger?

"How shall we, that are dead to sin . . ." More literally from the Greek, "How shall we who have died to sin once for all . . ." When we accepted Jesus as our Savior, we died to sin once for all. So why are we still living "therein"?

Don't forget for a moment just who is asking this. It is Paul, who in these first few chapters of Romans has emphasized so strongly that we are justified by faith, not by our own ability to avoid sin. It is Paul, who has emphasized the finality of justification by faith. It is this same Paul who now cries out to us for the Christian life. If salvation is a reality and we, who were dead, are now alive; if when we accepted Christ as our Savior we died to sin, why then are we still living in sin? If we as Christians have any sensitivity and if we are allowing the Holy Spirit to speak to our hearts at all, we know that Paul is speaking to us, because this all too often is where we are. Paul is saying to each of us that it is no little thing to sin after we become a Christian. "God forbid. How can it be so?"

Notice that Paul doesn't say, "Shall *you* continue in sin?" He says, "Shall *we* continue in sin?" He identifies himself with the problem. Why? Because, as we will see, even Paul found himself in this unhappy place from time to time. There is a constant danger, when we get on a little further in our Christian life, that we sort of stand in a high church tower and blast down on everyone else: "Look at you!" But we don't see this kind of spiritual pride in the heroes of faith in the Bible. When Daniel prayed for the Jewish people, he identified himself with them and said, "We have sinned" (Dan. 9:1-19). This is true wherever there is a moving of the Holy Spirit, wherever a real person of God is speaking. It isn't "you." It isn't "them." It's "we." How can *we* continue in sin?

In chapter 6, Paul deals specifically with the problem of sin in the believer's life. He will show that how we live our lives as Christians is of utmost importance, even though we are justified entirely by God's grace apart from any righteousness of our own. Before we begin our study of this important chapter, it would be good to note a few other New Testament passages that stress the importance of how we conduct ourselves as Christians. These passages will show clearly that Paul's emphasis on personal holiness in chapter 6 is in no way isolated from the rest of New Testament teaching.

The apostle Peter says that Christ died on the cross so that "we, being dead to sins, should live unto righteousness" (1 Pet. 2:24). Notice those same key words that Paul uses: *dead* and *live*. Jesus died on the cross not just so that we can go to heaven someday, but also so that we can be two things in this present life: dead to sin and alive to righteousness.

In 2 Corinthians Paul describes Christians as "Always bearing about in the body the dying of the Lord Jesus, that the life also of Jesus might be made manifest in our body. For we which live are always delivered unto death for Jesus' sake, that the life also of Jesus might be made manifest in our mortal flesh" (2 Cor. 4:10-11). We are not to wait till we die and go to heaven to start living the Christian life;

rather, in this present life, we are to bear about in our body both the death and the life of Jesus.

Jesus Himself spoke in similar terms: "If any man will come after me, let him deny himself, and take up his cross, and follow me" (Matt. 16:24). If we are true disciples of Jesus, we will deny ourselves. This is in the context where Jesus had begun to tell His disciples about His approaching death, and Peter had reacted strongly, saying that Jesus would never die. Jesus responded by going even further, saying that not only would He have to suffer death on a cross, but His disciples, if they truly were His disciples, would also be called upon to "take up their cross." Any Christian who would live a life of joy and of usefulness in this poor, lost world must deny himself and take up his cross daily.

Echoing Christ's words, Paul describes himself as being "crucified with Christ" (Gal. 2:19; see also Gal. 6:14). As Christians, we must in some way identify ourselves with the crucified Christ.

Even if there were no sixth chapter of Romans, these verses put together remind us that the Christian life is not just to be an easy thing. We must always understand that our salvation has nothing whatsoever to do with our works. But we must never forget that, having accepted Jesus as our Savior, we have a calling: It is a calling in this present life, first to die and then to live.

This brings us back to Romans 6:

What shall we say then? Shall we continue in sin that grace may abound? (6:1)

Because we are saved only on the basis of Christ's finished work, without any works on our part, does that mean we should just continue in sin?

God forbid. How shall we, that are dead to sin, live any longer therein? (6:2)

If it is true that, in the past, we accepted Jesus as our Savior, how can we, in the present, live any longer in sin? We died to sin, in the past tense, when we accepted Christ as our Savior:

Know ye not, that so many of us as were baptized into Jesus Christ were baptized into his death? (6:3)

Verse 2 tells us that we have died to sin, and verse 3 tells us when this death occurred: It occurred at the moment when we accepted Christ and were baptized by His Holy Spirit "into His death." This undoubtedly refers to the baptism of the Holy Spirit, rather than water baptism. In 1 Corinthians 12:13 Paul says, "By one Spirit are we all baptized into one body . . . and have been all made to drink into one Spirit." It seems very plain that in both of these passages Paul is speaking of the baptism of the Holy Spirit that occurs for all true Christians at the moment they accept Christ as Savior. Paul will state very strongly in 8:9 that all who have truly accepted Jesus as Savior are indwelt by the Holy Spirit. If we haven't been baptized by and are not now indwelt by the Holy Spirit, we are not truly Christians. Living in a day when so many like to view the Bible as just a collection of ideas and abstractions, we must keep on reminding ourselves that our salvation rests upon two historical points: the moment in space and time at which Jesus died on the cross; and the moment at which we by faith accepted Him as our Savior. At the moment that you accepted Christ as your Savior, you were baptized by the Holy Spirit into His death.

Perhaps it is easy to emotionally withdraw from the idea of being "baptized into Christ's death." We like to think of eternal life. We like to think of the wonder of being indwelt by the Holy Spirit. We like to think of being united with Christ, of having God the Father as our Father. We like to think of the great promises such as, "He who believes on the Son has life" (John 3:36). But this coin has two sides, says Paul. We need to be assured that we have everlasting life. This is God's promise to us based on Christ's finished work. But we must not forget that Jesus said, "You must take up your cross daily and follow me."

This is far too little emphasized by evangelical Christians today. We like to think of identifying with Jesus in terms of being with Him in the heavenlies (Eph. 2:6), or of His being the bridegroom and our being the bride, or of His being the vine and our being the branches. But let us never forget, as Christians, that if we are going to understand the Christian life we must also understand and then practice our identification, in this present life, with Christ's death.

Paul develops this thought further:

Therefore we are buried with him by baptism into death: that like as Christ was raised up from the dead by the glory of the Father, even so we also should walk in newness of life. (6:4)

At the same time that we accepted Jesus as our Savior, we were buried with Him in baptism by the Holy Spirit. Or, as we saw in Galatians 2:19, we were "crucified" with Him. We were buried with Him by baptism into death in order that, "like as Christ was raised up from the dead by the glory of the Father . . ." This is the introduction to what I have marked in my own Bible as "b." Throughout chapter 6 in my Bible I have marked all the "deaths" with the letter "a" and all the "being alive's" with the letter "b." It makes an interesting pattern. Verse 2 would be an "a," because it refers to the fact that we died when we accepted Christ as our Savior. Verse 3 says, "We were baptized into Christ's death," so that's an "a" as well. The first part of verse 4 would be "a" again: "Therefore we were buried with Him by baptism into death." But that death is for a purpose; we don't just stay dead. And that brings us to the second part of verse 4, which is a "b": Having been buried with Christ by baptism into death, we may now "walk in newness of life." "Should walk in newness of life" is more accurately translated "may walk in newness of life." It isn't just something we ought to do, but something that by God's grace is a very real possibility for us.

This is the key to understanding the Christian life. Many people seem to view the Christian life as some sort of gloomy struggle. It's as though the deaths of 6:2-4a were the end of the matter. Certainly there are the deaths, but the deaths are for a purpose. We don't just die in order to die. There is no asceticism here. We die in order to live—and not just in the future life, mind you, but in this present life as well.

At the very moment when we accept Jesus as our Savior, our guilt is gone, and we stand justified forever in God's sight. But there is still this present life to deal with, and if there is to be real life in the present, it must be preceded by a death. We might think of the death we as

Christians are to die as being parallel to Christ's death. I would hesitate to make this parallel except that Christ Himself did so: "If any man will come after me, let him deny himself, and take up his cross, and follow me" (Matt. 16:24). Jesus didn't die on the cross just to die on the cross. Jesus died on the cross in order that we might be redeemed. Likewise, we are not called upon to die daily just in order to be dead; we are called upon to die daily in order that we might experience the reality of being alive with Christ. Jesus has risen from the dead in space and time and history and now we, on the basis of this, having been baptized into His death, may walk in newness of life in space and time and history. This is the key to the Christian life.

In verse 5, Paul returns to the theme of Christ's death.

For if we have been planted together in the likeness of his death, we shall be also in the likeness of his resurrection. (6:5)

If we were united with Christ in the likeness of His death, we shall also, like Him, someday be raised physically from the dead. But this isn't just something for the future. It means something for the present as well, as we saw in verse 4—"that we may walk in newness of life" right now.

Knowing this, that our old man is crucified with him, that the body of sin might be destroyed, that henceforth we should not serve sin. (6:6)

"That the body of sin might be destroyed" could be translated, "That the body of sin might be made powerless." Notice again the emphasis on the physical body. This doesn't mean that only the body is sinful. There are sins of the spirit as well as sins of the body. But Paul is trying to show us that he's talking not about some mystical, abstract thing, not about something merely in the world of ideas: He's talking about something that is right down in the tough, historical, space-and-time stuff we know so well, including the problems of sin related to our physical body.

We will see this emphasis on the physical body again in verse 12: "Let not sin therefore reign in your mortal body." And in 8:23 he will speak of the future "redemption of our body," when our bodies are raised physically from the dead. But in verse 6 Paul is emphasizing that we don't have to wait for that future moment when our bodies are raised physically from the dead. Even in this present life, "having been crucified with Christ," we can experience the reality of "the body of sin" being "made powerless," in order that "henceforth we should not serve sin."

Paul isn't just telling us what we *should* be; he's telling us what we *may* be. "Even so we may also walk in newness of life" (6:4). It is relatively easy to set a standard. A lot of people set standards. The problem is in keeping them. Paul isn't telling us merely about a standard, he's telling us how to keep the standard. The possibility of our actually keeping the standard for Christian living is based upon two past facts: the fact of Christ's finished work at Calvary; and the fact of our having individually accepted Him as our Savior. In that moment when we took Christ as our Savior, we were buried with Him by baptism into death. And because we died with Him, "God forbid" (verse 2) that we should continue to live in sin.

For he that is dead is freed from sin. Now if we be dead with Christ, we believe that we shall also live with him. (6:7-8)

It is wonderful to know that, having accepted Christ as our Savior, we, like Him, shall someday be raised physically from the dead; but what Paul is hammering away at here is that the certainty of our future resurrection means something for our lives right now.

Think of it this way: Jesus died in history. Jesus rose from the dead in history. We accepted Christ as our Savior in history. We will be raised from the dead at some real, historical moment in the future. "Now," Paul is saying, "live like it!" Through faith, we are to live now on the basis of what has happened in the past, as though we were already in the future. Jesus died in history. Jesus rose from the dead in history. We accepted Christ as our Savior in history. We shall, in the future, be raised from the dead. Now the call is, by faith, to live in the present as though we were already in the future. This is the Christian call. It is sobering and beautiful and wonderful all at the same time.

Knowing that Christ being raised from the dead dieth no more; death hath no more dominion over him. (6:9)

When Jesus died and rose from the dead, that was the end of death as far as He was concerned. As He said from the cross, "It is finished" (John 19:30). When Jesus rose from the dead, death was finished.

For in that he died, he died unto sin once. (6:10a)

Literally the Greek is, "He died unto sin once for all." We have noted the "once for all" nature of Christ's death several times already, and that is what is meant here as well. Verse 9 says, in so many words, that Christ died to death once for all; now verse 10 says that He died to sin once for all. This doesn't mean that Jesus ever sinned. It means simply that His struggle with temptation (Heb. 4:15) is past. The battle is finished.

. . . but in that he liveth, he liveth unto God. (6:10b)

Jesus died once for all, but now He continues to live "unto God." He died, not just to die, but to be alive to God. Likewise, our calling as Christians is never primarily a negative thing. The basic Christian call is a positive thing. The first commandment, said Jesus, is to "love the Lord thy God with all thy heart, and with all thy soul, and with all thy mind" (Matt. 22:37). The word *don't* does not appear in this commandment. It is true that loving God means there are certain things we will want to avoid doing. These are, for instance, spelled out for us in the Ten Commandments. But our primary calling as Christians is a positive thing. So often Christians act as though the Christian calling is merely to have sort of an unhappy life and say no to this and no to that. But that isn't the point. There are certain negative things that are involved, which cause pain, but the calling is primarily a positive one. The calling is to be alive to God. The negative commands relate to things that hinder you from being alive to God. "He liveth unto God." And the only way to be alive to God is to be dead toward something else.

What are we to be dead to? According to what Jesus told Peter in Matthew 16:24, we are to be dead primarily toward ourselves. If we're to be Christ's disciples, we must deny ourselves, take up our cross, and follow Him. Being alive to God does not mean being dead to a series of rules; it means being dead toward self. And this death to self is not just so that we might suffer but so that we might be alive to God.

Christians constantly say to me, "I can't seem to find a reality in my Christian life." If there is to be a reality to our fellowship with God, there is a price to be paid. In order for Jesus to be alive to God, He had to die. In order for us to be alive to God in our daily walk, a daily death is needed. We must die daily to selfishness, to self-centeredness, to self-sufficiency. The death isn't the important thing. The being alive to God is the important thing. But if I'm going to be alive to God, there first must be the death.

Jesus died and rose from the dead. We died with Christ. We will someday be raised physically from the dead. But we are to walk in the present in light of that future truth. We will not be raised physically from the dead in the future if we have not died with Christ in the past. And in the present life we are to be experiencing this, both in terms of dying daily to sin and of living daily to God.

Do you want to be alive to God? Not just in the sense of being justified. Not just in the sense of one day having your body raised from the dead. Not just in the sense of one day being in heaven. Do you want the reality of being alive with God today, as a Christian? Then there must be a death. You can be active in Christian work. You can be a missionary. You can be a pastor. You can be a theology professor. You can be a thousand things. But if you want the reality of being alive with God and in fellowship with Him day by day, there must be the daily death. There is no other way.

Paul does not, however, just tell us what to do; he also tells us how to do it. We are now coming to the how.

Likewise reckon ye also yourselves to be dead indeed unto sin, but alive unto God through Jesus Christ our Lord. (6:11)

Every word here is precious. "Likewise," just as Christ died to sin and now lives unto God (verse 10), we are to "reckon" ourselves dead to sin and alive to God. You'll remember that word *reckon* from our discussion of Abraham in chapter 4. Reckoning has to do with faith. By faith, we are called to reckon, or consider, ourselves dead to sin but alive to God. When we grasp the simplicity and truth of what Paul is saying, it is like the breaking of chains in our Christian life. "Likewise reckon ye also yourselves to be dead indeed unto sin, but alive unto God." Our sense of being alive to God does not depend on the reality of our coming physical resurrection, although Paul has indeed said much about this wonderful reality. Our aliveness to God is deeper than this. Even deeper than the reality of our coming resurrection is the reality that Jesus, having died once for all, now lives to God. On the basis of this wonderful reality, we are by faith to reckon ourselves to be dead to sin and alive to God in this present life.

Now, if we are honest at all, we cry out within ourselves, "But how?" "I will try to reckon myself dead to sin and alive to God, but where will I get the strength to do so?" The last phrase of verse 11 is our shout of hallelujah: "Through Jesus Christ our Lord!" It is always "through Jesus Christ our Lord." We are not asked to live to God in our own strength. We'll see this phrase again in 6:23 and 7:25; it's like the "Hallelujah Chorus" in Handel's *Messiah*: "Through Jesus Christ our Lord." Then in 8:13 it's, "through the Spirit," and in 8:37, "through him that loved us." The similar wording of these verses isn't accidental. They are the cords that bind these great chapters together. Chapter 6, chapter 7, chapter 8—they roll out with a rolling of drums, and these verses tie these great chapters together. The Bible never says that we can live perfectly in this life; but neither, on the other hand, does it ever suggest that we have to be bound with the chains of our sinful past. There is a power that breaks those chains, and it is the power of the shed blood. It is the power of the living Christ. Jesus died, but He is alive. His work is finished. He is the living Christ. Through this finished work of Christ and the reality of who He is and what He is doing for us now, there is the possibility of a truly Christian life—"through Jesus Christ our Lord."

Let's give those verses a closer look: "Alive unto God through Jesus Christ our Lord" (6:11). "But the gift of God is eternal life through Jesus Christ our Lord" (6:23). Then there is the cry of 7:24, "Oh wretched man that I am! who shall deliver me from the body of this death?" followed by the joy of verse 25: "I thank God through Jesus Christ our Lord." In 8:13, there is the same thought, with the emphasis on the Holy Spirit. Then in 8:37: "In all these things we are more than conquerors through him that loved us," referring again to Christ.

Paul isn't just talking about an abstraction, about a standard without meaning in the present life. He's talking about something that is possible, and he has told us the basis on which it is possible: It is possible through Jesus Christ our Lord, through who He is and what He did upon the cross, through what He is and what He is doing for us now.

So how do I lay hold of all this? The answer is in verse 11: "Likewise reckon ye also yourselves . . ." We lay hold of it through the "reckoning" of faith. Let me repeat again what a calling this is: Jesus died in history. Jesus rose physically from the dead in history. We died when we accepted Jesus as our Savior, once for all. We will be raised in history in the future. Through faith we are now to live on the basis of all these great truths. We are to live as though we already have been physically raised from the dead.

Let not sin therefore reign in your mortal body . . . (6:12a)

There are three key words in verses 11-13: In verse 11 we saw that the key word was *reckon*; in verse 12 the key word is *reign*; and in verse 13 the key word will be *yield*. "Let not sin therefore reign in your mortal body." Paul is not saying that you are ever going to be perfect in this life; but there's an overwhelming difference between failing to be perfect, and letting sin reign in your life.

First of all, there's a difference between temptation and sin. Jesus "was in all points tempted like as we are, yet without sin" (Heb. 4:15). It is possible to be tempted without falling. Temptation is not sin. We can be tempted without sinning.

Secondly, there is a difference between not being perfect in this present life and letting sin rule your life. Paul is saying, don't let sin be king in your mortal body. Notice the emphasis on the physical body, as we saw in verse 6. Paul surely has in mind the sins of the spirit as well as the sins of the body, but it is all in the context of this present life, while we are living in our mortal body. "At this present time," Paul is saying, "don't let sin be king."

. . . that ye should obey it in the lusts thereof. (6:12b)

Paul now introduces the theme of slavery to sin, which he will deal with more strongly beginning in verse 16.

Neither yield ye your members as instruments of unrighteousness unto sin: but yield yourselves unto God, as those that are alive from the dead, and your members as instruments of righteousness unto God. (6:13)

Here is our third key word: *yield*. We have died to sin. We are, in the present tense, alive from the dead. We have, in the present tense, everlasting life (John 3:36). All right, then, let's yield ourselves to God!

The word *instruments* is the Greek word for "arms" or "weapons." Don't yield yourselves as "arms of unrighteousness" to sin, but yield yourselves and your members as arms or weapons of righteousness to God. Sadly, it is all too possible for a Christian to give himself to the devil and become a weapon in the devil's battle against God. When you and I let sin reign in our mortal body, when we yield ourselves to the devil, he uses us with saber-like sharpness in his battle against God.

If we are sensitive at all and love the Lord, this should make us weep. There is no room for mere exegesis here. There must be some tears. To have been purchased with the blood of Jesus Christ on Calvary's cross, to already have eternal life, to already be indwelt by the Holy Spirit . . . and to then yield ourselves as a weapon of the devil . . . There are some things we do as Christians that may seem morally neutral, but in most of the choices we make we are either yielding to the power of Christ or we are letting sin reign in our mortal body as we yield ourselves to the devil.

Yet, for the Christian, this yielding to the devil is so unnecessary.

For sin shall not have dominion over you: for ye are not under the law, but under grace. (6:14)

As Christians we have the possibility of living by faith, on the basis of the blood and in the power of the Spirit. Therefore, it isn't necessary that sin should have dominion over us. As Paul will say later, ". . . that the righteousness of the law might be fulfilled in us, who walk not after the flesh, but after the Spirit" (8:4). If we were just living under the law, in the sense of being told, "Don't do this. Here is what God wants of you, now do it," Paul is realistic enough to know that we would have no chance of succeeding. But that isn't the point. We are not under the law in this sense. Christ has kept the demands of the law for us. We are under grace. The finished work of Christ and the indwelling of the Spirit are ours. It is possible for us to yield to the power of Christ. Therefore, it isn't necessary to always be in defeat. It isn't necessary to be on the devil's side.

What then? shall we sin, because we are not under the law, but under grace? God forbid. Know ye not, that to whom ye yield yourselves servants to obey, his servants ye are to whom ye obey? (6:15-16a)

Being under grace does not diminish the demands of the law. In response to God's grace, we should want to obey Him. However, when we fail to do so and instead yield ourselves as the weapons of Satan (6:13), we in fact become his slaves.

Know ye not, that to whom ye yield yourselves servants to obey, his servants ye are to whom ye obey; whether of sin unto death, or of obedience unto righteousness? (6:16)

When we yield ourselves to the devil as his slave, we begin to produce death. "The wages of sin is death" (6:23a). Why should we yield ourselves to working for the devil's wages when, by wonderful contrast, the "gift of God is eternal life through Jesus Christ our Lord" (6:23b)!

People often tell me they can't understand why 6:23 is here and not somewhere in the first four chapters. Verse 23 is in chapter 6 because, while it is true concerning justification, it is also true concerning sanctification. "The wages of sin is death," and the horrible reality is that, though we as Christians are alive from the dead, it is entirely possible for us to be death-producing machines—grinding out death and more death, living contrary to the reality of the universe, living contrary to our calling, yielding ourselves to the devil and therefore producing death in this poor world.

Each of us has great significance, as Christians and also as human beings. Each choice we make has an effect upon all of history. The effects of our choices are real, they are not just part of a dream of God, as the Hindu would say. Each choice we make as a Christian and as a human being has a reality in history, and it affects all those about us. When you and I yield ourselves as slaves to the devil, we are death-producing machines. We can be perfectly orthodox. We can be in a "separated" church that tries to keep itself pure from the world. We can say the creeds and confessions and catechisms forward and backward. We can be all these things and yet be death-producing machines. We become death-producing machines when we "yield ourselves to obey" Satan rather than the Lord.

When you yield yourself to God you are His slave, but this is beautiful and good because God is not a tyrant. We were created for the purpose of loving the Lord our God with all our heart and soul and mind (Matt. 22:37). He is not a tyrant; He is a loving God. To yield ourselves as a slave in this sense, as the creature yielding ourselves to the God who is there—this is beautiful. This kind of slavery produces life.

We produce either death or life as people around us either accept or reject God because of what we say to them and how we live before them. To realize that our words and actions are that significant should make us tremble. We can be either a death-producing machine or a life-producing machine for those who are still lost. And, as we have seen, we can produce either death or life in the ongoing battle between God and the devil, depending on which side we support on any given day. "Know ye not, that to whom ye yield yourselves servants to obey, his servants ye are to whom ye obey; whether of sin unto death, or of obedience unto righteousness?"

Paul has said that some believers yield themselves as servants of sin. He now expresses thanks for those who have indeed become obedient servants of God.

But God be thanked, that ye were the servants of sin, but ye have obeyed from the heart that form of doctrine which was delivered you. (6:17)

The believers in Rome had been slaves of sin, but then they had obeyed God "from the heart." Theirs was a true profession of faith, a true conversion, and it was because of "that form of doctrine which was delivered you," or, in the more literal sense of the Greek, "that form of doctrine whereto you were delivered." What was it that broke our absolute slavery to the devil? It was a certain "form of doctrine" that did so. Today there are great efforts to tone down the content of all religions, including Christianity. The resurgence of fundamentalism in reaction to this trend notwithstanding, we face a loss of content, clarity, and truth claims. This is one of the hallmarks, perhaps *the* hallmark, of our age—thinking of religious things as merely meeting psychological needs and therefore having no real content.

This is not the biblical view. The biblical view is that there is a truth, a reality, in the universe, and that it is possible to state this truth in words that humans can understand. The Bible claims to give, and in fact does give, sufficient answers to the basic questions about life in the real world. I'm not saying for a moment that we can ever exhaust this truth or understand any part of it completely; but we can understand it *truly*. It is the content of the gospel, this truth about God, mankind, and history, this "form of doctrine," which saves us. This is why Paul could so boldly proclaim to people of all intellectual levels in his day, "I am not ashamed of the gospel" (1:16). The gospel has content. It is not merely something to meet psychological needs.

Our slavery to sin was broken by the truth of the gospel. And it was broken when we "obeyed" that truth, that "form of doctrine." It wasn't just believing the gospel that saved us, but also "obeying" it. Salvation involves an obedience to the truth. It is not just obedience to God. It is also obedience to the universe as it is. When a man isn't a Christian, he is trying to live in a universe that isn't there. There is a truth in the universe, and when we accept Christ as our Savior, when we bow before the God who is there, we obey the truth of God, which is also the truth of the universe.

Our obedience to the gospel has freed us, absolutely, from the power of sin. And we can experience this freedom in the reality of our daily walk.

Being then made free from sin, ye became the servants of righteousness. (6:18)

In God's sight, on the day when He declared you justified, you were made free from sin and you became the servant of righteousness. "Now," says Paul, "live this way." The way you were freed absolutely from sin is the way to be freed now from its prevalence in your daily life. First, there is the acknowledgment of sin; then the laying hold of the blood of Jesus; and then the thankful heart and mind. These are the realities. It is through Jesus Christ our Lord, in the power of the Spirit, "reckoning ourselves in faith to be dead indeed unto sin but alive unto God through Jesus Christ our Lord" (6:11). This is what I would describe as being the "creature glorified."

Later, in 8:18-39, we will consider the subject of glorification, which is the aspect of salvation that we will enjoy forever in heaven. But even in this life we can in a sense be the "creature glorified." We have to be creatures anyway, because we can't be anything else. We are not the Creator, we are only a part of His creation, only creatures. When the humanist tries to set himself up as God, he is fooling himself. He is just a creature. He is a creature bound by human limitations, and he is a creature bound by his own sin. When, however, we freely choose to love God, we are His creatures by choice. We willingly deny ourselves (Matt. 16:24) so that we can be alive to God (Rom. 6:10).

Being the creature glorified, being God's creatures by choice, means not only rejecting the bad things about ourselves, but also not relying on the good things about ourselves, so that we want only to be alive to God, so that we want only to put ourselves in His hands and be truly His slaves. I have known people who have sought to live their Christian lives on this level, and I've always been intrigued by how hard other Christians make it for them to do so. I'm thinking of a Christian friend who is a great singer. She understands that she must be willing to be dead to the using of that voice for her own importance, even in what would seem to be God's service, in order that she might be quiet and learn what God really wants her to do. Many of her fellow Christians have made it hard for her to remain true to that decision. They tell her again and again that she ought to be using her voice in some "big" capacity for God. But our greatest human talent may have nothing to do with our greatest usefulness to God. If we could only learn this, we would be saved from ever so much pride and ever so much failure. We must be dead to the big things, even those that seem to be good, if we're to be alive to God.

There is no proof whatsoever that our greatest natural talent is going to be the key to our service. It may be so, but it also may not be so. If a person can speak to hundreds or thousands of people, he or she may need to die to self and be willing *not* to speak to hundreds or thousands of people. It is only after we are the creature glorified, in the sense of being dead to self in that which seems to be good as well as that which is bad, that we're ready to be alive and useful in God's service. "In that he liveth, he liveth unto God" (6:10). The Christian's chief calling is to love God and to be in fellowship with Him. If we are seeking to be big in the eyes of the world, we will not be alive to God.

The Christian life does not mean always being as active as possible. The Christian life means being quiet and still in our fellowship with God, so that we can be alive to Him.

If someone were to ask me what is the thing that most Christians never seem to learn, I would say this is it. Our calling as Christians is not primarily to find some particular ministry on the basis of some natural talent we possess. Our calling is to be dead to all things good and bad alike, in order to be quiet before God. And then what? And then comes the wonder. Then comes the possibility, through faith, of seeing myself as though already alive and raised from the dead, stepping back into this space-and-time historical life in the power of the Spirit, to live for the glory of the Lord, yielding myself to His hand as a weapon sharpened for His use, yielding myself to be a slave of my lovely Lord. This is what Paul is talking about. We are creatures, but we may be the creature glorified. It is possible to live now, through faith, at this one burst of moment, as though I were already raised physically from the dead.

The Bible never suggests that we will ever come to this place once for all. But can't we understand that life is only one moment at a time? On this point the existentialist speaks truthfully. There is a moment. It is the present. The calling is not for tomorrow. The calling is for this moment and every moment, because life is only a succession of moments. It is our calling in this moment, through the finished work of Christ, in the power of the Spirit, through faith, to be dead to that which is good as well as that which is bad, as though I were already in the tomb.

If suddenly a great catastrophe were to happen, if the place where you live were to be shaken with a giant earthquake and your house were to fall down upon you, you would be dead, sealed beneath the bricks and mortar. You would not be interested in and you would not be called upon to use your fleshly talents one bit. You would be dead to the whole thing. That's the way we are to live our Christian lives: As the creature glorified, in faith making our rational and moral choices, yielding ourselves to God. We can then step forth from the bricks and the timber that have buried us, as it were. We step forth with our resurrected bodies, as it were, and in this burst of the moment, we can descend down the narrow streets through the darkness, out into our world. In that moment we are yielded to God.

Paul said he knew of a man (most Bible scholars think it was Paul himself) who went to the third heaven, where God is, then came back again (2 Cor. 12:1-4). If you and I were transported to heaven right now, and we saw its glory and purity and wonder and joy, and then came back to this poor, sordid world, do you think we would ever look at the world in the same way again? Why, the richest among us would be poor, and all our earthly joys would seem like sorrows. Well, that's the way we're to live. This moment, through faith, reckon yourself to be what you will be when Jesus has raised you from the dead. This is the Christian life. To think that the Christian life is personal activity in the light of personal talent—a speaking talent, a singing talent—to think that this is all there is to it, how bad, how poor this is compared to God's real claim to be Master of our life.

Let me say it as soberly as I know how: There is no real Christian work done except as people are dead to both good and bad at that moment and are yielded only to God. People may be saved, work may be done, hospitals built, churches enlarged, organizations founded, denominations begun. But it's all defective. None of us are perfect and we have no perfect moments, when compared with the perfection of Jesus Christ. But here and there across church history, we see a flaming fire, when men and women were truly yielded to God. This is the difference between what is mundane in Christianity and what is living and what is breathing and what has shaken the souls of men.

Do you want to enjoy life? This is the only time and the only way you will ever really enjoy it. It is the very opposite of asceticism. It is not death for death's sake. It is death for life's sake. It includes service for the Lord, but it also includes the enjoyment of this present life. This is the way God intended us to live. What is the chief end of mankind but to glorify God and enjoy Him forever? There is no real glorification of God and no real enjoyment of Him, even amid so-called "Christian work," no real basic and profound enjoyment of God's present world, except as we die moment by moment, purposely yielded to God on the basis of Christ's blood, in the power of the Spirit, through faith. Then we step back into the present world in order to glorify and enjoy our God.

When we come to this place of being totally yielded to God, we will not only enjoy Him more deeply, we will find far greater enjoyment in all our natural human relationships as well. When man sinned, the great relationship of man to God was broken. But there was broken also the relationship of man to himself, of man to other men, of man to nature. At some great future moment, at the resurrection of all Christians, all these relationships will fall into perfect and glorious place; but through faith we can know something of this healing even in this present life. As we live moment by moment "unto God" as the creature glorified, all of our human relationships begin to fall substantially into place—not perfectly, mind you, but substantially and really. Your relationship with yourself, your relationship with other people, your relationship with nature: These relationships, all of them secondary to our relationship with God Himself, will be enjoyed to the extent that in that moment we are dead to all things by choice, and flamingly alive to God, in fellowship with Him and loving Him. This is what Paul is saying, and he is saying nothing less.

Paul doesn't just give us this standard for our Christian life; he also gives us the how: "through Jesus Christ our Lord" (verses 11 and 23). By the grace of God, may we know something of the reality of this, and may we increasingly help each other, that through the reality of being dead to all things we might be alive to God; that through faith we might live now as though we already had our resurrected body; and that in this moment, moment by moment, we might bring forth not death but life, to the glory of God—so that we might truly enjoy God and all that He puts before us.

Being then made free from sin, ye became the servants of righteousness. I speak after the manner of men because of the infirmity of your flesh: for as ye have yielded your members servants to uncleanness and to iniquity unto iniquity; even so now yield your members servants to righteousness unto holiness. (6:18-19)

There again is the word *yield*. Before you were saved, you yielded yourself absolutely as a slave to sin, as a slave to rebellion against God. Someone might say, "Look at that woman over there, that prostitute walking the streets; I have never yielded myself the way she has." But Paul is talking about yielding ourselves to the slavery of sin and rebellion against the God who made us. This speaks to things like prostitution, but it includes all other sins as well, everything that involves rebellion against God—intellectual and moral and practical rebellion.

"Even so now yield your members servants to righteousness unto holiness." Holiness is a calling. It is a command. One of the great weaknesses of many of the creeds, even the creeds that I love best, is the lack of emphasis on what I would call the "conscious side" of our faith, especially in terms of sanctification and the work of the Holy Spirit. Certainly we must guard against any teaching that claims the possibility of absolute perfection in the Christian life. But we should not overreact by failing to teach the necessity of consciously yielding ourselves to the Holy Spirit. This yielding is a command. It is a privilege. It is a calling. It is a duty. It is a joy.

And it is not a mechanical thing. We of all people should know it is not mechanical. We must reject the twentieth-century concept of man as a machine. We live in a world of real personalities. God is a personal God. Our relationship to Him is above all individual and personal. We are not machines. He is not a machine. He calls upon us to act in our capacity as moral and rational creatures, to yield ourselves to Him.

For when ye were the servants of sin, ye were free from righteousness. (6:20)

Before we came to faith in Christ, we were free from all righteousness, but the end of this freedom was absolute death. As James explains, "When lust hath conceived, it bringeth forth sin: and sin, when it is finished, bringeth forth death" (James 1:15). Before you became a Christian, you may have thought yourself free and independent, but in reality you were bringing forth death. You were a death-producing machine, to yourself and to everyone and everything else. You were a rebel in God's creation, bringing forth death to yourself and to other people.

A better translation of the Greek would be, "For when ye were servants of sin, you were free as far as righteousness is concerned." In other words, before you were saved, you certainly were no slave to righteousness! It had no claim upon you at all. In fact, you never really did anything righteous. There were comparative "goodnesses," but no real righteousness. You were completely free from righteousness.

What fruit had ye then in those things whereof ye are now ashamed? for the end of those things is death. (6:21)

"What fruit were you having?" asks Paul. And the answer must be, "I was having plenty of fruit!" Before becoming Christians, we did many things of which we can now only be ashamed. Before coming to Christ, much to our shame, we were totally "free from righteousness" (verse 20).

But now being made free from sin, and become servants to God, ye have your fruit unto holiness, and the end everlasting life. (6:22)

Before you were a Christian, you were totally free from righteousness. Now, in Jesus Christ, you are also totally free, absolutely free—but this time it is freedom from sin! Through justification, the guilt is gone. We have become slaves to God. That's what we should be now, after we have accepted Christ as our Savior. And our new life in Christ should produce fruit. ". . . ye have your fruit unto holiness, and the end everlasting life." Paul is choosing his words carefully here. Before we were Christians, the "end" of our way of life was "death" (verse 21). Now, the end of what we are and what we should be, is "everlasting life" (verse 22). It is not just by chance that the last word of verse 21 is "death" and the last word of verse 22 is "life."

Then comes the well-known verse 23. As we have noted, it isn't a mistake that it is in this particular place rather than with the earlier section on justification.

For the wages of sin is death; but the gift of God is eternal life through Jesus Christ our Lord. (6:23)

If, in considering the last few verses, you have come to the point of despair, wondering, "Am I really a Christian at all?" Paul now quiets your heart. He reminds you that in the absolute sense, in God's sight, having accepted Christ as your Savior, you are now free from sin and your ultimate destiny is everlasting life, "through Jesus Christ our Lord."

Paul quiets our hearts, but he reminds us that as Christians we are producing something all the time, and that it's possible, even after becoming a Christian, to offer ourselves to the devil's service. Even as a Christian, I can choose the wrong side in the battle of the heavenlies.

The key to producing life rather than death is in yielding ourselves to God. "Neither yield ye your members as arms of unrighteousness unto sin; but yield yourselves unto God, as those that are alive from the dead" (verse 13). "Know ye not, that to whom ye yield yourselves servants to obey, his servants ye are to whom ye obey?" (verse 16). "As ye have yielded your members servants to uncleanness and to iniquity unto iniquity; even so now yield your members servants to righteousness unto holiness" (verse 19).

We tend to think of yielding as a passive thing, yet repeatedly in these verses it is a command: "Yield yourselves." Perhaps an illustration would shed some light on the active nature of this yielding.

When the angel came to Mary and said, "You are going to bear the Messiah," Mary had three options. She could have said, "I won't," and she wouldn't have borne the baby. She could have said, "I'll do it in my own strength," and she wouldn't have borne the baby Jesus. But she had a third possibility, which she chose. She said, "Behold the handmaid of the Lord; be it unto me according to thy word" (Luke 1:38). She handed her body to the Lord to be the womb out of which the body of the Messiah would be born, and He was born.

You and I have the possibility every moment of our lives to hand ourselves to the Lord, to be that out of which He will bring forth all that is wonderful. "Yield yourselves" (6:13) is an "active passivity." People are naturally afraid of that which is only passive, but we should be afraid of that which is only active as well. Our calling is to active passivity. God will bring about our sanctification, but we are called to be active partners in the process as we yield ourselves to Him.

And as we do so, we will discover the possibility of a truly Christian life, both now and in eternity, "through Jesus Christ our Lord."

10

THE CHRISTIAN'S STRUGGLE
WITH SIN: II
(7:1-25)

Through the years there has been quite a debate among Christians concerning the question of to whom Paul addressed chapter 7 of Romans. Some Christians believe, to varying degrees, that sinless perfection can be achieved in this life, subsequent to a "second work of grace" or a "baptism of the Holy Spirit," or some such terminology. Those who hold such beliefs obviously cannot apply chapter 7 to Christians, because Paul presents himself here as being far from perfect.

Certainly, knowing to whom Paul is writing this chapter would make a great difference in how we understand and apply it. Is it written to the unsaved person, or to the Christian, or perhaps to both? In considering this question, the first thing to notice is where this chapter is placed. It is not placed in the section on justification (1:18—4:25), but in the section dealing with sanctification (5:1—8:17). From its location, we would naturally expect that it is written primarily to the Christian.

I would suggest, however, that the ultimate answer to this question is found in something we have been seeing throughout our study of

Romans. We have seen that the principles that apply to justification apply to sanctification as well. There are not three separate salvations but just one. In this larger context, we should expect to find that chapter 7 applies not just to the unbeliever and not just to the believer, but to both.

That chapter 7 applies to believers as much as to unbelievers is also suggested by comparing Paul's message in this chapter with something he says in Galatians, which as we have noted is somewhat parallel to Romans. In Galatians Paul says, "For the flesh lusteth against the Spirit, and the Spirit against the flesh: and these are contrary the one to the other: so that ye cannot do the things that ye would" (Gal. 5:17). This, as we shall see, is exactly what Paul says in 7:14-24. Anyone who thinks that Romans 7 applies only to the nonbeliever has to explain why Paul said exactly the same thing in Galatians, where clearly he is writing to Christians.

We must assume, therefore, that the principles Paul will explain in chapter 7 apply to believers and nonbelievers alike. When I have accepted Christ as my Savior, I am born again. I have passed from death to life. There is a future salvation, which Paul will speak of in chapter 8, wherein I will find perfection. But in the present life I am not perfect, and the battle continues. I am still a rational and moral creature. I am called to love God. Sometimes I do love Him, and sometimes I don't. Therefore, while Paul's argument in chapter 7 certainly applies to the nonbeliever, it applies to me and to all believers as well. As we begin our study of chapter 7, let's allow it to speak to our hearts.

In chapter 6 we saw that *reckon*, *reign*, and *yield* were key words. From 7:1 to 8:17 we will find that a key word is *law*.

Know ye not, brethren, (for I speak to them that know the law,) how that the law hath dominion over a man as long as he liveth? (7:1)

Here we see the key word law occurring twice, and we also see a key concept we discovered back in chapter 4: ". . . as long as he liveth." Paul is continuing his comparison of life and death. If you were to circle these two words, as I have done in my own Bible from

4:17 down through 8:17, you would be surprised how many times they occur.

For the woman which hath an husband is bound by the law to her husband so long as he liveth; but if the husband be dead, she is loosed from the law of her husband. (7:2)

Continuing with the themes of law and life and death, Paul says that, according to the law, a woman must stay married to her husband as long as he lives, but after he dies she is free to remarry.

So then if, while her husband liveth, she be married to another man, she shall be called an adulteress: but if her husband be dead, she is free from the law; so that she is no adulteress, though she be married to another man. (7:3)

Paul is writing to people who know the law, its constraints and limits. Now he is about to draw a profound application from this simple illustration of the law's reach into marriage.

Wherefore, my brethren, ye also are become dead to the law by the body of Christ; that ye should be married to another, even to him who is raised from the dead, that we should bring forth fruit unto God. (7:4)

Two things happened when we accepted Christ as our Savior: We became dead to the law, and we became married to Christ. Before we accepted Christ as our Savior, the law had a proper hold over us. But when we accepted Christ, the law's hold over us was broken—broken as completely as though the husband had died and now the wife is free.

Paul presses his illustration only as far as it logically applies. A widowed woman might choose not to remarry. But in terms of our spiritual life, there is no such thing as neutrality. The only way to be free from the bondage of the law is to be "married to another," that is, to Christ. As we saw in chapter 6, as Christians and as human beings we are always yielding ourselves to something. We are always slaves to something. We are not allowed to be neutral. Likewise, the only way for us to be free from the law is to accept Christ as our Savior, and if we have accepted Christ as our Savior, we are in fact dead to the law.

Now, just who is this Christ to whom we are married? It is "him who is raised from the dead" (7:4). We should never fasten our mind exclusively on the dead Christ. We should never live exclusively under the shadow of the cross. Jesus died once for all, and it was finished. The death of Jesus is very important, but He is not still dead. When we have accepted Christ as our Savior, we are not married to a dead Christ, we are married to a living Christ. If a bride were married to a dead man, she could produce no children. But if she is married to a living man, she can produce children. We are married to a living Christ in order "that we should bring forth fruit unto God" (7:4).

Having accepted Christ as our Savior, we are united with Christ, not in a vague or unproductive sense; we are united with a resurrected, living Christ, and as the bride of this living Christ we have the high and wonderful calling of bringing forth fruit to God. Christ is the vine, and we are the branches, abiding in Him, bringing forth fruit. We are to be like Mary, yielding herself to God and thereby, in an active passivity, bringing forth the body of the Messiah from her own body. This is where we are to live. The law's hold over us has been broken, not just so that we can be free from the law but so that, being united to the resurrected Christ, we will bring forth fruit to God.

As Jesus said, "If you abide in me, you shall bring forth much fruit." If the bride is going to bring forth children, it isn't sufficient for her merely to give herself to the bridegroom on the wedding day. She must give herself in love time after time, and that's when children are born into the home. We are to give ourselves to Christ, not just once on the day when we accept Him as our Savior, but over and over again, constantly, moment by moment. And when we do that, He will bring forth fruit through us.

Eastern mysticism is quite popular in our day, but the mysticism of Christianity is far higher. The mysticism of the East demands a loss of personality. In Hindu mythology, when Shiva fell in love with a mortal woman, he put his arms around her and she was gone. Not so with Christianity. When we become Christians, we do not in any way lose our personality. God created us as rational and moral beings, and as He reveals His truth to us He addresses us as rational beings. The bride, who has said yes to the bridegroom on their marriage day, continues to say yes or no to him throughout their married life, and out of her choices of saying yes or no there will be the birth or non-birth of children. Likewise we, as rational and moral beings, have the high calling of saying yes or no to God each day of our lives. We have the high calling of giving ourselves in love to Christ, as He produces the fruit through us. This is what, in the last chapter, we called the "creature glorified."

Christian mysticism is based on the reality of what theologians call our "mystical union" with Christ. God the Father becomes our Father; we are indwelt by the Holy Spirit; but, according to the New Testament, there is a mystical union between the individual believer and Jesus Christ—not a mystical union that diminishes our own personality, but quite the contrary. Remaining rational and moral beings with a call to love God, we who have had the chains of the law broken now have the high calling of giving ourselves to Jesus Christ. As we do this He produces His fruit in us. "Abide in me, and ye shall bring forth much fruit."

It is simply not possible for us to bring forth this fruit in our own strength. You remember we were told in 6:11 that we should "reckon" ourselves to be dead to sin. We were then told in 6:13 to "yield" ourselves as instruments of righteousness to God. No finer picture could be given of the love of the bride giving herself to the bridegroom than the word *yield*. No finer word could be used of Mary giving herself to the work of the Spirit so that He produced the Messiah in her than the word *yield*. It is active passivity. "Yield yourself," says Paul. To whom? Yield yourself to the one to whom you are married—to the resurrected, living Christ.

For when we were in the flesh, the motions of sins, which were by the law, did work in our members to bring forth fruit unto death. (7:5)

"Motions" is more accurately translated "passions." Before we became Christians, the "passions of sin," which were aroused by the law, brought forth fruit "unto death." "The wages of sin is death." Before we were saved, the very law itself produced death.

But now we are delivered from the law, that being dead wherein we were held; that we should serve in newness of spirit, and not in the oldness of the letter. (7:6)

Having been freed from the law and the death it produces, we are now not just to be free, but to serve. How do we do this? Through the agency of the Holy Spirit, thereby knowing the power of Christ. We are not saved just for the sake of being saved, not just to be somehow neutral. We are saved so that we might become one with Christ, and that He might bring forth fruit through us. We are saved to serve, "not in the oldness of the letter . . . but in newness of spirit." If we are going to bring forth fruit, we can't do it in the old way. As we have seen over and over again, the principle holds true both before and after we're saved: We can't save ourselves by keeping the law; and as Christians, after we're saved, we can't bring forth fruit to God merely by keeping the law. We can't do it in our own strength, but only "through Jesus Christ our Lord."

Too often we give new Christians the impression that they can automatically begin exhibiting Christian character. If we try on our own to develop Christian character, we will never make it. It is no more possible to keep the law in our own strength after we become a Christian than it was possible for us to be saved in the first place by keeping the law. It would be like a little branch taking off and saying, "I am the branch and I will bring forth fruit." Such a thing simply does not happen. The little branch needs the connection with the vine. It would be just as if a bride would say, "I'm married now, so I can have children," and then would go her own way, without her husband. There is no birth unless the bride gives herself to the bridegroom. When she does give herself to the bridegroom, from the two of them comes the child. And that's exactly what Paul is saying to us here. If our attitude is, "Now that I am a Christian, I can keep the law," we'll fall flat on our face.

What shall we say then? Is the law sin? (7:7a)

Paul knew that this question would arise among the believers in Rome, and we hear the same question raised today. There are those who teach that, after we have accepted Christ as our Savior, we are completely done with the law. Paul does not say this. The law has its place. The law isn't bad; the law is good, but in its place. Paul discusses this at length in Galatians. For instance, he asks, "Having begun in the Spirit, are ye now made perfect by the flesh?" (Gal. 3:3); that is, "Are you now made perfect by your own human efforts to keep the law?" The answer is obviously no. You couldn't be saved this way, and as a Christian you can't live this way. It is not honoring to the resurrected Christ, who waits patiently to be our bridegroom, to try to produce the fruit ourselves without Him.

What shall we say then? Is the law sin? God forbid. Nay, I had not known sin, but by the law: for I had not known lust, except the law had said, Thou shalt not covet. (7:7)

Paul is apparently telling of his own pre-conversion experience. "I would not have known I was a sinner," says Paul, "except for the law." Actually, the words "lust" and "covet" are from the same Greek root, and both could be translated "covet." It is interesting that, in giving this personal example, Paul quotes the only one of the Ten Commandments that deals exclusively with an internal manifestation of sin. It was this Tenth Commandment that showed Paul that he was a sinner. It is possible to fool ourselves and think we are keeping the first nine commandments, because we can think of them as merely external. Of course, none of them are merely external, as Jesus clearly showed, but we could mistakenly think of them in that way. But there is one of the Ten Commandments that is in no way external. It is totally, intrinsically internal: "Thou shalt not covet." In the Jewish religion as it had developed by the time of Christ, there was a constant tendency to make individual laws external and therefore keepable. But there was one commandment that Paul knew he could not keep, and that was, "Thou shalt not covet." Whenever he thought about that commandment, he realized he was a sinner who needed salvation. The law is useful as a schoolmaster to bring us to Christ (Gal. 3:24). However, if we try to live in our own strength in the light of the law, we've missed the whole point.

It is good, in the long term, that the law shows us our sinfulness and our need of salvation. In the short term, however, this new self-awareness can be a very disagreeable experience.

But sin, taking occasion by the commandment, wrought in me all manner of concupiscence [coveting]. For without the law sin was dead. For I was alive without the law once: but when the commandment came, sin revived, and I died. And the commandment, which was ordained to life, I found to be unto death. For sin, taking occasion by the commandment, deceived me, and by it slew me. Wherefore the law is holy, and the commandment holy, and just, and good. (7:8-12)

The law is good because it shows us how far short of perfection and goodness we fall. But precisely because it does show us how imperfect and sinful we are, when we seriously look at the law, we cannot honestly think of ourselves anymore as basically good. In that sense, the law "kills" us (verse 11). You'll recall that Jesus said He had come not to save the righteous but to save sinners (Matt. 9:13), meaning that only those who realize they are sinners will respond to His offer of salvation. That is somewhat parallel to what Paul is saying here. He is not saying that there was ever a time when he hadn't sinned. Rather, he is saying that, when he began to look at himself in the light of the law, he gained a new understanding of just how sinful he really was. In that sense, the law killed Paul and will kill anyone who gives it serious consideration. The law is a schoolmaster to bring us to Christ. When we see ourselves in the light of the law, we are killed by the realization of our sinfulness, and thus we are ready to hear the gospel.

Was then that which is good made death unto me? God forbid. But sin, that it might appear sin, working death in me by that which is good; that sin by the commandment might become exceeding sinful. (7:13)

The law was given so that sin "might appear sin," so that it might be seen to be "exceeding sinful." It is through the law that a man comes to realize his guilt and therefore his need of a Savior. And, of course, even as Christians we need constantly to see our sinfulness and our need of grace. The Ten Commandments have a purpose for us. The commandments of the New Testament have a purpose for us. The Sermon on the Mount has a purpose for us. It is wrong for the Bible-believing Christian to read the Bible's many commandments and then just go home and go to bed. Being under grace is not a license to care-lessness and indifference. When I read the great moral teachings of Christ, it should bring me to my knees as I realize all the times when I have been a hearer rather than a doer of His Word (Matt. 7:24-29). I need constantly to bring my shortcomings under the covering of Christ's blood. I need the fresh cleansing and forgiveness. I need to go back to my bridegroom's arms, so that He might bring forth fruit in me.

Let's recall again what we learned in chapter 6: It is possible for the Christian to be a slave of the devil, to give himself as a weapon into the hands of the devil in his battle against God. To avoid doing this, we must let the law speak to our hearts. This is 10,000 miles away from any notion of sinless perfection. When I read the Ten Commandments and the Sermon on the Mount, it should bring me as a Christian to my knees again to claim the blood of Christ, to be for-given and to say thank you for Christ's finished work. And I shouldn't just stop there. This is only the front hallway, so to speak. Having been brought to my knees by this fresh awareness of my sin, I need to give myself anew to the Savior, so that He might fulfill the requirements of the law in me.

Sin is shown to be really sinful whenever I truly understand the law, whether that be when I first turn to Christ for justification, or later on in my Christian life. We Bible-believing Christians, who believe we have been forgiven and have the assurance of eternal life, can become hard and complacent toward sin. We can forget the sinfulness of sin. We need to be constantly brought up short to the awful fact of what sin is. We need to realize that when we sin as Christians, we receive the wages of sin, which is death. Not that we'll be lost again, but we begin producing death to all those around us. We constantly need, through a tender conscience and through the work of the Holy Spirit, reminders of the awfulness of sin.

We can put our emphasis so much on the "once-for-allness" of salvation, which is so wonderful and beautiful, that we forget that salvation is a flowing stream that includes an ongoing process of sanctification—a process that is not automatic, but that involves clear choices on our part. As I study the Ten Commandments and the Sermon on the Mount, as I look at the commandments of Paul and look at the example of Christ's life, the sinfulness of sin will become apparent if I am sensitive and letting the Holy Spirit speak to me. I will flee to the shed blood to claim God's cleansing in this moment, to commit myself anew to Christ. Then and only then comes the wonderful promise of verse 4, that through my marriage to Christ, He will "bring forth fruit unto God" through me.

For we know that the law is spiritual: but I am carnal, sold under sin. (7:14)

The law is spiritual. It has a good purpose. I am free from the law when I accept Jesus as my Savior, in the sense that it no longer binds me (7:1-4). I am no longer condemned by the law. Still, however, the law sets before me the character of God. The law sets before me what it means to love God. And as I look at the law, I realize that "I am carnal, sold under sin." The problem is not the law. The problem is me.

Beginning with verse 15, Paul describes his own ongoing struggle with sin even after becoming a Christian.

For that which I do I allow not: for what I would, that do I not; but what I hate, that do I. (7:15)

The word translated "allow" is really "know." "For that which I do I know not." In other words, "I don't understand why I do the things I do."

If then I do that which I would not, I consent unto the law that it is good. (7:16)

Paul has asked, "Is the law sin?" (7:7) and has shown that in fact the law is good, especially in that it shows us our sinfulness and therefore our need for Christ. Now Paul is saying the same thing from a slightly different angle: Whenever Paul does something wrong and then realizes that it is wrong, he is in essence acknowledging that some kind of law is needed.

As we have seen, even the most blatant materialist and the most outspoken atheist make certain moral judgments against others and then sin against those same moral principles themselves—and they know that they are doing this (2:1). They know they are violating their own conscience. They know they should be doing better. Now, in 7:16, Paul says that this very realization that we should be doing better shows us that the law is good and is a necessary thing—even as it condemns us.

Man is a rational and moral being. No one can live as though the world were completely amoral. There are those who try to live this way, but ultimately everyone has to have some kind of moral standard. In verse 16 Paul is saying, "Even if a man wants to say that the law is evil, the very fact that he desires to do better demonstrates that the law is good." Even the nonbeliever knows that he should not covet. The very fact that he knows this, and the very fact that the law says, "Thou shalt not covet," shows that the law is good. Even those today who try to deny all moral absolutes hold up self-sacrifice as a moral virtue. Whenever anyone acknowledges something to be a moral virtue, they are acknowledging that we need moral absolutes. They are acknowledging that the law is good. A man who rejects the Bible recently said to me, "Well, what we need to do is to show people a sense of love." Everyone has within themselves this sense that there are some things they simply should do. And surely this condemns them, because they know that they don't live up to their own standards. People can talk of self-sacrifice, but I'd like to be in their homes for a few days and see how self-sacrificing they really are! None of us can perfectly live up to our own standards. Our own standards condemn us as surely as the law condemns us.

Paul continues to describe his personal struggle with sin:

If then I do that which I would not ... Now then it is no more I that do it, but sin that dwelleth in me. (7:16a, 17)

Paul is not looking lightly upon sin, as if to say, "Oh well, I can sin as a Christian and it really doesn't matter, because I'm not the one doing it." Paul is not saying any such thing. Rather, he is saying, "When I constantly do those things that I don't want to do, I'm just like a slave." When we sin, we become separated both from God and from ourselves, so that with Paul we feel like saying, "I'm not the one doing this! I'm just a slave to sin." A person going through a nervous breakdown will seem extremely separated from himself, but all of us feel that way sometimes, especially in the area of good desires. Even the most amoral people have good moral desires, and when they find themselves unable to live up to those good desires, they like Paul feel separated from themselves and enslaved to sin. "It is no more I that do it, but sin that dwelleth in me."

Paul develops this as he goes on.

For I know that in me (that is, in my flesh,) dwelleth no good thing. (7:18a)

All humans have good moral desires within themselves. They all like to do good things for other people. They all want a better world. Yet, contrary to their good desires, they find themselves enslaved to sin. When Adam sinned, he didn't stop being the moral and rational creature God had made him to be. He continued being a moral and rational creature. It is because man *does* have a conscience that he is condemned, because as he makes moral judgments against others, he doesn't live up to those standards himself (2:1). God writes down those judgments and holds them up to judge him. As people have good desires but don't live up to them, they are condemned.

For I know that in me (that is, in my flesh,) dwelleth no good thing: for to will is present with me; but how to perform that which is good I find not. (7:18)

Notice again, it is "I," it is Paul himself who has this struggle. Nonbelievers have this battle, but so do we who are Christians. Paul wants to do what is right; it's the "how" that escapes him.

For the good that I would I do not: but the evil which I would not, that I do. Now if I do that I would not, it is no more I that do it, but sin that dwelleth in me. (7:19-20)

Here again we see Paul the slave to sin. It is the conflict that each of us knows only too well—the conflict between our ideals and the reality of what we are. The most debased man or woman in the world has ideals, and there's a conflict between the ideal and the reality.

I find then a law, that, when I would do good, evil is present with me. (7:21)

"Law" in this particular verse does not mean the Law of Moses, but simply a principle of life, similar to a law of nature—something that is true for all people. Ever since Adam committed that first sin, this is where we humans are.

For I delight in the law of God after the inward man: But I see another law in my members, warring against the law of my mind, and bringing me into captivity to the law of sin which is in my members. (7:22-23)

Paul's struggle against sin has given him a divided personality. On the one hand he "delights" in God's law, but on the other hand there is "another law in my members" that is constantly warring against his delight in God's law. Through Christ we have become justified before God. His Word informs, calls, corrects, and encourages us. Yet in our body, we are still part of a fallen world. Legally, our problem of guilt before God has been resolved, but factually we are still waiting for the full redemption that will be ours only when Christ returns. Till then, our battle with sin continues. It is truly a "captivity" to sin, and Paul longs for deliverance.

O wretched man that I am! who shall deliver me from the body of this death? (7:24)

Our problem with sin isn't just some theoretical problem, and Paul's language in this verse brings it right down to the physical level, here in this space-and-time historical world in which we live: "Who shall deliver me from the body of this death?"

Paul will now answer that question, in words that should by now have a familiar ring:

I thank God through Jesus Christ our Lord. So then with the mind I myself serve the law of God; but with the flesh the law of sin. (7:25)

The answer, for Paul, can be found only "through Jesus Christ our Lord." The law is not enough. There must be a yielding to the power of Christ. Paul comes back to what he said in 6:11: "Likewise reckon ye also yourselves to be dead indeed unto sin, but alive unto God through Jesus Christ our Lord." And again in 6:23: "For the wages of sin is death, but the gift of God is eternal life through Jesus Christ our Lord." As we have seen, this verse applies in a special way to that time in the past when we first put our trust in Christ. But it applies to us also in the midst of the battle, in the reality of our everyday lives as Christians. It applies not just in our ivory towers or at Bible conferences, but it applies to me when I walk out into the dark streets of Lausanne. "O wretched man that I am," but then, "I thank God through Jesus Christ our Lord."

As we have followed Paul through this seventh chapter, we have seen him wrestling with the same problems that we wrestle with every day. The picture he paints is certainly not one of the possibility of sinless perfection, but neither is it one of hopeless defeat. For we, like Paul, can, "thank God through Jesus Christ our Lord"—once for all for our justification, but then also as a moment by moment thing as we pursue sanctification.

We need the power of Christ for our lives, whether for justification or for sanctification, and it is only possible to have this power through Jesus Christ, and the agency by which we acquire this power is the indwelling Holy Spirit.

There shouldn't be a chapter break after 7:25, for the thought flows right on. As we come to chapter 8, we'll find that we are introduced in a flaming way to the agency of the Holy Spirit, who is the point of contact between us and the power of the resurrected Christ.

11

LIFE IN THE SPIRIT
(8:1-17)

෮

s we look at the first seventeen verses of Romans 8, we
should keep in mind that it is the conclusion of Paul's teaching on sanctification, which began at 5:1. Throughout our
study of Romans, and especially in chapters 6 and 7, we have seen that
the law is not enough to save us, and it is not enough to sustain us after
we have been saved. Both before and after we become Christians we
need the power of Christ through the agency of the Holy Spirit who
lives within us. In chapter 8, Paul introduces us to the Holy Spirit
specifically as the agent of Christ's power in our lives.

Chapter 7 has shown that the law itself is not bad but good (7:14).
The law is good, for it shows us that we are bad. And since we are
what we are, even after we have accepted Christ as our Savior, it is not
enough merely to try in our own strength to keep the law. Therefore,
we have found that the key to the unity of these chapters on sanctification is the word *through*. "The wages of sin is death, but the free gift
of God is eternal life *through* Jesus Christ our Lord" (6:23). Before
that, we read, "Likewise reckon ye also yourselves to be dead indeed
unto sin, but alive unto God *through* Jesus Christ our Lord" (6:11).
And then chapter 7 concludes with Paul's great exclamation, "O

wretched man that I am! who shall deliver me from the body of this death? I thank God *through* Jesus Christ our Lord" (7:24-25). We can sum up these verses quite simply: We can live the Christian life only *through* the power of Jesus Christ. We need the power of the resurrected Christ (7:4). He is not the dead Christ. He is the living, ascended, and glorified Christ, and it is only through His power that we can live the Christian life. "I thank God *through* Jesus Christ our Lord."

But what does all of this mean? When Paul says, "I thank God through Jesus Christ our Lord," are we just to somehow imagine Christ or try to follow His example? No, there is something much deeper than this, because the power of Jesus Christ is ours to draw upon through the agency of the indwelling third person of the Trinity, the Holy Spirit. As we have seen, this is the true Christian mysticism. We learned in chapter 6 that we are to die to ourselves, but then, through faith, we are to live in this present life as though we had already been raised from the dead. This is mysticism of the highest order. It does not deny the validity of the present seen world. It does not, like Hinduism, consider history as merely the dream of God. Nor is it like some kinds of monasticism, which would acknowledge the reality of the present world but find very little value in it. Unlike these so-called mysticisms, true Christian mysticism means that, within this present life, living in the real world, I have the holy calling to be the creature glorified. It means that, through faith, I am to die to all things both good and bad, but then to take my resurrected body, as though I had already been raised physically from the dead, and step back into this present world, to serve in the power of the indwelling Spirit.

Chapter 7 built on this concept. I am to be committed to Christ as my bridegroom. I am to let this glorified, living Christ bring forth the fruit unto God through me.

As we think about becoming the creature glorified, we can think of it as happening in three steps. The first step, which we dealt with in chapter 6, involves imagining that we, like Paul, have gone to the "third heaven," the heaven where God is. If, after seeing the purity and beauty and wonder of heaven, we were to come back to this world, how poor this world would seem by comparison.

The second step, which we considered while looking at chapter 7, goes far beyond this first step. It isn't as though we are just to imagine this, but in reality we are to be willing to be dead to all things, including things that seem to be good in themselves, so that we might be alive to God and in fellowship with Him, and then step back as though with resurrected bodies into this present space-and-time historical world.

We have already considered to some extent the third step in experiencing the reality of the creature glorified: We must realize that we don't have to do it in our own strength. Chapter 7 deals with this in terms of Christ being the bridegroom and we individually being His bride (7:4). It is the strength and work of the resurrected Christ that is bringing forth fruit in us. Now in chapter 8 we will find that the agency whereby this can happen is the Holy Spirit who indwells us. This is the "how" of becoming the creature glorified. We become the creature glorified "through Jesus Christ our Lord" (6:11, 23; 7:25), and this happens "through the Spirit" (8:13).

You may remember the great apostolic benediction, "The grace of the Lord Jesus Christ, and the love of God, and the communion of the Holy Ghost, be with you all" (2 Cor. 13:14). All too often this is something that's just rattled off as sort of a period at the end of a church service, signaling that it's time to get up and go home. But this is a profound statement and should always be said with deep worship: "The grace of the Lord Jesus Christ, the love of God, and the communion of the Holy Spirit." The French translate it as, "the communication of the Holy Spirit." There is to be a communication of the Holy Spirit with the individual Christian in the present life, and in a sense the Holy Spirit's communication carries with it the entire Trinity. In a sense the Spirit is the Trinity's *agent* in communicating with us humans. If I am going to walk in this present life according to my high calling as a Christian, I need a strength higher than my own strength. I need the power of Christ. How is this power of Christ to be mine? It's not enough just to imagine that I have this power. It's not even enough to take the second step and reckon myself dead to sin and alive to Christ. There must also be a communication of the power of Christ to me through the agency of the Holy Spirit who indwells me.

To borrow the fervent expression of Paul in 6:2, "God forbid" that we should talk about these things as just cold theological truths. There is a deep calling here to our whole person—to the will, to the mind, to the emotions. Through the agency of the Holy Spirit, there is a point of contact between the whole Trinity and the whole person. As moral, rational beings, beings who think and act and feel, we are to experience the reality of the indwelling Holy Spirit in our thoughts, in our actions, and in our emotions. The Holy Spirit indwells us, and He is personal. He is the line of contact, the means of communication between the whole Trinity and the whole person.

"Through Jesus Christ our Lord" now begins to take on real meaning. Don't you see how far away this is from the current theological trend of turning all things into merely abstractions and ideas? You see how far away this is from the new transcendentalism, which deals only with myth and the nonhistorical. We are indwelt by the Holy Spirit. He is the agent in our present space-and-time historical relationship with God. "Where is your Christian character?" We must rebuff such a question. Our strength as Christians is not in our Christian character. It is in the power of Jesus Christ crucified, raised, ascended, glorified, the living Christ. And how is this power to be laid hold of? Are we merely to think about it? No! We are indwelt by the Holy Spirit, and He is the agent who brings us in touch with the whole Trinity.

Through the indwelling of the Holy Spirit, our relationship with Christ, as Paul describes it, becomes a glorious reality: "Wherefore, my brethren, ye also are become dead to the law by the body of Christ; that ye should be married to another, even to him that was raised from the dead, that we should bring forth fruit unto God" (7:4). The Spirit who indwells us is our point of contact with the resurrected Christ. Paul has shown us the need for this power of Christ, whereby we might bring forth fruit to God. Now, in chapter 8, he is introducing us to the agent, the indwelling Holy Spirit.

Just before His ascension Jesus said, "All power is given unto me in heaven and in earth" (Matt. 28:18). He also said, "Ye shall receive power, after that the Holy Ghost is come upon you" (Acts 1:8). We are promised the power of the resurrected Christ, through the agency of the Holy Spirit. The church was told to wait for the coming of the Holy Spirit (Acts 1:8), because this was to be their means of communication with the power of the resurrected Christ. The power is not something within ourselves. It isn't as if at Pentecost the Church became something great within itself. It is not that any individual Christian becomes something special within himself or herself. The power is always the power of the resurrected Christ. Having accepted Christ as my Savior, I am invited moment by moment to draw upon His power. Since I can trust Christ to have conquered the darkness of death at Calvary, to have saved my soul, and to someday open the doors of heaven and receive me there, I am now invited, moment by moment, through faith, to know His resurrected power in my present life.

This eighth chapter, which deals so specifically with the Holy Spirit, is also the one that makes very plain that we're not perfect yet. The day of final redemption is still in the future, but that does not change the fact that we are called, through faith, in the present life, to draw upon the present reality of the power of the crucified, risen, victorious Christ.

Law, *life*, and *death* have been key words in this section on sanctification. In chapter 8 Paul will continue to emphasize all three of these key words.

There is therefore now no condemnation to them which are in Christ Jesus, who walk not after the flesh, but after the Spirit. For the law of the Spirit of life in Christ Jesus hath made me free from the law of sin and death. (8:1-2)

If we have accepted Christ as our Savior, we will never have to face the prospect of eternal condemnation. This first verse of chapter 8 should remind us of the first verse of chapter 5, with which Paul introduced this section on sanctification: "Therefore being justified by faith, we have peace with God through our Lord Jesus Christ." He is really saying the same thing here in 8:1, and he will return to this great theme in verses 18-39: Eternal life is forever. Eternal life is eternal. If we have taken Jesus as our Savior, our condemnation is past forever.

For the law of the Spirit of life in Christ Jesus hath made me free from the law of sin and death. (8:2)

We just heard Paul ask, "Who shall deliver me from the body of this death?" (7:24). And now comes the answer: "The law of the Spirit of life in Christ Jesus has [once for all!] made me free from the law of sin and death" (8:2). Because I have accepted Jesus as my Savior, my condemnation is past. I am once for all free from the law of sin and death.

For what the law could not do, in that it was weak through the flesh, God sending his own Son in the likeness of sinful flesh, and for sin, condemned sin in the flesh. (8:3)

The law is good (7:14), but there is something it cannot do. It cannot save me. Why? Because it "was weak through the flesh." The law is all right in itself, but it is weak through the flesh, that is, through my flesh and your flesh. We can't keep the law. Therefore "God, sending his own Son in the likeness of sinful flesh and for sin, condemned sin in the flesh." We couldn't keep the law, but Christ did.

"God sending his own Son in the likeness of sinful flesh, and for sin [by a sacrifice for sin], condemned sin in the flesh." By emphasizing that Christ condemned sin specifically "in the flesh," Paul seems to be reminding us again that he is talking about our present life, in our present bodies. He's talking about life in the real world of real people like you and me.

God sending his own Son . . . condemned sin in the flesh: that the righteousness of the law might be fulfilled in us, who walk not after the flesh, but after the Spirit. (8:3b-4)

We were saved, not just to go to heaven, but also "in order that the righteousness [the righteous demands] of the law might be fulfilled in us." There was something that we as humans could not do (verse 3a), so God sent His own Son in the likeness of sinful flesh to do it (verse 3b). And then verse 4 spells out exactly what God sent His Son to do: "In order that the righteous demands of the law might be fulfilled in us." We are saved in order to go to heaven, but we are also saved in order to keep the law, something we could not have done previously and something we cannot do even now in our own strength—but something we *can* do through the power of Christ and with the help of the indwelling Holy Spirit.

God saved us so that we can one day be with Him forever in heaven. But He also saved us *in order* that "we may walk in newness of life" (6:4), *in order* that "we should bring forth fruit unto God" (7:4), and *in order* that "the righteous demands of the law might be fulfilled in us" (8:4). We can do all these things, not in our own power, but through Christ and through His indwelling Spirit.

. . . who walk not after the flesh, but after the Spirit. (8:4b)

This latter half of verse 4 emphasizes that sanctification involves a conscious involvement on our part. Salvation and the gift of the Holy Spirit are once-for-all things (verses 1-4a). But if salvation is going to have any reality in my everyday life, I must think also about walking according to the Spirit (verse 4b). We have seen over and over again that the Bible does not deal with us as machines. We have significance. We have choice. We must have the indwelling of the Holy Spirit. But having the indwelling of the Holy Spirit does not then make it automatic. There is a conscious side to sanctification. We are indwelt by the Holy Spirit. That is wonderful. But now the call is to walk according to the Spirit.

. . . who walk not after the flesh, but after the Spirit. For they that are after the flesh do mind the things of the flesh; but they that are after the Spirit the things of the Spirit. For to be carnally minded is death; but to be spiritually minded is life and peace. Because the carnal mind is enmity against God: for it is not subject to the law of God, neither indeed can be. (8:4b-7)

A more contemporary translation would be, ". . . who walk not according to the flesh but according to the Spirit. For they that are according to the flesh mind the things of the flesh, but they that are according to the Spirit, the things of the Spirit: For the minding of the flesh is death, but the minding of the Spirit is life and peace." We are always "minding" something, and the minding is produced either by the flesh or by the Holy Spirit. There is no such thing as neutrality where our relationship with God is concerned.

So then they that are in the flesh cannot please God. But ye are not

in the flesh, but in the Spirit, if so be that the Spirit of God dwell in you. Now if any man have not the Spirit of Christ, he is none of his. And if Christ be in you, the body is dead because of sin; but the Spirit is life because of righteousness. But if the Spirit of him that raised up Jesus from the dead dwell in you, he that raised up Christ from the dead shall also quicken your mortal bodies by his Spirit that dwelleth in you. (8:8-11)

"If any man have not the Spirit of Christ, he is none of his." Once you have accepted Christ as your Savior, you are indwelt by the Holy Spirit once for all. It is simply not possible to have accepted Christ as Savior and not be indwelt by the Holy Spirit, whom Paul calls here "the Spirit of Christ" (compare Phil. 1:19; 1 Pet. 1:11). We need the power of Christ, and the agency of this power is the Holy Spirit. "If Christ be in you . . ." (verse 10). And how is Christ to be in us? Through the agency of the "Spirit of Christ" (verse 9).

Paul describes the Holy Spirit as coming from Christ but also as coming from God the Father. In verse 9 he also calls Him the "Spirit of God," while in verse 11 he calls Him "the Spirit of him that raised up Jesus from the dead," which of course refers to God the Father. It is interesting to compare Paul's understanding of the Trinity with the way Christ Himself spoke of His relationship with the Father and the Spirit. In John 14 Jesus says that both He and God the Father will "come unto" and "make our abode with" anyone who loves them (John 14:23). But just a few verses previously, He says that He will ask God the Father to "give you another Comforter, that he may abide with you forever" (14:16). The Comforter is, of course, God the Holy Spirit, and Jesus says that the Holy Spirit "dwelleth with you, and shall be in you" (14:17). He then concludes by promising that "I will not leave you comfortless: I will come to you" (14:18). How will God the Father and God the Son "come" to us and "make their abode" with us (verse 23)? They will do this in the person of this Comforter, the Holy Spirit, the one who comforts (verses 16-18). There is a unity in the ministries of the three persons of the Trinity. Paul emphasizes this unity of the Godhead, and it is important that we see this as we read Romans 8.

"He that raised up Christ from the dead shall also quicken your mortal bodies" (8:11). Here again is the emphasis on the physical body. We'll see this again in verse 13: "But if ye through the Spirit do mortify the deeds of the body . . ." Our redemption is not just some far-off, transcendental thing relating only to the world of ideas. It has to do with the full person. Just as our future salvation will involve the full redemption and resurrection of the body, so also in this present life our redemption is to mean something in terms of our physical bodies. It is the very antithesis of the emphasis on the transcendental in much of modern theology.

Verse 12 picks up the emphasis of verse 4, ". . . who walk not after the flesh, but after the Spirit."

Therefore, brethren, we are debtors, not to the flesh, to live after the flesh. (8:12)

In verses 5-11, Paul has been reminding us that salvation is an absolute thing. We were born again, once for all. We have received and are indwelt by the Holy Spirit, once for all. This being so we are now to understand that we are debtors "not to the flesh, to live after the flesh." We should feel no obligation to live according to the flesh. We should build our lives on a different foundation: On the basis of being indwelt by the Holy Spirit; on the basis of the promise of the Father and the Son that "We will come to him, and abide with him" (John 14:23); on the basis of the fact that we have not been left orphans. "All of this being true," says Paul, "surely now we will understand that we are not in any way obligated to live after the flesh" (8:12).

The fact that we are indwelt by the Holy Spirit is wonderful indeed, but it demands a conscious response on our part. If we are truly going to be keepers of the law in the present life, the conscious call for us is to walk in the Spirit just as we already live in the Spirit. "Therefore, brethren, we are debtors, not to the flesh, to live after the flesh." "Therefore," says Paul, "on the basis of everything I have reminded you of concerning salvation" (verses 5-11), "you should be seeking to live according to the Spirit and not according to the flesh." Paul will strengthen his "therefore" as he begins each of the next three verses with "for."

For if ye live after the flesh, ye shall die: but if ye through the Spirit do mortify the deeds of the body, ye shall live. (8:13)

The best way to read this is, "If you through the Spirit cause the wicked deeds of the body to die . . ." We've seen that word *through* several times already, beginning in 6:11, where we learned that we are "dead indeed unto sin, but alive unto God through Jesus Christ our Lord." Now, in 8:13, we see that the Holy Spirit is the agency whereby we can get rid of the evil doings of the body and experience the life of the resurrected Christ. It is through the Spirit, not through our own strength, that we can do this.

Then the next "for":

For as many as are led by the Spirit of God, they are the sons of God. (8:14)

Who are the sons and daughters of God? They are all those who are led by the Spirit of God, all those who "walk" according to the Spirit (verse 4). The call is always the same. We are to abide in Christ, as the branches abide in the vine. There is to be fruit in the Christian life. If there is no fruit, if there is no evidence that we are abiding in the vine, then perhaps there is no reality to our profession of faith. It is fine to say, with the apostle John, that "as many as received him, to them gave he power to become the sons of God" (John 1:12). That's a great truth. On the day when we accepted Jesus as our Savior, wonder of wonders, we became the children of God. But if we truly became the children of God, we were at that moment indwelt by the Holy Spirit; and if we were indwelt by the Holy Spirit, surely there will be some evidence of this in our lives. "If we live in the Spirit, let us also walk in the Spirit" (Gal. 5:25). It is a call for a conscious effort on our part: We should be "led by the Spirit" (Rom. 8:14); we should not "grieve" the Spirit (Eph. 4:30); we should not "quench" the Spirit (1 Thess. 5:19). Paul has shown us the wonder of the Spirit's work in helping us keep the law; and yet he is also showing clearly that there must be a conscious involvement on our part: "Walk . . . after the Spirit" (8:1); be "led by the Spirit."

Paul's first two "for's" concerning our conscious involvement in sanctification have been words of exhortation. His third "for" is a word of comfort and encouragement.

For ye have not received the spirit of bondage again to fear; but ye have received the Spirit of adoption, whereby we cry, Abba, Father. (8:15)

We have received the Holy Spirit, and we are to let Him lead us. If we are truly saved, there should be some evidence of this in our lives. But Paul isn't saying these things to make us grovel in sorrow, searching our hearts and beating our chests, wondering, "Am I really a Christian?" We will see that the rest of this chapter is a great cry of victory and assurance. If you are indwelt by the Holy Spirit, then indeed you should walk in the Spirit and you should be led by the Spirit. At the same time, interwoven with these reminders is the tremendous realization that, having accepted Christ as Savior and being indwelt by the Holy Spirit, God is our Father. He loves us and cares for us.

The word "Father" in this verse is the Greek word for father, while "Abba" is the Aramaic word for father. There is a very precious and a very important distinction between the two words. The Greek word "father" can be used like our English word "father." It can have either a harsh or a gentle meaning. But the word "Abba" in the Aramaic is rather parallel to our word "Daddy." It is a gentle term. Each language, surely, has a gentle word for "father," which cannot have a harsh meaning. Having issued a ringing call to live out our faith in our everyday lives, Paul seeks now to quiet our hearts. I don't know about you, but I need this kind of encouragement. Only the person with a heart of iron could not need encouragement after hearing the cry to "be led by the Spirit," and to "walk in the Spirit." It's a glorious challenge, but it can also leave us discouraged as we see how far short we fall. When this happens we need assurance, and Paul gives us the assurance we need. If we have accepted Christ as our Savior, God the Father, the Creator, the very one we have sinned against, can now be called "Daddy."

Paul has pointed out the absolute gap between being saved and being lost. He has reminded us of the importance of recognizing that we are indwelt by the Holy Spirit—the importance of, moment by moment, living according to the Spirit. How marvelous this is! But if, as we contemplate all of this, our hearts begin to fail us, how gentle is our God! How tenderly He picks us up and says, "Don't you understand this is not to cause you to fear, it's not to break your heart. It isn't to crush you to the earth. Quite the contrary, it's to assure you that I have come to you and that I am your papa, your daddy."

Paul wants us to understand the wonder and glory of being indwelt by the Holy Spirit. He wants us to do some heart searching as to whether or not we are living up to this highest of callings, this greatest of challenges. And yet at the same time, he wants to give us the greatest possible comfort. For the transcendent God of the universe is the one who in the stillness of the night, or when I have fallen in the mud, takes me by the hand and invites me to call Him Daddy.

This wonderful word of assurance introduces us to the rest of the chapter, because as we shall see Paul goes on and talks about our future glory (8:18-25), then about the assurance that, once we have accepted Christ as our Savior, we are saved forever and we can never, never be lost again (8:26-39). And here, it seems, he is already looking forward to this. Have we fallen? Are our lives shattered? God waits to pick us up. This does not minimize the challenge to share day by day in Christ's victory over sin. At the same time, however, there is His gentleness.

I'm sure that each of us, if we can remember our daddies at all, can remember times when we fell and he picked us up and put us back on our feet. Surely the word *daddy* brings many precious memories. And who is this one who may be called, "Abba"? He is the Creator of the universe, the "Father" of the Trinity.

The Spirit itself beareth witness with our spirit, that we are the children of God. (8:16)

As Christians we can have at least three assurances that we are truly God's children. The first assurance is the absolute one, built upon the promise of God in Scriptures such as, "He that believeth on the Son hath everlasting life" (John 3:36). On that wonderful day when we accepted Jesus as our Savior, immediately we had this flaming, certain assurance from the infinite God who cannot lie: "He that believes on the Son has everlasting life."

Our second assurance that we are children of God is the fruit that we should see in our lives. We should see fruit, and we should see some motion of the Spirit in our lives.

The third assurance is the one we read of in verse 16, an assurance as deep as the deepest running stream from the heart of the earth, deep and wonderful: The Spirit Himself bears witness with our spirit that we are the children of God. We can cry "Abba, Father" (verse 15) because of the Spirit's assurance "that we are the children of God" (verse 16).

And what is this great assurance? It is not merely an external thing based upon an external promise. It isn't even based just on the evidence of the fruit we are bearing as Christians. Rather, it is the fact that somewhere deep inside of us, we who have accepted Jesus as our Savior—at times it is as wonderful as the rolling sea—somewhere, deep inside of each of us, there is the witness of the Holy Spirit to our own spirit that we are the children of God.

When we're broken, when we have fallen into sin, when Satan our adversary has beaten us again, sometimes this third assurance becomes feeble indeed. At such times, we can go back to the great objective promises, the great nails in the wall that constitute our first level of assurance—the promises of Scripture that if we have accepted Jesus as our Savior we are the sons of God: "He that believeth on the Son hath everlasting life."

That particular verse has always been a favorite of mine. I sometimes describe it as being tied to the mast of a ship. When the waves arise and I am beaten and buffeted, I can always go back and say, "Yes, Satan, I have fallen again, but I have the oath and the promise of God, based on His holiness, based on His eternal justice, based on His flaming holiness so that He cannot lie. Based on the finished work of Jesus Christ, I have this sure promise: 'He that believeth on the Son hath everlasting life.' I have believed, therefore I have everlasting life! You cannot loosen me from that certainty!"

But then there are those more intimate moments when I have that third level of assurance, when I know through the testimony of the Holy Spirit to my spirit that I am a child of God.

None of these three assurances are to be despised. Each has its place, and we should go from assurance to assurance in our personal lives. We go from assurance to assurance for ourselves, and we help each other to claim these three assurances. ". . . the Spirit of adoption, whereby we cry, Abba, Father. The Spirit himself bearing witness with our spirit that we are, in this present life, the children of God."

And if children, then heirs; heirs of God, and joint-heirs with Christ; if so be that we suffer with him, that we may be also glorified together. (8:17)

Here again we see the Trinity: God the Father is our Father; we are indwelt by the Holy Spirit (verse 16); and we are joint-heirs with Jesus Christ. The entire Trinity assures us of our salvation. Paul will conclude these first eight chapters by showing us that, once we have been saved, we will always be saved (8:26-39). We will find in those verses that the assurance that this is so is based upon the work of the whole Trinity. And here, in verse 17, Paul is introducing this wonderful truth. The whole Trinity assures us that we "are joint-heirs with Christ" of eternal life.

. . . if so be that we suffer with him . . . (8:17b)

It is wonderful to be able to say that I am a joint-heir with Christ. It is wonderful to be able to identify with Christ in this way. Jesus is in heaven, and we are told elsewhere in Paul's writings that already, right now, in God's sight, we are in the heavenlies with Christ (Eph. 2:6). We could spend a great deal of time exploring the wonders of our identification with Christ even in this present life. But we are not in the world of glory yet. We're in the world that hates God. We're in the world that crucified Christ. So, when I talk about the wonders of identification with Jesus Christ, I must also immediately understand what this means considering the world's current attitude toward Christ.

In our generation, people everywhere are saying lovely things about Jesus, but it is not the Christ of Scripture that they are talking about. The orthodox Jew, for instance, may say that Christ was a good man. Muslims may say the same thing. On every side, people speak good things of someone they call Jesus Christ, but it is not the Jesus Christ of Scripture. When I turn to the Jesus Christ of Scripture, what do I discover that the world did with Him? It killed Him! Our identification with Christ in the present life means identification with the Christ whom the world will not accept. Let us be courageous as we read Christ's accurate warnings of what the world would do to Him (Matt. 16:21-24). Let us be even more courageous as we consider Christ's warning that "a disciple is not above his master" (Matt. 10:16-24), meaning that the world may do the same to us.

It is very romantic and idealistic to speak of being a "joint-heir with Christ" only in terms of the present loveliness and future glory that this entails. It is wrong to invite people to accept Jesus as their Savior and tell them the wonders of identification with Christ, without telling them that identification with Christ will also mean suffering in this present evil world. We need not be morose about this. We need not glory in the prospect of martyrdom. But we must be realistic. Jesus taught that, as prospective disciples, we should count the cost. If a man is going to build a tower, Jesus says, he must count the cost, (Luke 14:27-30). A king, Jesus says, does not go to war unless he considers whether or not he can win the battle (Luke 14:31-33). The Word of God is not an idealistic, romantic book at all. It says, "Count the cost."

. . . if so be that we suffer with him, that we may be also glorified together. For I reckon that the sufferings of this present time are not worthy to be compared with the glory that shall be revealed in us. (8:17b-18)

Yes, identification with Christ also means suffering with Christ. Should I draw back, then? I often look at the young people—and the older ones too—who accept Christ as their Savior through our work; although I am so thankful for each one of them, I also know that, because most of them come from non-Christian families, there will be persecution. It is wonderful to see them come and accept Christ as Savior, but I know that in many cases it will mean divided families. I know of a Jewish girl in London who has been put out of her home because of her belief in Christ. Her books, including her Bible, have been burned and her bank account has been taken from her. How do you think I feel about that? Do you think we should have a heart of stone and have no compassion for those we are enlisting in the battle? It's wonderful as we see these people being rescued "as brands from the fire" (Zech. 3:2; cf. Jude 23). But must we not pause? Must we not understand that, when a person truly accepts Jesus as his or her Savior, it means war? Must we not comprehend that he or she will have the enmity of the world? Must we not comprehend that, if we are really living in the power of the Spirit, there will be sorrow?

How dare we, then, invite people to accept Jesus as Savior? How dare we? First of all, we dare do so because it is the truth. It is the truth of the universe. God exists. Secondly, we dare invite people to accept Christ because without Him they are lost. It often seems to me that the neoorthodox and modernist Bible teachers of our day have counterfeited and reinterpreted every meaningful Christian term. But once while listening to a young man's prayer, I realized that there are at least two words that can never be counterfeited. Those are the words *lost* and *hell*. How dare we invite people to accept Jesus as Savior when we know it will mean war and often suffering, divided homes and separation from the whole twentieth-century mentality? How dare we? We dare to do so, first of all, because it is truth; and secondly, because unless they do accept Jesus, they are eternally lost. Nothing else could make it worthwhile, but this makes it worthwhile.

We dare proclaim the gospel because it is truth. We dare proclaim it because apart from the gospel people are lost. And thirdly, we dare proclaim the gospel because we know the wonderful end of the story:

. . . if so be that we suffer with him, that we may be also glorified together. For I reckon that the sufferings of this present time are not worthy to be compared with the glory which shall be revealed in us. (8:17b-18)

No sufferings amount to anything when compared with the truth; no sufferings amount to anything compared with the lostness of the lost; and no sufferings amount to anything compared with the glorious future aspect of salvation. And to this we are now introduced.

You remember we saw, in speaking of Romans 1:16-17, that the "salvation" Paul speaks of there is not just justification: It is justification (1:18—4:25); it is sanctification (5:1—8:17); and now we are beginning to learn about the future aspect of salvation, which is glorification (8:18-39). Is there suffering in connection with salvation? Yes, there is suffering. Are there tears? Yes, there are tears. Is there a cost? Yes, there is a cost. "Joint-heirs with Jesus Christ" includes identification with Him in His suffering. But the sufferings of this present time (verse 18) are not worthy to be compared with the glory that will follow. "Not worthy to be compared!" It's like a song, like a shout of victory, a triumphant blowing of the trumpets. It's the call to war and the call to glory: "Not worthy to be compared," small dust in the balance, not to be thought of.

We should weep for ourselves, and we should weep even more for those who accept Jesus as Savior through our testimony, as we see them being turned out of homes or being separated from the whole twentieth century in which we live. Yes, there must be some tears. And yet all the tears are "not worthy to be compared with the glory that shall be revealed in us."

When will this glory be revealed in us? At Christ's Second Coming. Paul speaks of this in 2 Thessalonians: "So that we ourselves glory in you in the churches of God for your patience and faith in all your persecutions and tribulations that ye endure" (2 Thess. 1:4). If you visit Thessalonica, you can look up at Mount Olympus and see the lake stretched out before you and you will see a white tower. It was from this place, in the great persecution under Nero, that many of these very people Paul wrote to in Thessalonica were taken to their deaths. That's what he's talking about. It must have been terrible for Paul to preach to the people in Thessalonica and then see them dragged off to the stakes and to the lions.

Only once, as far as we know, was Martin Luther tempted to turn aside from his Reformation teaching, and that was when the Protestant martyrs were burned in the old medieval square in front of the town hall in Brussels. When Luther heard that they had been killed because of his teaching, he almost turned aside. We Christians would have hearts of stone if we didn't feel as Luther felt. But should we turn aside? Martin Luther pressed on, thank God. It was truth he was battling for in Europe, and it was truth that Paul was battling for in the Roman Empire. Those to whom Luther preached and those to whom Paul preached were lost before they accepted Christ as their Savior.

In Paul's day, in Luther's day, in our own day, there is also the glory that lies ahead. The comfort Paul offered to the church at Thessalonica in this grievous moment was the same that is portrayed in Romans 8. He held out to them God's promise of "rest with us" (2 Thess. 1:7a). And when would the Thessalonians, along with Paul, find their "rest"? In this world? No; they would find their ". . . rest with us, when the Lord Jesus shall be revealed from heaven with his mighty angels" (verse 7b). For the world, Christ's future appearance will mean judgment. But to those who have come to God through Him, it will be a time of rest with God.

That's exactly what Paul is saying in Romans 8. Will you have rest? Do you sometimes say, "I can't go on any longer"? Don't be ashamed. I say that sometimes. "I just can't go up the hill any longer." Do you say it for yourself? Do you say it for some of those you have led to Christ, who now suffer persecution for Jesus' sake? Where shall we look for rest? Paul directs our eyes to a single point, to the glory that lies ahead.

This introduces us to the future aspect of salvation (8:18-25). It's a small section; there's much more prophecy in other portions of the New Testament. But these few verses strike as a great hammer upon glowing metal, showering sparks in all directions. The past aspect of salvation, if we have accepted Jesus as our Savior, is our justification: The guilt of our sin is gone. The present aspect of salvation is sanctification, which is salvation from the power of sin. Then there is the future aspect, glorification, which will be salvation from the very presence of sin, and which will take place at the Second Coming of Christ.

PART THREE

GLORIFICATION

(8:18-39)

12

BELIEVERS RESURRECTED,
CREATION RESTORED
(8:18-25)

क

In our study of Romans 1—8, we have learned about the past aspect of salvation, by which we stand justified before God (1:18—4:25). We have learned about salvation's present reality in our lives, the ongoing process of sanctification (5:1—8:17). Verse 17 of chapter 8 speaks of our being "glorified together," which introduces us to this final section. Romans 8:18-25 speaks of our glorification, the aspect of salvation which is still in the future:

For I reckon that the sufferings of this present time are not worthy to be compared with the glory which shall be revealed in us. (8:18)

We looked at this verse at the end of the previous section and noted the reality of the suffering Christians endure in this present life. We looked at 2 Thessalonians 1:4-7, where Paul wrote words of comfort to Christians who were at that very time enduring persecution. Such persecution continued, and in about the year 96, the aging apostle John is still feeling the effects of this persecution as he endures life in a sort of Roman concentration camp on the isle of Patmos. In the book of Revelation he writes, "I John, who also am your brother, and companion in tribulation, and in the kingdom and patience of Jesus Christ, was in the isle that is called Patmos, for the word of God, and for the testimony of Jesus Christ . . ." (Rev. 1:9). What is John's comfort amid his suffering? It is "the patience of Jesus Christ," by which I believe he means the patience we can gain from looking forward to Christ's return. Just as Paul commended the Thessalonians for their "patience" (2 Thess. 1:4), and then reminded them that they would find "rest with us, when the Lord Jesus shall be revealed from heaven" (verse 7), so also John found his hope in patiently awaiting Christ's return. There is only one real answer amid tribulation, whether in the day of the Thessalonians, in the day of John on Patmos, or in the rest of church history including our own day; the only adequate answer to tribulation is our hope in the coming of Christ in glory.

John actually saw something of Christ in glory right there on Patmos. But in Romans 8:18-25, Paul will tell us that all Christians are to live in expectation of one day seeing the Lord just as John saw Him. If we today are living as we should live as Christians, we do not need to seek tribulation. We will surely suffer some sort of persecution as we find ourselves running counter to the whole twentieth-century mentality. Yet no matter how great the sufferings are, whether it be the young woman in London put out of her home; whether it be another person who has gone back to his home in El Salvador and is probably facing persecution right now; whether it involves our brothers and sisters in countries with open and obvious persecution of Christians; or whether it be each one of us, with our own friends, with our own family: Whatever our sufferings might be, we can find comfort in these words: "For I reckon that the sufferings of this present time are not worthy to be compared with the glory that shall be revealed in us."

Paul invites us to open the door and walk through, as in just a few brief verses he gives us a glimpse of our Lord's return and of the glorious future aspect of our salvation. Remember, Paul is still exegeting the theme verses of 1:16-17, which he concluded by saying, "the just shall live by faith." And now in this section he shows us that we can live by faith right up to the gates of glory.

We have also noted, in reference to the theme passage, that we need never be "ashamed of the gospel" as a belief system (1:16), nor need we ever be ashamed of the day-to-day practice of our faith, for "hope maketh not ashamed" (5:5); we should never be ashamed of our hope in Christ, for it will never disappoint us. In these verses on glorification, Paul will reassure us once more that our hope for a future salvation will never disappoint us or make us ashamed. He will end this section with these words of encouragement: "For we are saved by hope: but hope that is seen is not hope: for what a man seeth, why doth he yet hope for? But if we hope for that which we see not, then do we with patience wait for it" (8:24-25).

Our hope in Christ is an unbroken line, from the time we believed in Him and were therefore freed from guilt; down through our experiences as Christians in this present life as we see the wonders of God's sanctifying work through the indwelling Holy Spirit; then stretching on to the fulfillment of that hope in the coming of Christ as Paul will now describe it.

When Paul speaks of the "glory which shall be revealed in us" (verse 18), the Greek is actually "in reference to us." It is not just a glory that will be revealed *to* us, but a glory that will be revealed surrounding us, in the context of us. In verses 19-23 he will tell us what this glory is, and why the sufferings of this present time are not worthy to be compared with it.

For the earnest expectation of the creature waiteth for the manifestation of the sons of God. (8:19)

"Creation" is a more contemporary word for *creature*, and I will translate it as such from here on. "Earnest" in this verse would be better translated "constant." We should constantly be looking forward to this future glory. Jesus told us we should be always eagerly expecting His return (Luke 12:35-37). The early church certainly waited for the Lord's return. They expected Him to return in their own generation. Some of the more liberal Bible scholars of our day would say that because He didn't return in their own generation, they were wrong. Not at all. Each generation is to wait. It is to be our constant expectation. "The constant expectation of creation awaits the manifestation of the sons of God."

What is this "manifestation of the sons of God" that all creation looks forward to? It is the physical resurrection of the believer's body, as Paul will state specifically in verse 23. Of course, we all long for the day when we will receive our resurrected bodies. This should be our constant hope and expectation, but Paul says that the whole creation longs for our resurrection. And why do all do so?

For the creature was made subject to vanity [futility], not willingly, but by reason of him who hath subjected the same in hope. Because the creature itself also shall be delivered from the bondage of corruption into the glorious liberty of the children of God. For we know that the whole creation groaneth and travaileth in pain together until now. And not only they, but ourselves also, which have the firstfruits of the Spirit, even we ourselves groan within ourselves, waiting for the adoption, to wit, the redemption of our body. (8:20-23)

As Christians, we have "the firstfruits of the Spirit." If one apple appears on a tree, I know that it will soon yield a full harvest of apples. The fact that I now have new life through the indwelling Holy Spirit is my guarantee that one day I will have the total "redemption of [my] body." In a moment we will see this same idea expressed by the word *earnest*. The Holy Spirit is the earnest, or guarantee, of the future complete redemption of our body.

Yet even though as Christians we now have the firstfruits of the Spirit (verse 23a), we still groan (23b), waiting for the redemption of our body, and the whole creation groans right along with us (verse 22). What is this groaning all about? It is the same groaning we heard from Jesus as He stood before the tomb of His friend Lazarus (John 11:33, 38). Jesus wept at Lazarus' tomb (John 11:35), but I think He was also angry: angry against all the suffering and abnormalities that have come upon the world because of sin; angry not just against the devil, but against all the results of sin. And "even we ourselves," though we "have the firstfruits of the Spirit," groan just as our Lord did, as we see all the suffering around us and within us.

Creation groans, and we ourselves groan, waiting for something. We're waiting for the redemption of our body. And the redemption of our body is, in the words of verse 19, "the manifestation of the sons of

God," the revealing of the sons of God. Certainly we are to show forth Jesus Christ in this present life; but on resurrection day, in the moment when our bodies are changed and become like Christ's glorious body, in the moment when we are changed in the "twinkling of an eye" (1 Cor. 15:52), there will be a manifestation of the sons of God far beyond anything we could imagine in this present life. And it won't be just we humans who are raised to glory. All creation as well will at that moment be "delivered from the bondage of corruption into the glorious liberty of the children of God" (8:21).

Isn't this present life a life of suffering and groaning? Troubles, sorrows, persecution, sick children, people killing each other, people maligning each other; a great portion of the world today are slaves to other men; a great portion of the world today are displaced from their homes. Are we so foolish or hardhearted as to say that this is not a world of suffering? And yet, according to Paul, it all points forward specifically to the future redemption of our body and the subsequent restoration of all creation at Christ's return.

Even we ourselves groan within ourselves, waiting for the adoption, to wit, the redemption of our body. (8:23b)

Throughout these first eight chapters of Romans we have noticed a recurring emphasis on the physical body. In 1:24 we read about those who, because of their rebellion against God, have been reduced to "dishonouring their own bodies between themselves." As sin has entered the world, it has involved our physical bodies. Then, you will recall, we learned in chapter 4 that Abraham believed that God could bring life out of his and Sarah's dead bodies (4:19). And just as Abraham believed that life could come from his dead body, we were called, in chapter 6, to pursue sanctification in the area of our physical bodies as in all areas of our lives. "Our old man was crucified with him, that the body of sin might be made powerless" (6:6). "Let not sin therefore reign in your mortal body" (6:12). Then in chapter 7, "Who should deliver me from the body of this death?" (7:24). The emphasis continues in chapter 8: "If Christ be in you, the body is dead because of sin; but the Spirit is life because of righteousness" (8:10); and 8:13: "If you live after the flesh, you shall die, but if you through the Spirit do make to die the doings of the body, you shall live." Certainly throughout these chapters Paul shows how salvation relates to our whole person, but we can't help noticing this recurring emphasis on the physical body.

Our bodies suffer because of the Fall. If we accept Christ as our Savior, this is to mean something in the present life in regard to our bodies. Surely those of us who have been Christians for any length of time have seen some victories over sin in the area of our physical bodies. Yet we must surely long for more victory still. We still feel the weight of the Fall in terms of sickness and in terms of our bodies getting older. We must say we have seen some victory, but we long for more. We still "groan within ourselves, waiting for the adoption, to wit, the redemption of our body" (8:23), not just in the area of sickness, not just in the area of physical death, but in the area of being all that we should be. We long for the day when Christ will be completely honored and praised in our body as well as in our mind and spirit.

We often speak of God's care for the whole personality. When God made man, He intended that our whole personality would love and praise Him. The first commandment, to "love the Lord thy God with all thy heart, and with all thy soul, and with all thy strength, and with all thy mind" (Matt. 22:37), applies not just to the spirit but to the whole person, including the body. Surely all of us at times long for all aspects of our being, including our body, to be blended together in a whole to the praise of God. And Paul answers that the day will come when we will, indeed, be able truly to praise God with our full being.

Do you "groan" over the state of fallen creation, as it is manifested both within yourself and in the world outside? Well then, "My beloved," says the Lord, "I'm coming, and your body will be redeemed" (8:23). There will come a day when we will be able to praise Him as we should. Meanwhile, our calling is to "present our bodies a living sacrifice, holy, acceptable unto God" (12:1).

Here in Romans Paul speaks of the redemption of our body. In Ephesians, he says that those who believe have been "sealed with that Holy Spirit of promise, which is the earnest of our inheritance until the redemption of the purchased possession" (Eph. 1:13b-14). We are God's "purchased possession," purchased by Christ's own blood. And

God has "sealed" us with the indwelling Holy Spirit, who is the "earnest" or promise that He will one day redeem us in full.

In English law, it used to be the custom that when a portion of land was purchased, the person who was selling the land handed, in the presence of witnesses, a handful of his soil to the person who was buying it. That handful of soil was the "earnest," or promise, that the whole had been purchased. When you and I are indwelt by the Holy Spirit, this is an earnest of the fact that the whole has been purchased by the blood of the Lamb. The earnest is already ours. He dwells within us in the person of the Holy Spirit. He is the proof that the whole has been purchased. And what is the whole? The whole is the redemption of our bodies. Because the Spirit indwells us, we can be sure that the Lord has purchased our whole being, and that He will one day claim it by raising us from the dead (8:23).

Meanwhile we wait, and all creation waits.

Because the creature itself also shall be delivered from the bondage of corruption into the glorious liberty of the children of God. For we know that the whole creation groaneth and travaileth in pain together until now. (8:21-22)

The indwelling Holy Spirit is the firstfruits, the earnest or guarantee that God will one day completely redeem us by raising us from the dead (8:23). But then, our own complete redemption will in turn be an earnest or guarantee for the redemption of all creation. As James expresses it, we are "a kind of firstfruits of [God's] creation" (James 1:18). Paul says that right now the whole creation looks forward to the day when our redemption will usher in "deliverance from the bondage of corruption." Meanwhile, they "groan and travail in pain together until now."

To understand how our complete redemption will be the guarantee for the complete redemption of all creation, we must look at some other parts of Scripture, beginning all the way back in Genesis 3 with the story of the curse. Immediately after Adam and Eve commit the first sin, God speaks first of all to the serpent, saying that one day a Redeemer will come to undo the damage that the serpent has done: "I will put enmity between thee and the woman, and between thy seed and her seed; it shall bruise thy head, and thou shalt bruise his heel" (3:15). There will be a Redeemer who will win a complete victory over Satan. Romans 8:18-25, coming after this victory of Christ over Satan at the cross, promises on the basis of that victory the coming total redemption of all creation from the damage done by original sin.

Genesis 3 describes the damage that would come to all creation because of mankind's sin. After speaking to Satan, God turns to Eve and says, "I will greatly multiply thy sorrow and thy conception; in sorrow thou shalt bring forth children" (3:16). Eve's own body will now be against her. Sin will bring not just mental suffering but physical suffering as well.

God then speaks to Adam of another devastating change in the physical world as the result of sin: "Because thou hast hearkened unto the voice of thy wife, and hast eaten of the tree, of which I commanded thee, saying, Thou shall not eat of it: cursed is the ground for thy sake" (3:17). Adam has committed the sin and he will suffer as a result, but the ground will also suffer. Adam and Eve's first sin brought abnormality to themselves and to the entire external creation as well. The suffering wasn't just in the minds of Adam and Eve. The whole creation would suffer right along with them. The fields where Adam planted his crops would now bring forth "thorns and thistles" (3:18).

The first sin brought abnormality to the physical human body, as signified by the woman's pain in childbearing. It brought abnormality to all nature as well, signified by the ground's producing thorns. Then in Genesis 3:19 we read of a third abnormality: ". . . till thou return unto the ground; for out of it wast thou taken: for dust thou art, and unto dust thou shalt return." The third abnormality resulting from sin was physical death.

Looking back at Romans 8, we find a wonderful reversal of this process. It's true, says Paul, that "creature was made subject to futility" (8:20). But he immediately goes on to say that "creature itself shall be delivered from the bondage of corruption" (8:21). And when will this happen? It will happen when the third part of the curse has been overcome, when redeemed humanity, as the "firstfruits," has experienced the reversal of the curse of death in the "redemption of our body" (8:23). When this third external abnormality has been overcome, then will come the cry, as Paul expresses elsewhere, "O death, where is thy sting? O grave, where is thy victory?" (1 Cor. 15:55). The firstfruits of our physical resurrection will set in motion the redemption of the whole creation.

Because the creature itself also shall be delivered . . . For we know that the whole creation groaneth and travaileth in pain together until now. (8:21a, 22)

From the very beginning, all creation has suffered right along with mankind. And from the very beginning it has had a share in God's unfolding plan of redemption. When God judged wicked humanity in the Flood, all but a designated few of the animals died along with them. When Noah and his family and all the rescued animals came out of the ark, God made the covenant of the rainbow with humans and animals alike: "And God said, This is the token of the covenant which I make between me and you and every living creature that is with you" (9:12). The covenant was not only between God and man, but between God and every living creature as well.

When at the Exodus God killed all the firstborn of Egypt while delivering Israel, the firstborn animals of Egypt died right along with their masters, while the animals of the Israelites were saved along with them (Ex. 12).

The story of the Exodus and the first Passover of course points forward to the death of Christ, the Passover "Lamb of God, which taketh away the sin of the world" (John 1:29). We could also consider the Passover to be a promise: It is a promise that, on the basis of the finished work of the Lord Jesus Christ, not only will believing mankind be redeemed, but all creation will be redeemed along with them. Satan will not be allowed a victory in the world of humans, and Satan will not be allowed a victory in the world of the total creation. The Seed of the woman shall bruise the serpent's head (Gen. 3:15). As the lamb of the Passover enabled the beasts of the Israelites to come out of Egypt alive, so eventually the work of Christ will send forth all creation into its glorious liberty. "Because creation itself also shall be delivered from the bondage of corruption into the glorious liberty of the children of God."

God is concerned about His whole creation, and we should be concerned about it as well. Our greatest sorrow should be reserved for lost and suffering humanity, but we should weep as well for the sufferings our sin has brought upon all of creation. You'll find many modern artists who, though having no understanding of the Bible, at least understand and portray in their work the suffering of nature. The artist who pictures nature all rough and raw surely understands it better than the romanticist who looks at nature as though it were a piece of flawless beauty. Tennyson, who writes of "nature, red in tooth and claw," sees nature as it truly is. When Picasso paints the cat with the bird in its mouth, he is painting nature in all its reality. Mankind sinned, they rebelled against their Creator, and all nature bore the curse along with them. Mankind kept on sinning, and the Flood destroyed animals as well as people. Noah believed God, and the ark carried the animals as well as the humans. At the Passover, the blood of the lamb on the doorposts saved animals as well as people.

Then in Romans 8 we find these great ringing words of promise for all creation: "The constant expectation of creation waiteth for manifestation of the sons of God. For creation was made subject to vanity, not willingly, but by reason of him who hath subjected the same in hope, because creation itself also shall be delivered from the bondage of corruption into the glorious liberty of the children of God. For we know that the whole creation groaneth and travaileth in pain together until now. And not only they, but ourselves also, which have the firstfruits of the Spirit, even we ourselves groan within ourselves, waiting for the adoption, that is, the redemption of our body" (8:19-23).

This "redemption of our body" will be the firstfruits; when, "in the twinkling of an eye . . . the trumpet shall sound, and the dead shall be raised incorruptible" (1 Cor. 15:52), this will be only the firstfruits of the tremendous redemption of all creation. Satan will not be allowed a victory in creation any more than in the world of humans. And all upon what basis? Upon only one basis: "The seed of the woman," that is, Jesus Christ our Lord, "shall bruise the serpent's head" as He wins His victory over hell and death at Calvary.

In Revelation, John paints a wonderful picture of redeemed creation: "Every created thing which is in heaven, and on the earth, and under the earth, and such as are in the sea, and all that are in them, heard I saying, Blessing, and honor, and glory, and power, be unto him that sitteth upon the throne, and unto the Lamb for ever and ever" (Rev. 5:13). This is the song of redeemed creation, not even just every animate thing, but every created thing. We know very little of the total praise of creation to God. As someone has rightly observed, because of the curse on nature it is impossible to reason from nature to nature's God. But there will be a day when that no longer is true. There will be a day when, once again, the "morning stars will sing together" just as they did at creation (Job 38:7). How beautiful the birds sing now. But what will creation be like in its song of redemption! And we will be the firstfruits of all this: raised from the dead (8:23); reigning with Christ upon the earth (Rev. 5:10); and then will come the song of redeemed creation (Rev. 5:13).

Edward Hicks (1780-1849), the primitive American painter, did almost all of his paintings on one single theme: redeemed creation. Hicks was primitive in his style, but his subject matter certainly was not primitive, for it was taken from the very heart of all history and all creation: There was a curse on creation, but there will come a day when the curse is lifted. Isaiah described and Hicks expressed in his paintings that "The wolf and the lamb shall feed together" (Isa. 65:25). As certainly as the ark carried the animals along with the humans; as certainly as the firstborn of the Israelite beasts were saved along with their masters; as certainly as all this there will come a time when all creation will be redeemed, when all created things will raise their voices to praise God as He was meant to be praised.

Do you love nature now? What will it be then! In the art museum in Neuchatel, there are three murals by the Swiss painter Paul Robert (1851-1923) on the theme of the Second Coming of Christ. The murals proclaim that when Christ returns He will be Lord over everything. One of the murals depicts the relationship of Christ to the world of industry; one shows His relationship to the world of the arts and other intellectual endeavors; and one shows His relationship to the world of agriculture. The mural on Christ and agriculture is set in the valley between Neuchatel and La Chaux de-Fonds. I wish you could see this part of Switzerland in spring. There's no place like

Switzerland, with its wildflowers blowing in the breeze. But Paul Robert painted the scene even more beautiful than it is now, more beautiful than eye has ever seen, because it will be so when Christ returns.

. . . the glory which shall be revealed in us. . . . the glorious liberty of the children of God. . . . the redemption of our body. (8:18b, 21b, 23b)

Is this all just a hopeless dream, or can we be sure that Christ will someday return for us? The apostle Peter would say to us that Christ's return is as certain as His first coming to this earth. Speaking to a crowd in Jerusalem, Peter declared that "those things, which God before had showed by the mouth of all his prophets, that Christ should suffer, he hath so fulfilled" (Acts 3:18). Jesus came to earth and died on the cross and rose again. Those are undeniable facts of history, and they happened just as "all of [God's] prophets" said they would happen. But Peter goes on to call the people to repentance and faith, so that they would be ready to meet the Lord "when the times of refreshing shall come from the presence of the Lord; and he shall send Jesus Christ" (verses 19b-20a). Peter is now talking about the same future events that Paul has been talking about in Romans. He goes on to describe these great future events as the "times of restitution of all things" (verse 21a). Surely he has in mind the future redemption of all creation that we have been hearing about from Paul. And how certain can we be that these wonderful things will come to pass? Peter calls it the "times of restitution of all things, which God hath spoken by the mouth of all his holy prophets since the world began" (verse 21). God's prophets predicted Christ's first coming, and Christ came. The prophecies were fulfilled literally and completely. These same inspired prophets of God have predicted Christ's Second Coming, so we can be certain that those predictions will come true as well—literally and completely. If we believe that Christ lived on this earth and died for us and rose again, we can trust the prophets' word that He will return for us someday.

Not just in our imaginations but in real, space-time history—at a particular point of time in a particular geographic place—the times of restitution and refreshing will come. That took place in part in the ark bearing humans and animals across the flood, and with the Passover lamb saving the Israelites and saving their animals as well. Satan is not going to have a victory. The future fulfillment of prophecy will be as certain as the fulfillment of prophecy already past. If we believe in the past finished work of Jesus Christ, the flaming word is that, just as surely as Christ lived on our earth and died on the cross and rose from the dead, just as surely as all this took place, there will one day be the restitution of all things.

As we think about our coming complete redemption and with it the restoration of creation, we need to look ahead for a moment to Romans 8:29, which we will consider again in the final chapter of this study. We read that Christ is "the firstborn among many brethren." And in Colossians 1:18, Paul describes Christ as the "firstborn from the dead." We will one day be raised from the dead (Rom. 8:23), but Christ has already been raised from the dead. Therefore He is the firstborn among many brethren. Paul speaks in similar fashion in 1 Corinthians 15, the great passage on the physical resurrection of the dead: "But every man in his own order: Christ the firstfruits; afterward they that are Christ's at his coming. Then cometh the end, when he shall have delivered up the kingdom to God, even the Father; when he shall have put down all rule and all authority and power" (1 Cor. 15:23-24). Christ is the firstfruits, the firstborn from the dead (Col. 1:18), in relation to redeemed humanity.

But Paul also sees Christ as the firstborn from the dead in relation to all creation; just a couple of verses earlier in Colossians he describes Him as "the firstborn of every created thing" (Col. 1:15). It's exactly the same terminology in both places. And so that this cannot be misunderstood, Paul goes on to say that God allowed Christ to die on the cross, "by him to reconcile all things unto himself" (verse 20). All things, every created being. Jesus died not just to save lost sinners, but to restore the broken creation as well.

With all this in mind, we read on down through this section in Romans 8 again and feel the force of it: "For I reckon that the sufferings of this present time are not worthy to be compared with the glory that shall be revealed in reference to us. For the constant expectation of creation waiteth for the manifestation of the sons of God. For creation was made subject to vanity, not willingly, but by reason of him who hath subjected the same in hope. Because creation itself also shall be delivered from the bondage of corruption into the glorious liberty of the children of God. For we know that the whole creation groaneth and travaileth in pain together until now. And not only they, but ourselves also, which have the firstfruits of the Spirit, even we ourselves groan within ourselves, waiting for the adoption, that is, the redemption of our body. For we are saved by hope: but hope that is seen is not hope: for what a man seeth, why doth he yet hope for? But if we hope for that we see not, then do we with patience wait for it" (8:18-25).

And we wait; for it still lies ahead.

In conclusion, we turn back to our key verse: "For I am not ashamed of the gospel of Christ: for it is the power of God unto salvation" (1:16). The gospel, the good news of Christ's death and resurrection on our behalf, is the power of God unto the whole salvation, including the resurrection of the body of the believer and the restoration of all creation.

And yet, we still wait. But don't forget the next verse: "For therein is the righteousness of God revealed from faith to faith: as it is written, The just shall live by faith." We are called to live by faith. And in the present life we won't be disappointed, we won't be made ashamed of the faith and the hope we have placed in Christ (5:5). And finally, when we are glorified, when God's glory is revealed in reference to us (8:18), we certainly will feel no shame whatsoever for having lived a life of faith, as our salvation through Christ is brought to glorious completion.

13

ETERNAL LIFE IS FOREVER
(8:26-39)

જાજ

In Part 1 of this book we have learned about the past aspect of salvation. When we accepted Christ as our Savior, we were justified. If we have done this, our guilt before God is gone. In Part 2 we learned of salvation's present aspect, whereby in this life, through the power of Christ and through the indwelling Holy Spirit, we can experience ongoing salvation from the power of sin. In the first chapter of Part 3 we learned of a glorious future salvation in the resurrection of the Christian's body, bringing with it the restoration of all creation. In this glorified state, we will be free of the very presence of sin, and we together with all creation will no longer suffer the consequences of sin.

This is all very wonderful, but it raises a crucial question: What good is all this—thinking especially now of our future salvation—what good is all this if you or I won't be there? What if, even though we have accepted Christ as our Savior, we could be lost again? All these are wonderful things: this marvelous future salvation, the wonder of the resurrection of the body, the wonder of the restored creation; but if it would be possible that we who have accepted Christ as our Savior could be lost again, what joy is it to even think of these things?

It becomes kind of like showing a child a Christmas tree and then putting him out in the cold.

As we consider 8:26-39, we will be asking the question, What assurance do we have that we who have taken Christ as our Savior *will* be there? Just how secure is our salvation? Let's start by reading 1:16 again: "For I am not ashamed of the gospel of Christ: for it is the power of God unto salvation to every one that believeth; to the Jew first, and also to the Greek." The question before us right now is, Just how great is this "power of God unto salvation"? We have noted that "salvation" in this verse refers not just to justification, but to sanctification and glorification as well. It is salvation past, present, and future. So, just how great is God's power to save us? Can He save us in the future as well as in the past and present? Having read about the wonders of salvation's future aspect, can I be sure that I will be there?

As Paul concludes his description of salvation in Romans 1—8, he answers this question. And his answer is not just purely academic. It is not just some nice, flowery words. Rather, his answer gives us the assurance we need. It is an answer that brings us joy, so that we don't have to go to bed every night reviewing the events of the day and wondering, Am I still saved or am I lost?

Paul draws his discourse on salvation to a conclusion in 8:26-39, but rather than seeing a gradual winding down of his message we see Paul ending with tremendous force and with a definite theme. The theme of these final verses is that eternal life is forever. Jesus said, "My sheep hear my voice, and I know them, and they follow me: And I give unto them eternal life; and they shall never perish" (John 10:27-28a). Would Jesus give us eternal life only to take it back again if we sinned too much? Paul's answer, and as we shall see the answer of our Lord as well, is that such a thing could never happen. Eternal life is not a conditional gift. Eternal life is forever.

We find a key to unlocking this theme when we notice a parallel between Paul's introduction (1:1-15) and his conclusion (8:26-39). Paul's description of salvation began with the Trinity. In the first four verses of chapter 1 we meet all three persons of the Trinity—God the Father, God the Son, and God the Holy Spirit. We will see now that Paul ends just where he began. He assures us of our eternal salvation on the basis of the ongoing work on our behalf of all three persons of the Trinity. We are assured of our salvation by the work of the Holy Spirit (8:26-27), by the work of the Father (verses 28-32), and by the work of the Son (verses 33-34). Paul will then conclude in verses 35-39 with a sort of culmination and conclusion of these three guarantees of salvation.

He tells us first of the work of the Holy Spirit on our behalf.

Likewise the Spirit also helpeth our infirmities. (8:26a)

What could possibly separate us from God and cause us to lose our salvation? It would be our "infirmities," that is, our human weaknesses and tendency to sin. But there is someone who helps us amid these weaknesses.

Likewise the Spirit also helpeth our infirmities: for we know not what we should pray for as we ought: but the Spirit itself maketh intercession for us with groanings which cannot be uttered. And he that searcheth the hearts knoweth what is the mind of the Spirit, because he maketh intercession for the saints according to the will of God. (8:26-27)

The Holy Spirit guarantees us that once we have accepted God's gift of salvation through Christ, we will never be lost again. As we have seen, the Spirit is the "earnest of our inheritance until the redemption of the purchased possession" (Eph. 1:14). As He indwells us in this life, the Spirit guarantees our eternal life. We are "sealed" for all eternity by the Holy Spirit (Eph. 1:13). These are wonderful words of assurance, but they could also be made to sound somewhat impersonal and legalistic. But as Paul in 8:26-27 describes the Spirit's present, continual interceding for each of us individually, it is like a flaming fire that could never be impersonal. What does the Holy Spirit do for us? He "makes intercession for us with groanings which cannot be uttered." The whole creation "groans" under the terrible weight of the consequences of our sin (8:22). "Even we ourselves groan" (verse 23) as we live in this fallen world. But amid all this suffering and amid all our longings there is someone else who groans. It is "the Spirit himself," making "intercession for us with groanings which cannot be

uttered" (verse 26). You won't be lost again. If you have accepted
Jesus as your Savior, you'll be there on resurrection day. Weak and
infirm though you may feel, faltering though your love may often be,
you'll be there. For it does not rest upon you, it rests upon the work of
the whole Trinity. The Holy Spirit would have to fail for you to be lost
again. His intercession for you would have to be of no avail. Well
might the sun grow dark or the universe turn into a chaos, but this one
thing you can know for sure: The Holy Spirit is interceding before
God's throne on your behalf, and He will not fail in His work of intercession. Some people talk of the "perseverance of the saints" as
though it were some mechanical thing. But it isn't like this at all. It is
a living, vibrant thing as "the Spirit himself makes intercession for us
with groanings which cannot be uttered."

The security of our salvation is also guaranteed by God the Father
(8:28-32). It is guaranteed by the fact that He has chosen us (verses
28-30) and by the fact that He has sent Jesus His Son to redeem us
(verses 31-32).

**And we know that all things work together for good to them that love
God, to them who are the called according to his purpose. (8:28)**

This is one of the Bible verses that everyone seems to know and
everyone seems to misquote. People will often just sort of shrug their
shoulders with an attitude of fatalism and say, "Oh well, all things
work together for good," implying that this applies to all people, no
matter who they are or what they believe. This is exactly what this
verse does not say. What it says is, "We know that all things work
together for good to them that love God, to them who are the called
according to his purpose." There is a limitation. All things do work
together for good, but only for a certain group. The group this principle works for is those who "love God" and who are "the called according to his purpose."

You'll recall we saw this same limitation in 1:16. The gospel is the
"power of God unto salvation," but only "to everyone who believes."
It is universal, in that it applies to all kinds of people, here designated
by Paul as "Jews and Greeks." But it is limited to those from among
all people who believe. Now supposing you read Romans 1:16 like

this, "For I am not ashamed of the gospel of Christ: for it is the power of God unto salvation to everyone." Period. Full stop. That would be a tragic lie. People are being lost forever by being taught such things in our generation. Salvation is open to all classes of humanity, all nations, all colors of skin, living under all flags. It is open to all. But it is limited in every case to those from each class who believe on Jesus Christ as Savior.

Romans 8:28 has exactly the same limitation: "All things work together for good to them that love God, to them who are the called according to his purpose." Paul now describes the tremendous calling that is our from God the Father.

For whom he did foreknow, he also did predestinate to be conformed to the image of his Son, that he might be the firstborn among many brethren. Moreover whom he did predestinate, them he also called: and whom he called, them he also justified: and whom he justified, them he also glorified. (8:29-30)

If you have been called by God (verse 28), if you have believed in Him, you can rest in the assurance that He has predestined you for complete salvation. He has justified you. Right now He is sanctifying you, beginning the process of conforming you to the image of Christ. And He will one day glorify you.

Paul speaks of this matter of predestination in Ephesians: "Blessed be the God and Father of our Lord Jesus Christ, who hath blessed us with all spiritual blessings in heavenly places in Christ: According as he hath chosen us in him before the foundation of the world, that we should be holy and without blame before him in love: Having predestinated us unto the adoption of children by Jesus Christ to himself, according to the good pleasure of his will, to the praise of the glory of his grace, wherein he hath made us accepted in the beloved" (Eph. 1:3-6). Such is the greatness of our infinite God that, while remaining in complete control of all human history, He was able to create humans outside of Himself who would have true significance. Those of us who have freely chosen Christ as our Savior can be assured that God, in His sovereignty, "chose" us and "predestinated" us "before the foundation of the world." Yet as we have seen, both our initial salvation (1:18—

4:25) and our sanctification (5:1—8:17) involve significant choices on our part. According to the Bible, there is no ultimate conflict between God's sovereignty and our human free will. After we have accepted Jesus as our Savior, the Word of God shines through and says that, wonder of wonders, God the Father has chosen you.

Have you accepted Jesus as your Savior? Then you may be sure of this, that God the Father has chosen you. We have seen that for you to be lost again, the Holy Spirit would have to fail. But now we see that, for you to be lost again, God the Father would have to have failed in His choice of you. You many recall the old story about the man who is walking down the street and comes to a church and sees over the church door a sign that says, "Whosoever will." He goes in, but then he begins to be afraid and someone takes him down into the basement, shows him those gray foundation stones holding up that great building, and on one of the stones he finds written the words, "Chosen before the foundation of the world." When you have accepted Jesus as your Savior, you can be sure. The Holy Spirit intercedes for you, and God the Father has chosen you.

"For whom he did foreknow, he also did predestinate to be conformed to the image of his Son" (8:29). God created man in His own image (Gen. 1:27). Man has revolted. The image is distorted. Go into the place of wealth or down into the place of poverty, it doesn't matter which. It isn't a question of wealth or poverty. Go to the universities or go down into the uneducated portion of the world. It isn't a question of education. Wherever one turns one sees mankind, meant to be the image-bearer of God—but what a distorted image! Marred and soiled, often speaking more of the devil than of God. Mankind's morality twisted, mankind's rationality contorted, believing all sorts of strange things, whether it be in the jungles of a primitive society or in the jungles of the modern university. Love, completely distorted. Man, created to be the image of God, to think, to act, to feel, to be rational and moral, to have real significance in the area of rationality and morality and beauty and love—and now look at mankind. The German concentration camps exhibited all this, but "nice" people exhibit it too. The woman walking the street for her living, yes, but the nice people too. "In the image of God," yet how terribly we sometimes reflect that image. Yet God the Father has "predestinated us to be conformed to the image of his Son," this Son of God, this marvelous one.

By faith we experience this conformity to Christ to some degree even in this present life. That's what sanctification, our present salvation (5:1—8:17), is all about. But the final goal, which we will see only in eternity, is full conformity to the image of His dear Son.

Moreover whom he did predestinate, them he also called: and whom he called, them he also justified: and whom he justified, them he also glorified. (8:30)

Observe the steps in salvation that Paul describes in these verses: 1) "Whom he did foreknow . . ."; 2) ". . . he also did predestinate" (verse 29); 3) "Whom he did predestinate, them he also called"; 4) "And whom he called, them he also justified"; 5) "And whom he justified, them he also glorified." If God has chosen you, you're as good as in heaven now! If God has justified you, rest quietly, beloved, you will be in heaven.

Too often God's choosing is presented in such a cold theological fashion. It is treated as though it were merely a process of selection and elimination. But when Paul wrote these words, he had only one purpose: to give you assurance. If the idea of predestination is presented in such a way that it decreases your assurance, then it isn't being presented the way the Bible teaches it. The Bible only teaches about God's choosing in order to give you assurance of your salvation. If you have accepted Jesus as your Savior, your heart can be still. He'll carry you through the gates of glory.

Having spoken of God's assurance in choosing us for salvation, Paul now finds assurance in the fact that God sent His Son Jesus to die for us.

What shall we then say to these things? If God be for us, who can be against us? He that spared not his own Son, but delivered him up for us all, how shall he not with him also freely give us all things? (8:31-32)

"He that spared not his own Son" should remind us of John 3:16: "For God so loved the world, that he gave his only begotten Son, that whosoever believeth in him should not perish, but have everlasting life." The infinite Creator God, who sovereignly chose us before the foundations of the world, is the same God who loved each one of us enough to send His Son to die for us. There is the total assurance of God's sovereign choice, plus the total assurance of His infinite love.

We have read about Abraham taking Isaac up the mountainside to sacrifice him to the Lord. God spared Abraham's son, but He didn't spare His own Son, "but delivered him up for us all." And if He has already done this much for you, "how shall he not with him also freely give us all things," including eternal life.

Are you afraid that you might be lost again? Don't be. The Holy Spirit intercedes for you. God the Father has chosen you and has sent His Son to die on Calvary's cross for you.

Notice the similarity in how these verses on our assurance from God the Father begin and end: "And we know that all things work together for good" (verse 28a); and then the section ends with, "How shall he not with him also freely give us all things?" (verse 32b). This should erase forever any hint of fatalism in the truth that "all things work together for good." This is not the face of fate, it is the face of your loving heavenly Father who chose you and sent His Son to die for you. If God did this for us, surely He will give us "all things." Therefore, we can know that "all things work together for good to them that love God."

Eternal life is forever. We are assured of this by the whole Trinity: by the work of the Holy Spirit (8:26-27); by the work of God the Father (8:28-32); and finally, by the work of God the Son, Jesus Christ our Lord.

Who shall lay any thing to the charge of God's elect? It is God that justifieth. Who is he that condemneth? It is Christ that died, yea rather, that is risen again. (8:33-34a)

"Rather" is better translated "much more." "It is Christ that died, yes much more, that is risen again." When Jesus died for us, He said, "It is finished." The debt for our sin was fully paid. But then, "much more," He rose again. He is the living Christ. And what is this living Christ doing now?

Who is even at the right hand of God, who also maketh intercession for us. (8:34b)

We have already learned that the Holy Spirit "maketh intercession for the saints" (8:27). And now we learn that Jesus "also maketh intercession for us." His priestly work of intercession on our behalf continues in heaven, on the basis of His finished work on the cross. He stands for us before the righteous Judge of the universe, before the very one against whom we have sinned. He pleads for us on the basis of His own character and on the basis of His finished work at Calvary. As Jesus pleads our case before this holy God, the very holiness of God now works for us. The holiness of God that must condemn us because we have sinned against Him, now works on our behalf. For Jesus pleads His shed blood, and God the Father, because of His holiness and His perfect justice, cannot ask any second payment for our sins. Jesus pleads for us on the basis of the complete forgiveness He has won for us at Calvary.

Jesus pleads our case, and therefore we can know that we will never be lost again. The security of our salvation rests not upon our good works, but upon Christ's work for us at Calvary and upon the work He is still doing for us, pleading our case before God the Father.

Is it possible to make too strong of a case for the belief that once a person is saved, he or she is always saved? It is impossible to make the case any stronger than the Bible makes it. Look at 1 John 2:1: "My little children, these things write I unto you, that ye sin not. And if any man sin, we have an advocate with the Father, Jesus Christ the righteous." Here again is Christ's ongoing intercession on our behalf. Will the sins we commit after becoming a Christian cause us to lose our salvation? No. Why? Because "we have an advocate with the Father," and this advocate, who petitions the Father for us, is "Jesus Christ the righteous." He is pleading for us not on the basis of our righteousness or lack of righteousness, but on the basis of His own perfect righteousness. And God, because of His holiness and justice, must accept that plea.

Just how effective is Christ's intercessory work on our behalf? The writer of Hebrews has much to say about the completeness of Christ's work of salvation. In one place he says, "Wherefore he is able also to save them to the uttermost that come unto God by him, seeing he ever liveth to make intercession for them" (Heb. 7:25). "Wherefore," that is to say, on the basis of His having finished His work on our behalf, Jesus is able to save those of us who believe in Him "to the uttermost." "Uttermost" in this context could have at least two meanings. I think the writer of Hebrews had both in mind. Jesus can save us "to the uttermost" in that He can save us regardless of any personal failings on our part. But "uttermost" in this context can also mean that He is able to save us forevermore.

Lost again? How? Through a failure on the part of the Holy Spirit? Through God the Father having been mistaken when He chose you or me for salvation? Through God the Father having been wrong in sending Christ to die for us? Through Christ's death at Calvary proving to be insufficient? Through Christ failing in His present efforts to intercede for us before the Father? Through God's failing to forgive us in response to Christ's intercession, even though Christ has paid our debt in full?

Lost again? No! Eternal life is forever. The Holy Spirit guarantees that eternal life is forever (8:26-27). God the Father guarantees that eternal life is forever (8:28-32). And Jesus guarantees that eternal life is forever (8:33-34). Having received all these assurances, you might say, "That's enough! Now I'm convinced that I'll never lose my salvation." But then, in verses 35-39, it's as if the Lord through Paul were saying, "No, wait a minute! I want you to understand in a way that you can't ever forget. Not just when you're sitting there reading this book, but during those times when you're feeling overwhelmed, when the waves are so high that you feel broken, when you crash to the earth, when Satan begins to throw things in your face." God says, "I want you to remember that eternal life is forever, even in the midst of the storm." And so he gives us these final great words of assurance:

Who shall separate us from the love of Christ? shall tribulation, or distress, or persecution, or famine, or nakedness, or peril, or sword? (8:35)

Remember, people were being killed for their faith even as Paul was writing this.

As it is written, For thy sake we are killed all the day long; we are accounted as sheep for the slaughter. (8:36)

Paul is quoting Psalm 44:22, and it is interesting to read that verse in its original context: "Yea, for thy sake are we killed all the day long; we are counted as sheep for the slaughter." And then the psalmist goes on to say, "Awake, why sleepest thou, O LORD? arise, cast us not off forever. Wherefore hidest thou thy face, and forgettest our affliction and our oppression? . . . Arise for our help, and redeem us for thy mercies' sake" (Ps. 44:23-24, 26). The psalmist says, "we are killed all the day long," then cries out to God to rescue His people. Paul, on the other hand, says, "Yes, it's true, 'for thy sake we are killed all the day long.' Yes, but Christ has died, and the victory is won. We don't need to cry out to God to come and rescue us." Yes, we are killed all the day long, but:

Nay, in all these things we are more than conquerors through him that loved us. (8:37)

Even amid trials as bad as the psalmist was enduring, we are more than conquerors. In our own strength? Of course not. We are more than conquerors "through him that loved us." We are "alive to God through Jesus Christ our Lord" (6:11). We have "the gift of God," which is "eternal life through Jesus Christ our Lord" (6:23). With Paul, we "thank God through Jesus Christ our Lord" (7:25) for our victories over sin in this life. And now in 8:37, "Nay, in all these things we are more than conquerors through him that loved us." The psalmist in distress cries out to God, "Awake!" But Paul says to us, "Be still." Yes, we may be suffering greatly because of our faith in Christ, and yet, "in all these things we are more than conquerors through him that loved us."

We noted that the verses explaining God the Father's assurance begin and end with "all things" (28a, 32b). And now in verse 37, "in all these things we are more than conquerors." And just how wide are these "all things"?

For I am persuaded, that neither death, nor life, nor angels, nor principalities, nor powers, nor things present, nor things to come, nor

height, nor depth, nor any other creature shall be able to separate us from the love of God, which is in Christ Jesus our Lord. (8:38-39)

Nothing in all the universe can separate us from God's love. It isn't just the things we see, it's also the things we don't see. Supernatural forces, demons, all the forces of hell, the entire hierarchy of evil. Isaiah says, "It shall come to pass in that day, that the LORD shall punish the host of the high ones that are on high, and the kings of the earth upon the earth" (Isa. 24:21). On the coming day of judgment, God will punish the rulers of this earth who have rebelled against Him, but He will also punish "the host of the high ones that are on high," by which He means our adversary the devil and all the angels who have chosen to serve him. Any of the evil hosts of Satan who try in any way to "separate us from the love of God" will be defeated. And where does that leave us? It leaves us as "more than conquerors through him that loved us."

Paul begins this final section by asking, "Who shall separate us from the love of Christ?" (8:35). And he ends by saying, "Nothing can separate us from the love of God" (8:39). This always reminds me of the passage in John 10 that we looked at earlier: "My sheep hear my voice, and I know them, and they follow me: And I give unto them eternal life; and they shall never perish, neither shall any man [anything] pluck them out of my hand. My Father, which gave them to me, is greater than all; and nothing is able to pluck them out of my Father's hand" (John 10:27-29). If we have truly trusted Christ for eternal life, he assures us that we will never perish, and that nothing can "pluck us out of his hand." Then, as though this was not assurance enough, he says that nothing can pluck us out of God the Father's hand either. If you have trusted Christ, nothing can separate you from His love, and nothing can separate you from God the Father's love. Once again, it is the whole Trinity assuring us of our salvation.

Let's read verses 35-39 as a unit now: "Who shall separate us from the love of Christ? shall tribulation, or distress, or persecution, or famine, or nakedness, or peril, or sword? As it is written, For thy sake we are killed all the day long; we are accounted as sheep for the slaughter. Nay, in all these things we are more than conquerors through him that loved us. For I am persuaded, that neither death, nor life, nor angels, nor principalities, nor powers, nor things present, nor things to come, nor height, nor depth, nor any other creature, shall be able to separate us from the love of God, which is in Christ Jesus our Lord."

Remember that these verses, like the rest of these first eight chapters of Romans, are simply an exegesis of Paul's theme verse: "For I am not ashamed of the gospel of Christ: for it is the power of God unto salvation" (1:16). Here in these final four verses we see just how powerful this salvation is. And the very last phrase of the very last verse of Paul's exegesis explains, in a way, the whole reason for the gospel, for we would never have had the gospel at all had it not been for "the love of God, which is in Christ Jesus our Lord."

Yes, if you have believed on Jesus as your Savior, go ahead and pull back the curtain. Dare to look ahead. Look ahead to the day when your body will be resurrected, when with your resurrected eyes you will see the glories of the redeemed, restored creation. Look ahead to the day when, free in your glorified state from the very presence of sin, you will live with your Lord forever.

And when the storms of life come, and we stumble, and we cry out, "Oh God, will I be there?" the answer is, Eternal life is forever; beloved, be still, you will be there. You do not need to worry. If you have accepted Christ as your Savior, you will be there. And this rests upon the work of the whole Trinity.

SCRIPTURE INDEX

GENERAL
INDEX

demnation of, 52; secrets of, 52-53; twentieth-century, 44; under God's wrath, 29-30, 54, 60-61, 63, 65, 69-70, 74-76, 82

Glorification, 165-69, 203-33

God, as Abba, 197-200, blasphemy against, 61-62; children of, 36, 143, 196-97; chosen by, 225-27; Creator, 31-32, 35; "foolishness" of, 36; idolatry of, 41-42; judgment of, 44-49, 52-54; law of, 38, 45, 78-80, 185-86, 191-93; the moral absolute, 80; oracles of, 63-64; peace with, 117-38; perfect standard of, 70, 79; rebellion against, 29-54, 71, 81-82, 113; reconciliation with, 136-37, 150, 219; revelation of, 38; righteousness of, ix, 13, 36, 64-65, 75-82, 122, 137, 220; slaves of, 163, 165, 170; wrath of, 29-54; 60-61, 63, 65, 69-70, 74-75, 82; yielding to, 161-72, 186

Gospel, the, definition of, 23-24, 29, 85; dunamis, 23; "foolishness," 36-37; proclaiming, 18, 21-25, 29, 36-37, 202; "unhumanistic," 81-82; universal, 77, 103

Grace, 37, 51, 61, 78-79, 82, 85-89, 92, 94-98, 100-103, 105, 107, 119, 121, 130-31, 137, 141-42, 146, 148, 150-52, 154, 161-62, 168, 173, 181, 189, 225

Greeks and Barbarians, 21, 24, 50

Guilt (keyword), 30; as taken by Christ, 19, 76-77; of nonbelieving Gentiles, 29-54; of nonbelieving Jews, 51-65; of the whole world, 67-71

Hammurabi, 87

Heaven, laying up treasure in, 48

Hell, 33, 99, 202, 216, 232

Hicks, Edward, 217

Hinduism, 176, 188

Holy Spirit, the, agent of the Trinity, 186-91; baptism of, 130, 134, 153-54; first-fruits of, 210-20; indwelling of, 133, 153, 177, 188-200, 210-13, 221; power of, 125, 161, 166; work of 17, 169, 181, 186-204, 223-24, 228; yielding to, 169

Homosexuality, 42-43

Humanism, 71, 74, 81-82

Incarnation, the, 16

Isaiah, the prophet, 41, 63

Jeremiah, the prophet, 42

Jews (nonbelieving), 51-65, 70-71; called to be missionaries, 56-57; circumcision and, 62-63; condemnation of, 62, 64-65,

67-71; in Ezekiel's day, 58-59; resting in the law, 55-65, 70-71; "righteousness" of, 95; unbelief of, 64; under God's wrath, 60-61, 63, 65, 69-70, 74-75, 82

Jews (Old Testament), justification of, 16, 83-113

John, the apostle, 53, 61, 125, 129, 196, 207-208, 216-17

John the Baptist, 83-84, 95

Jonah, 57-58

Judaism, umbrella of, 62, 69

Judeo-Christian tradition, 75

Justification, after the cross, 73-82; before the cross, 83-113; definition of, 23-25; 27-113; principles applying to, 173-74; result of, 117-38; steps of, 123-24, 148

Kierkegaard, Søren, 87, 109

The law, Christ, keeper of, 19, 181; doers of, 50-52; established by faith, 82-113; freedom from, 175-86, 190-92; giving of, 141, 147-48; judge, 50, 78; keepers of, 195-96; as a key word, 174-86, 191; and marriage, 175; of Moses, 70, 94, 106-107, 141, 147-48, 185; not justified by, 70-71, 81-82, 161-62, 187; part of the gospel, 29; resting in, 55-65, 70-71; righteousness of, 62, 96, 162, 192; righteousness without, 75, 79, 81-84, 104-7; schoolmaster, 83-84, 95, 106, 148, 179-80; work of, 31; wrath provider, 105-7

Life vs. death (keywords), 25, 107-8, 134, 137, 139-59, 170-71, 191-96;

Living by faith, ix, 24-25, 107, 112-13, 122, 126-27, 129, 131-34, 144, 156, 161, 191, 196-97, 208, 220

Lust (covet), 179

Luther, Martin, 25, 29, 82, 203-204

Mankind, condemnation of, 46-47, 49-52, 67-71, 79; conscience of, 30-33, 37, 45-47, 49, 51, 106; corruptible image of, 38-39; damnation of, 71, 74-75; deadness of, 139-48; "fools," 35-38; idolatry of, 41-42; judgment of, 46-47; "knowing God," 34-35; "lost," 49-50, 145, 202; "machines," 31-33, 36, 169-70; needing a Savior, 29-71; rational and moral beings, 31-33, 37, 41, 45-47, 52, 81, 176-77, 183, 226; rebellion of, 81-82, 113; "righteousness" of; 73-75, 81, 95, 151, 229; secrets of, 52-53; sin of, 214-16; unrighteousness of, 29-30, 44, 49, 64-65, 229; wisdom of, 37-38